**THE DOW JONES-IRWIN
GUIDE TO INTEREST**
*What you should know
about the time value of money*

THE
DOW JONES-IRWIN
GUIDE TO
INTEREST

*What you should know
about the time value of money*

LAWRENCE R. ROSEN

Editorial Advisor

Melvin Bloom, Ph.D.
Miami University

Dow Jones-Irwin
Homewood, Illinois 60430

© DOW JONES-IRWIN, INC., 1974

This publication is designed to provide accurate and
authoritative information in regard to the subject matter
covered. It is sold with the understanding that the
publisher is not engaged in rendering legal, accounting, or
other professional service. If legal advice or other expert
assistance is required, the services of a competent
professional person should be sought.

*From a Declaration of Principles jointly adopted by a Committee
of the American Bar Association and a Committee of Publishers.*

First Printing, April 1974
Second Printing, August 1974
Third Printing, October 1974
Fourth Printing, June 1977

Printed in the United States of America

Library of Congress Cataloging in Publication Data
Rosen, Lawrence R
    Dow Jones-Irwin guide to interest.
    1. Interest and usury. 2. Interest and usury—
Tables, etc. I. Dow Jones-Irwin. II. Title.
HG1628.R77   332.8'2   73–89120
ISBN 0–87094–067–8

Preface

The *Dow Jones-Irwin Guide to Interest* is meant to
help the public form an accurate picture of the financial
implications of everyday money decisions. It provides
quick answers to everyday questions about interest that
will be useful to savers, businessmen, home owners, car
buyers, and investors. Tables, graphs, and formulas with
examples of applications have been brought together by
the author to serve those who consider themselves "non-
mathematical" and others who, though perfectly cap-
able of performing complex mathematical calculations,
will welcome this quick reference source. Its unique
graphs make it possible to solve complicated money
problems in seconds.

The basic formulas and sample equations are given.
Readers whose last exposure to equation solving was in
the dimly remembered past of schooldays may be pleas-
antly surprised by the clarity and elegance of the simple
explanations. But no attention need be paid to the
"mathematics of interest." Anyone who can look up a
figure in a table and can read simple graphs—and who

at the same time has questions about present and anticipated money and interest issues—will find this *Guide* a handy sourcebook.

My special thanks to Melvin Bloom, Associate Professor of Mathematics of Miami University (Ohio) for his suggestions about and review of the text.

March 1974   LAWRENCE ROSEN

Contents

Appendix 2.   Logarithms, 161

Appendix 3.   Loan repayments, 187

Appendix 4.   Interest and dividend income, 203

Appendix 5.   Return on investment—discounted cash flow, 213

Appendix 6.   Mortgage "points," 217

1

How long does it take
a single investment to double
at various earnings rates?

It one invests $1,000 today at 4% simple annual interest, after one year the account is worth $1,040; after two years, $1,080.00, and so on. The formula is:

$$I = P \times i \times T$$

where:

> I = interest earned
> P = principal (e.g., $1,000)
> i = rate of annual interest (e.g., 4%, or 0.04)
> T = time in years (e.g., 1 year).

Thus, in the example given, after one year the interest earned (I) is $1,000 × 0.04 × 1, or $40.

The value of the account (S) is the original principal ($1,000) plus the interest earned ($40). Thus,

$$S = P + I$$

and since

$$I = P \times i \times T,$$
$$S = P + P \times i \times T, \text{ or}$$
$$S = P(1 + iT).$$

After two years, the value of the account, with 4% simple annual interest, is:

$$S = P(1 + iT)$$
$$= 1,000(1 + 0.04 \times 2)$$
$$= 1,000(1.08)$$
$$= 1,080.$$

This calculation fails to take into consideration, however, the interest earned in the second year on the $40 interest from the first year. Interest paid only on the original principal is called "simple interest."

Compound interest

Compound interest would be calculated as shown in the ten-year table.

Year	P Principal at beginning	I Annual interest earned during year at 4% (P × i × T)	S Value at end of year (P + I)
1............	1,000.	40.	1,040.
2............	1,040.	41.6000	1,081.6000
3............	1,081.6000	43.2640	1,124.8640
4............	1,124.8640	44.9946	1,169.8586
5............	1,169.8586	46.7943	1,216.6529
6............	1,216.6529	48.6661	1,265.3190
7............	1,265.3190	50.6128	1,315.9318
8............	1,315.9318	52.6373	1,368.5691
9............	1,368.5691	54.7428	1,423.3118
10............	1,423.3118	56.9326	1,480.2444

The formula for determining S, the value of an account after a period of years, n, (e.g., 10), started with an original investment, P (e.g., 1,000), at i annual compound interest (e.g., .04) is:

$$S = P(1 + i)^n$$
$$= 1,000(1.04)^{10}$$
$$= 1,000(1.480244)$$
$$= \$1,480.244$$

The value of $(1 + i)^n$ at various rates of i and for various values of n is shown in *Appendix 1;* Table 6, in the first column, shows how $1.00 will grow if left at the rate of 4% compounded annually. The result at the end of ten periods is $1.48.

If the tables were not available, the value of $(1 + i)^n$ could be determined by using logarithms, which are explained in Appendix 2. The method for determining the value x of $(1.04)^{10}$, that is, 1.04 multiplied by itself 9 times, is:

$$\text{Log } x = 10 \text{ log } 1.04$$
$$\text{Log } x = 10(0.017033)$$
$$\text{Log } x = 0.170330; \text{ and}$$
$$x = 1.48023, \text{ which is } (1.04)^{10}.$$

Growth of single investments

Refer to Graph 1, "How long it takes a single investment to double at various compound earnings rates." The dashed line shows that a single investment today of $1,000, with earnings compounded at 8% per year, will double after nine years.

This result can be checked by the formula:

$$S = P(1 + i)^n$$
$$= 1,000(1.08)^9$$
$$= 1,000(1.999004)$$
$$= \$1,999$$

GRAPH 1

How long it takes a single investment to double at various compound annual earnings rates

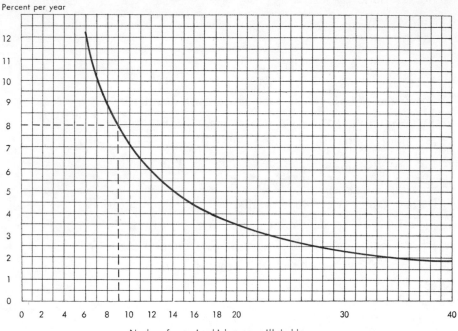

Shown in the accompanying table is the value of a lump sum investment of $1.00 after the expiration of selected periods of years at various rates of annual compound earnings.

Annual compound rate of earnings	Value of an investment of $1.00 after selected periods of years				
	1	5	10	15	20
4%	$1.040	$1.217	$1.480	$1.801	$2.191
6%	1.040	1.338	1.791	2.397	3.207
8%	1.080	1.469	2.159	3.172	4.661
10%	1.100	1.611	2.594	4.177	6.727

Thus, $1.00 invested today—with earnings at 8% reinvested annually—after 20 years would grow to $4.66. A hundred dollars would increase to $466, $1,000 to $4,661, and $10,000 to $46,610.

The formula, in review, is:

$$S = P(1 + i)^n$$

where

> S is the value after n years
> n is the number of years
> P is the original investment
> i is the compound annual growth rate.

Graph 2, "Single investments at 1% to 5% compound interest," and Graph 3, "Single investments, 4% to 14% compound interest," show the values for a $1.00, $1,000, and $10,000 original value ($P$) for periods of zero to 30 years.

EXAMPLE 1:

Refer to Graph 2. After 16 years, how much is $1.00 worth if it earns 3% compound annual interest? As the dashed line shows, the value would be $1.60.

The formula is:

$$
\begin{aligned}
S &= P(1 + i)^n \\
&= 1(1.03)^{16} \\
&= 1(1.604706) \\
&= \$1.60
\end{aligned}
$$

Using the graphs: examples

EXAMPLE 2:

Similarly, a $1,000 investment at 3% after 16 years would be worth $1,600 and an original $10,000 investment about $16,000.

GRAPH 2

Single investments at 1% to 5% compound

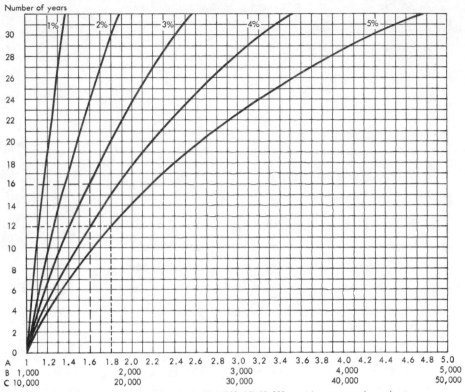

Number of years

Value of a single investment of (A) 1; (B) 1,000; (C) 10,000 at various compound growth rates

EXAMPLE 3:

A person has $10,000 today and estimates that he can earn 5% per year compounded. How many years will it take for his investment to reach $18,000 if no withdrawals are made?

To find the solution in Graph 2, the problem may be restated as follows: At 5% compound interest, how long does it take an investment of $1.00 (10,000) to increase to $1.80 (18,000), or to multiply by 1.8 (18,000 divided by 10,000)?

As the dotted line shows, it would take about 12 years.

EXAMPLE 4:

How long, at 5% compound interest, would it take $4,000 to increase to $7,200? Rephrased, the question is: how long would it take $4,000 to multiply itself 1.8 times. This would require the same length of time as it would take $1.00 to increase to $1.80, or 12 years.

Refer to Graph 3, "Single investments, 4% to 14% compound interest." One's goal is to have $50,000 at the end of 18 years. Assuming money can earn 8% compounded, how much must be invested today? Start on the left vertical side of the graph at 18

GRAPH 3

Single investments, 4% to 14% compound

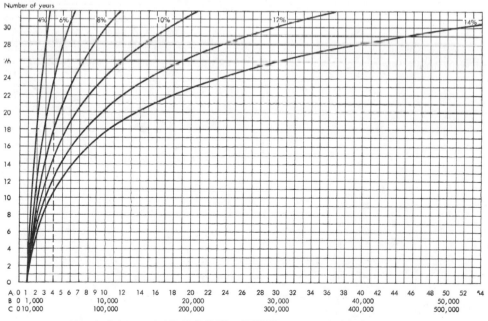

Value of a single investment of (A) $1; (B) $1,000; or (C) $10,000 at various compound growth rates

years, proceed—as the dashed line shows—horizontally to the 8% curve, then down vertically to the base. This shows that $1.00 will grow to $4.00 after 18 years at the 8% rate.

The problem then is as follows. Where x is the sum that must be invested today to reach $50,000 after 18 years at 8% compounded:

$$\frac{\$1}{4} = \frac{x}{50,000}$$
$$4x = 50,000$$
$$x = \underline{\underline{\$12,500}}$$

Hence, $12,500 invested today will be worth $50,000 at 8% compounded.

2
Present value of future income

A person owns a promissory note that he received from the sale of a car. The maker of the promissory note promises to pay $1,000 two years from today without interest. The owner of that promissory note needs cash today, however, and he takes it to his bank. He asks the bank to purchase the note for cash today.

Single-payment promissory note

The banker explains that he cannot pay $1,000 for the note; its present value is less than that. He says that the bank will buy the note at its present (or discounted) value, however. Bank practice, he further explains, requires him to receive a return when the note is finally collected equivalent to what the money would have earned if it had been invested at 10% compounded annually.

The problem, then, is to determine the present value of a note with a maturity value of $1,000 due two years hence and with a discounted interest rate of 10%. Where:

P = present value
S = maturity value ($1,000)

n = time from the present until maturity (2 years)

i = discounted interest rate (10%),

the formula is:

$$S = P(1 + i)^n \text{ and}$$
$$P = S(1 + i)^{-n}$$
$$= 1{,}000(1.10)^{-2}$$
$$= 1{,}000[1/(1.10)^2]$$
$$= 1{,}000(.82644628)$$
$$= \$826.44.$$

$826.44 is the amount the bank will pay.

The values for $(1 + i)^{-n}$ used in the formula are shown in Appendix 1.

EXAMPLE:

Graph 4, "How much money due in the future is worth today," may be used to find the present value of a future single payment. Assume $1,000 is due 9 years from today. What is the present value discounted at 12% compound interest?

As the dashed line shows, the present value is $360.

GRAPH 4

How much $1,000 due in the future is worth today

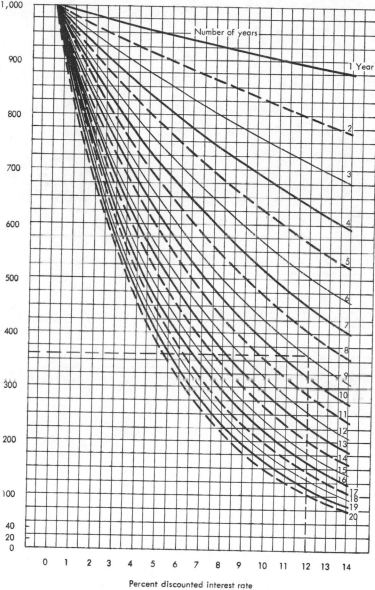

Value today

Percent discounted interest rate

3

Present value of a series of future payments

A car dealer sells a car on the installment plan. The buyer agrees to pay $100 a month for 36 months, without interest. However, the car dealer needs his money today to be able to buy more cars and pay his bills. He takes the promissory note of the purchaser to the bank and wishes to sell the note for cash.

The banker explains, as he did to the owner of a single-payment promissory note in Chapter 2, that the $3,600 of future payments is worth less than that today. The bank is willing to purchase the promissory note for cash by paying an amount that will earn the bank 12% interest on the price it pays.

Where:

A = present value

i = monthly discount rate or monthly compound interest rate

n = number of months of equal future payments (36)

R = amount of each regular future monthly payment ($100),

13

the formula for determining the present value (the amount the bank will pay) is:

$$A = R\left[\frac{1 - (1 + i)^{-n}}{i}\right]$$
$$A = 100\left[\frac{1 - (1.01)^{-36}}{.01}\right]$$
$$= 100(30.1075)$$
$$= \$3,010.75.$$

$3,010.75 is the amount the bank will pay, today.

The values of $\left[\dfrac{1 - (1 + i)^{-n}}{i}\right]$ may be found in Appendix 1, starting on page 81, under the column "Present worth of 1 per period: What $1 payable periodically is worth today."

Alternatively, Graph 5, "How much future monthly payments of $1.00 per month are worth today," may be used.

EXAMPLE:

An installment contract provided initially for 180 payments of $100 each without interest at the rate of one payment per month. Twenty-nine payments have already been made and the owner of the contract now wishes to obtain the present value from a bank. If the bank accepts to buy it at 8% discounted, how much will the owner receive?

Enter the graph at 151 months and, as the dashed line shows, at the 8% curve move horizontally to determine the value today, $95. However, $95 is the value for payments of 151 payments of $1.00 per month. The

GRAPH 5

How much future payments of $1.00 per month are worth today

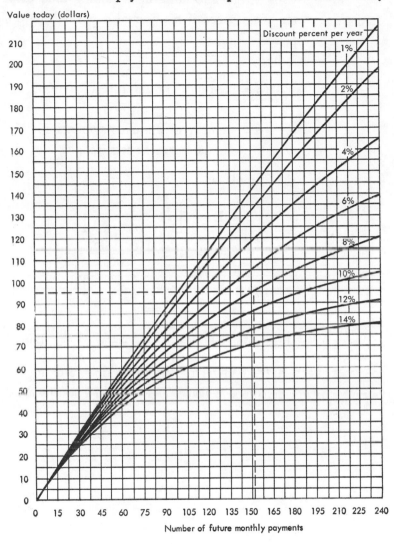

Value today (dollars)

Discount percent per year

1%
2%
4%
6%
8%
10%
12%
14%

Number of future monthly payments

value for payments of $100 per month is, therefore, $95 × $100, or about $9,500.

A person has a debt of $10,000 to repay in a single lump sum payment about 10 years from now. How

Sinking funds

much should he set aside each year over the next 10 years in order to build up a sinking fund of $10,000 ten years hence if his annual deposits earn 6% compound?

Where:

S = sum due in the future ($10,000)

i = annual interest (.06)

n = number of annual payments (10)

R = annual payment required,

the formula is:

$$R = S\left[\frac{i}{(1 + i)^n - 1}\right]$$
$$= 10,000\left[\frac{.06}{(1.06)^{10} - 1}\right]$$
$$= 10,000(.075867982)$$
$$= \underline{\$758.68} \text{ per year}$$

The value of $\dfrac{i}{(1 + i)^n - 1}$ may be found in Appendix 1 under the column titled "Sinking Fund: Periodic deposit that will grow to $1 at a future date."

4

Life expectancy of a $10,000 investment with equal annual withdrawals

A basic problem that faces investors—especially investors in a mutual fund periodic or automatic withdrawal plan—is the depletion of the investor's capital that occurs if the rate of withdrawal exceeds the rate of earnings on the capital. In such a case, the investor will eventually have no capital remaining.

The table here shows the length of time original capital of $10,000 will last, before being reduced to zero, if

Selected withdrawal and earning rates

a. annual withdrawals or redemptions are made at 6% ($600), 8% ($800), and 10% ($1,000) of the original capital; and
b. the original capital remaining after the withdrawals grows at compound interest rates of 4%, 6%, 8%, 10%, and 12% compounded annually.

17

Rate of annual withdrawal of original capital	Compound rate of growth of capital				
	4%	6%	8%	10%	12%
6%($ 600)	28	never	never*	never*	never*
8%($ 800)	17	23	never	never*	never*
10%($1000)	13	15	20	never	never*

Number of years before capital exhausted

* The original capital will increase.

To understand the examples here, refer to Graph 6, "How long will my capital last?" It answers the question for varying withdrawal and earnings rates.

EXAMPLE 1:

One has today $10,000 of original capital. It is invested to earn at 8% compound annual interest. If 10% of the original capital, i.e., $1,000 per year, is withdrawn—year after year—after how many years from today will the original capital be reduced to zero?

Answer: 20 years. And the answer remains 20 years if the original capital were $20,000 ($30,000) and the annual withdrawals were $2,000 ($3,000).

EXAMPLE 2:

The dashed line shows that if 7.5% of original capital (e.g., $10,000) is withdrawn annually ($750), and the original capital remaining grows at an annual compound rate of 6%, the $10,000 original capital will be exhausted in about 28 years.[1]

---

[1] The mathematical formula is:

$$x = \frac{i}{1 - (1 + i)^{-n}}$$

where: x = Percentage of original capital withdrawn annually
i = Annual compound earnings rate of remaining capital
n = Number of years before capital is exhausted.

EXAMPLE 3:

An elderly person can invest his money to earn 4%
and wishes to have an income (including exhaustion
of capital) of $10,000 per year for at least 13 years.
How much original capital is required?

1. On Graph 6 move vertically (see dotted line on
    graph) up from 13 years to the 4% curve and
    then across horizontally to the left margin.

    The point where the horizontal line intersects the

GRAPH 6

How long will my capital last?

(curves represent the annual compound earnings growth rate of the capital remaining
after each withdrawal)

Percent of original capital withdrawn annually

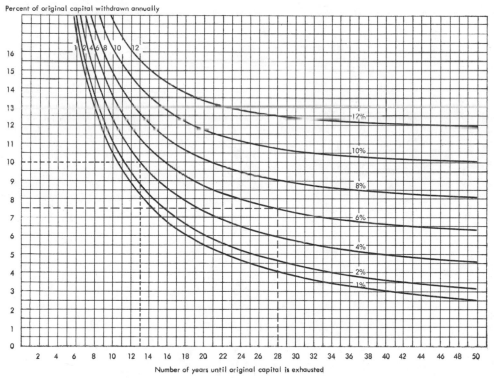

Number of years until original capital is exhausted

left margin of the graph is 10%. Thus, he may withdraw 10% a year of his original capital.

2. He can withdraw at the rate of 10% of his original capital. The remaining question is: How much original capital is needed? We know that 10% of x, the original capital, equals $10,000 per year. Therefore, $100,000 is required.

$$\text{(If } 0.1x = 10,000,$$
$$\text{then } x = 100,000.\text{)}$$

5

Mortgages, loans, and depreciation

Mortgages are a factor in most peoples' lives. The repayment of most loans secured by a first mortgage on real estate is by level or equal payments over the 20-, 25- or 30-year life of the mortgage. Each payment represents both an interest and a principal repayment. At the time of the final payment, the outstanding loan balance is extinguished.

Graph 7 shows how the interest portion of each payment on a $20,000 loan is predominant in the early years of payments and how in later years the proportion of each payment that is applied to reduction of principal increases.

Interest and principal amortization

Two types of questions frequently arise in connection with mortgage loans:

1. A person can afford to pay x dollars per month toward a loan. If interest is $y\%$, how much can he borrow today, assuming he may repay the loan over z years?

GRAPH 7

$20,000 loan at 2% amortized by annual payments of $2,226.53

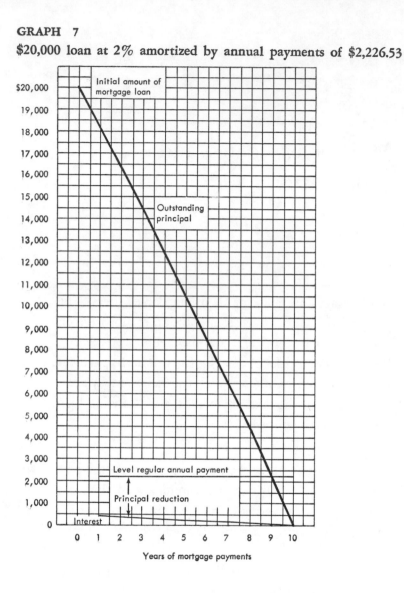

Years of mortgage payments

2. Someone wants to buy a house with a loan of *x* dollars; the interest is *y*%, and the repayment period is *z* years. How much are his annual repayments?

Both of these problems may be solved by using Graph 8, "Mortgage loan repayments."

EXAMPLE 1:

A person wishes to buy a house that will involve a mortgage loan of $20,000 with 6% interest over 20 years. How much are his annual loan payments?

Enter the Graph 8 on the base line at 20 years; move vertically to the 6% loan interest curve; then horizontally to 8.7%; 8.7% times the amount of the loan, $20,000, is the annual payment: $1,740.[1]

EXAMPLE 2:

A person can afford to pay $250 per month ($3,000 per year) on a mortgage loan. If interest costs are 8% and he can obtain a 22-year repayment period, what size loan may he secure?

Enter the graph at 22 years; move vertically to the 8% curve; then horizontally to 9.8%. Under these conditions, his annual repayment will be 9.8% of his original loan amount.

To find the loan amount (x):

$$0.098x = 3,000$$
$$x = \frac{3,000}{.098}$$
$$= \$30,612$$

He can borrow $30,612 and pay off the loan over 22 years at 8% interest by annual payments of $3,000.[1]

The maximum allowable depreciation rates which may be applied to real property under the U.S. Tax Reform Act of 1969 are as follows:

Depreciation allowances

• For buildings bought or constructed after July 24

---

[1] Solution by formula to these problems is shown in Appendix 3. Also refer to Appendix 3 for other loan computations, including discounts and add-ons.

24

GRAPH 8

Mortgage loan repayments

Annual payment as percent of original loan*

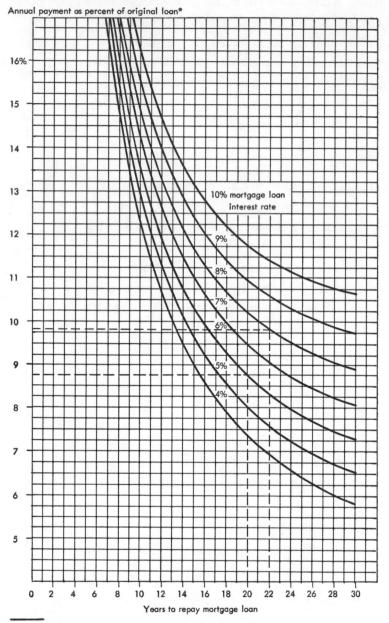

Years to repay mortgage loan

* Also referred to as "annual constant." See Appendix 3, Form 1, page 175.
For short term monthly installment loans, see Graph 50.

1969, if such buildings are *new residential rental property where at least 80% of the gross rentals come from dwelling units,* then 200% declining balance depreciation may be utilized;

- For *used residential* property with a useful life of 20 years or more, 125% declining balance may be used;
- For *other new* real property 150% declining balance may be used; and
- For *other used* real property only straight-line depreciation is allowed.

Depreciation is a bookkeeping entry and is not a cash expenditure even though it is a tax deduction. On the other hand, mortgage loan principal repayments are a cash expenditure, but not tax deductible.

To the extent that depreciation exceeds mortgage loan principal repayments, a tax-sheltered cash flow is created—that is, the owner receives cash in excess of his taxable income. Conversely, if loan principal repayments exceed depreciation, a negative situation results in that the owner's taxable income is greater than his cash receipts.

Graph 9 shows—as a percentage of the original loan —the reduction in outstanding principal that occurs as the result of each annual loan repayment.

EXAMPLE 1:

If the mortgage loan is for 30 years at 7.5% interest, as a result of the sixth annual level payment, the original loan principal is reduced by about 1.4%.

The graph also shows—as a percentage of the original depreciable amount—each year's allowable depreciation.

GRAPH 9

Mortgage loan principal repayments expressed as a percentage of the original loan

(depreciation expressed as a % of the original value of the depreciable asset)

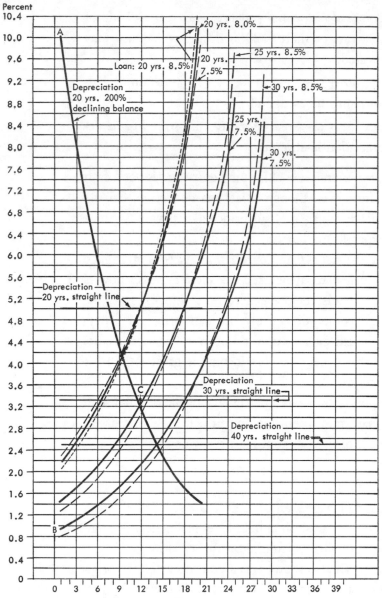

EXAMPLE 2:

If a building is depreciated over 20 years using the 200% declining balance method, what percent depreciation deduction may be made for the third year? As the graph shows, about 8.1%.

The original amount depreciable and the original loan amount may be nearly equal or quite different. Note that if such original amounts are quite different, the graph percentages for each apply to different original sums. If such original amounts are nearly equal, however, then the graph percentages may be directly compared to each other.

It is often the case that the original amounts (depreciation and mortgage loan) are approximately equal, as is shown in the following hypothetical case.

Property purchase price....................	$1,000,000
Value of land (not depreciable).............	300,000
Value of building (amount depreciable)......	$ 700,000
First mortgage loan at	
70% of purchase price...............	$ 700,000

Graph 9 gives an overall view of the relationship between various rates of depreciation and various mortgage loan terms. Graphs 10 through 18 are more detailed and should be used for particular cases:

Graph 10 7.5% loans and 20-year depreciation at 200%, 150%, and 125% declining balance and straight line

Graph 11 7.5% loans and 30-year depreciation.

Graph 12 7.5% loans and 40-year depreciation.

Graph 13 8.0% loans and 20-year depreciation.

Graph 14 8.0% loans and 30-year depreciation.

Graph 15 8.0% loans and 40-year depreciation.

Graph 16   8.5% loans and 20-year depreciation.
Graph 17   8.5% loans and 30-year depreciation.
Graph 18   8.5% loans and 40-year depreciation.

Tax shelters

Refer to Graph 9.
Assume:

a.   200%, 20-year, declining balance depreciation is used;
b.   the mortgage loan is for 30 years at 7.5%
and
c.   the original amount depreciable is equal to
the original loan.

Then, in the first year, what tax shelter exists?

The depreciation expressed as a percentage of the
original depreciable amount (e.g., $700,000) is
10%, or $70,000 (point A on the graph).
The portion of the loan payment that reduces the
principal of the original loan (e.g., $700,000) is
0.96%, or $6,720 (point B on the graph).
Hence, the tax sheltered cash receipts—the excess
of depreciation over loan principal repayment—
is 9.04%, or $63,280.

In the same example, after how many years would tax
sheltered cash receipts no longer be created?

When the depreciation line on the graph crosses
the loan line, the two are equal and no tax sheltered cash receipts would be created. This occurs
at point C, which is approximately the fourteenth
year.

The formula for determining the amount of principal repayment from any level annual loan payment is:

$$x = R\left[\frac{1 - (1 + i)^{n_2}}{i}\right] - R\left[\frac{1 - (1 + i)^{n_1}}{i}\right]$$

Where:

x = amount of principal repayment

R = level annual loan payment

i = loan interest rate

n_1 = number of years of the original mortgage less the number of the payment where one wishes to find x

$n_2 = n_1$ plus 1 year.

EXAMPLE 1:

There is a 20-year mortgage of $100,000, at 8% interest (i). How much of the eighth annual payment (of $10,185.22) reduces the outstanding loan (x)?

$$x = 10,185.22\left[\frac{1 - (1.08)^{-18}}{.08}\right] - 10,185.22$$
$$\left[\frac{1 - (1.08)^{-19}}{.08}\right]$$

$$= 10,185.22(7.9037759416)$$
$$- 10,185.22(7.5360780169)$$
$$= 10,185.22(7.9037759416 - 7.5360780169)$$
$$= 10,185.22(0.3676979247)$$
$$= \underline{\$3,745.12}$$

Straight line depreciation

The formula for determining the annual percentage of depreciation relative to the original depreciable amount for straight line depreciation is:

$$x = \frac{1}{n}$$

Where:

> x = annual depreciation percentage of original depreciation amount
>
> n = number of years or useful life.

EXAMPLE 2:

What is the annual percentage depreciation, if 20 years is the useful life?

$$x = \frac{1}{20}$$
$$= 5\%$$

Declining balance depreciation

The formula for determining the annual depreciation amount for declining balance methods is:

$$x_n = ry(1 - r)^{n-1}$$

Where:

> x_n = The declining balance depreciation in the Nth year.
>
> r = The rate of declining balance depreciation (relative to straight line) times the straight line rate.
>
> y = The original amount to be depreciated.

EXAMPLE 3:

> Assume: a.   200% declining balance
>
> b.   20 years
>
> c.   original amount depreciable is $100,000.

What is the depreciation percentage in the 5th year?

$$x_n = ry(1 - r)^{n-1}$$
$$x_5 = (2.0)(0.05)(100,000)[1 - (2.0)(0.05)]^{5-1}$$
$$= .1(100,000)(.9)^4$$
$$= .1(100,000)(.6561)$$
$$= \$6,561.00$$
$$= \text{or } \underline{6.56\%} \text{ of the original depreciable amount}$$

GRAPH 10

7.5% loans, 20-year depreciation

(mortgage loan principal repayments and depreciation expressed as a percentage of the original value of the loan & depreciable asset)

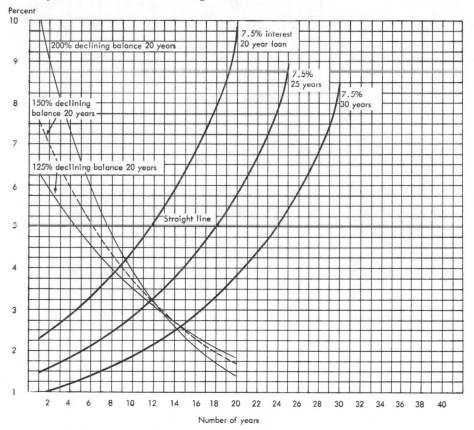

32

GRAPH 11

7.5% loans, 30-year depreciation

(mortgage loan principal repayments and depreciation expressed as a percentage of the original value of the loan & depreciable asset)

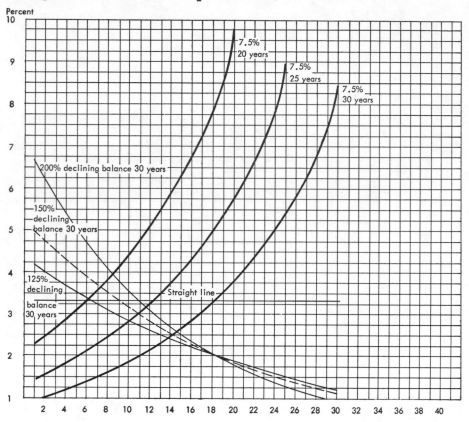

GRAPH 12

7.5% loans, 40-year depreciation

(mortgage loan principal repayments and depreciation expressed as a percentage of the original value of the loan & depreciable asset)

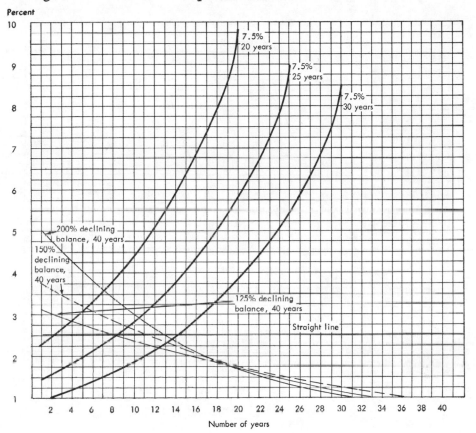

Percent

Number of years

34

GRAPH 13

8% loans, 20-year depreciation

(mortgage loan principal repayments and depreciation expressed as a percentage of the original value of the loan & depreciable asset)

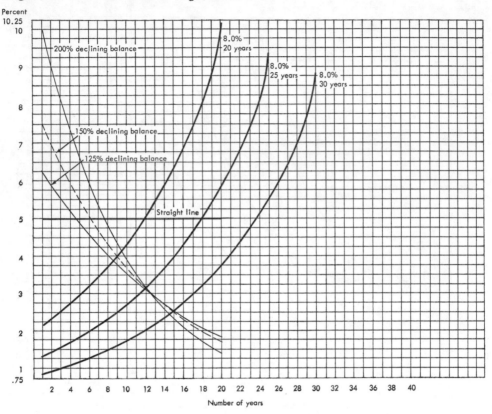

GRAPH 14

8% loans, 30-year depreciation

(mortgage loan principal repayments and depreciation expressed as a percentage of the original value of the loan & depreciable asset)

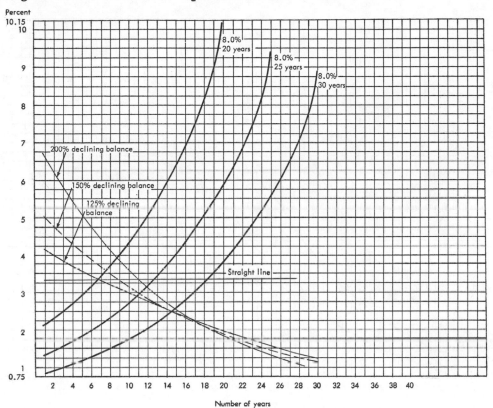

Number of years

36

GRAPH 15

8% loans, 40-year depreciation

(mortgage loan principal repayments and depreciation expressed as a percentage of the original value of the loan & depreciable asset)

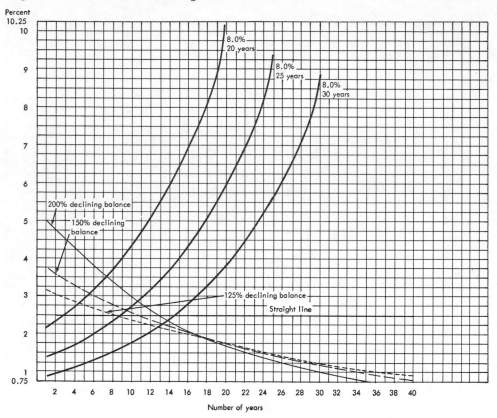

GRAPH 16

8.5% loans, 20-year depreciation

(mortgage loan principal repayments and depreciation expressed as a percentage of the original value of the loan & depreciable asset)

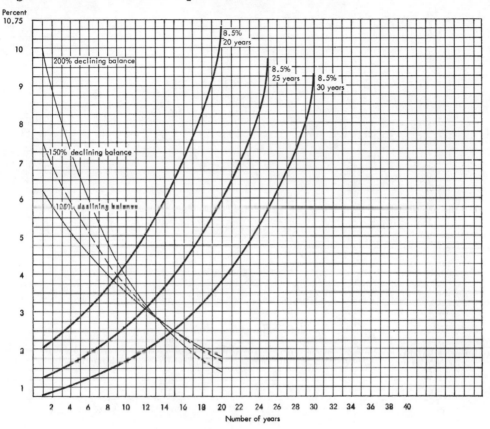

Percent

10.75

8.5%
20 years

200% declining balance

8.5%
25 years

8.5%
30 years

150% declining balance

120% declining balance

Number of years

38

GRAPH 17

8.5% loans, 30-year depreciation

(mortgage loan principal repayments and depreciation expressed as a percentage of the original value of the loan & depreciable asset)

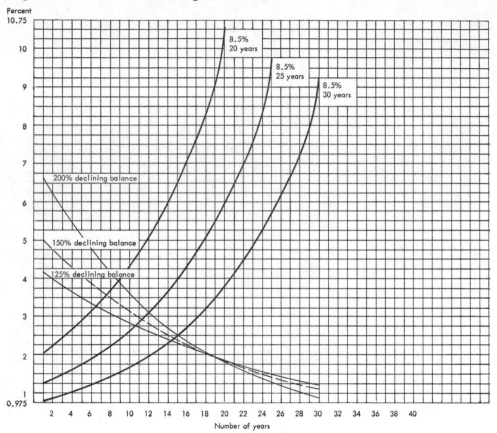

GRAPH 18

8.5% loans, 40-year depreciation

(mortgage loan principal repayments and depreciation expressed as a percentage of the original value of the loan & depreciable asset)

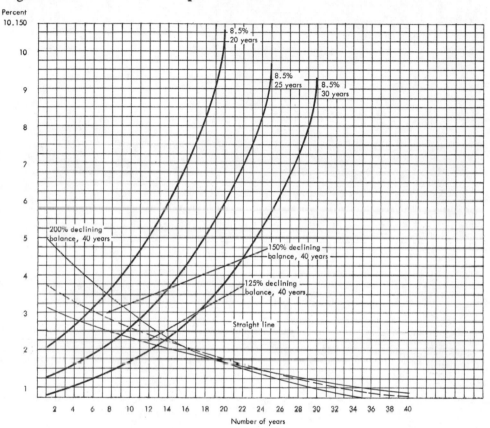

Percent

10.150

Number of years

6

Bond yields

Normally, bonds are bought and sold at prices other than their maturity value. The maturity value, or face amount, is the sum (usually $1,000) which the issuer of the bond promises to pay to the owner at the bond's maturity date. The maturity date may be 5, 10, 15 or 20 years, or some other interval from the date on which the bonds were issued.

The issuer of most bonds also promises to pay an interest rate to the owner, every year or every six months. The rate of interest (e.g., 6%) is expressed as a percentage of the bond face amount or maturity value. The interest may also be expressed in a dollar amount, as, for example, $60, which means that each annual interest payment is $60—equivalent to 6% of the $1,000 maturity value.

If today one buys for $1,000 a bond with a maturity value in 20 years of $1,000, and if the bond pays 6% per year (the interest coupon), then the yield to the purchaser is 6%. However, if the purchaser bought the

Computing yield to maturity

bond at a discount, that is, he paid less than $1,000, his yield to maturity will be greater than 6%. Similarly, if he paid a premium for the bond, that is, he bought it for more than $1,000, his yield to maturity will be less than 6%.

To determine yield to maturity, a complex calculation, the following formula is used:

where:

i = annual compound interest yield to maturity

A = purchase price of the bond

S = maturity value

n = number of years from purchase date to maturity

R = annual amount of bond interest paid to the owner

then,

$$A = R\left[\frac{1 - (1 + i)^{-n}}{i}\right] + S(1 + i)^{-n}.$$

Both the values of $\left[\dfrac{1 - (1 + i)^{-n}}{i}\right]$,

which is called "present worth of $1 per period or what $1 payable periodically is worth today," and the value of $(1 + i)^{-n}$, which is called "present worth of $1 or what $1 due in the future is worth today," are shown in Appendix 1, starting on page 81.

For example, to yield 10% to maturity (i), if the maturity value is $1,000 ($S$), the maturity date is 20 years (n) hence, the coupon interest is 8% ($80) ($R$): how much should I pay for the bond today (A) (neglecting brokerage commissions and transfer taxes)?

$$A = R\left[\frac{1 - (1 + i)^{-n}}{i}\right] + S(1 + i)^{-n}$$
$$= 80\left[\frac{1 - (1.10)^{-20}}{.10}\right] + 1,000(1.10)^{-20}$$
$$= 80(8.513564) + 1,000(.14864363)$$
$$= 681 + 149$$
$$= \underline{\$830}$$

The purchase price must be about $830.

Solving the equation for the purchase price when the yield to maturity is known is not difficult. It is, however, difficult to solve the equation for the yield to maturity (i). In practice, the yield to maturity (i) is precisely the unknown that investors often wish to determine. Graphs 19 through 48, developed by the author, simplify this problem of finding the yield to maturity. These graphs involved in excess of 30,000 separate calculations and plottings.

In this chapter, 30 graphs provide a quick way to determine yield to maturity. Each graph covers *each* period measured by years to maturity; for example, the year of purchase of a bond by an investor is 1974 and the maturity date of the bond is 1990. There are 16 years until maturity. Graph 34 would be used because it covers "Bond yield to maturity: 16 years."

The other inputs to the graph are the purchase price, in the left vertical column; and the coupon interest rates paid on the bond—the curves on the graph.

Simplified way of finding yield to maturity: graphs

EXAMPLE 1:

Years to maturity: 20
Coupon interest rate: 8%
Purchase price: $830.

Turn to Graph 38 (20-year graph). The dashed lines shows that the yield to maturity is 10%.

EXAMPLE 2:

> Years to maturity: 1
> Purchase price: $990
> Coupon interest rate: 3%

Turn to the 1-year graph, Graph 19. The dashed line shows the yield to maturity is 4%.

EXAMPLE 3:

> Years to maturity: 5
> Purchase price: $1,130
> Coupon interest rate: 8%

Turn to the 5-year Graph 23. The dashed line shows the yield to maturity is 5%.

EXAMPLE 4:

How much may be paid to purchase a bond whose maturity value 12 years hence is $1,000, if the coupon interest rate is 7% and the investor desires a yield to maturity of 8%?

Turn to the 12-year Graph 30. The dashed line shows the purchase price to obtain the desired yield would have to be $925.

Refer to Appendix 4 for additional information on bonds and other money and capital market instruments.

See Appendix 7 for mathematical methods of determining yield to maturity.

See Appendix 8 for comparing yield to call.

GRAPH 19

Bond yield to maturity: 1 year

Purchase price

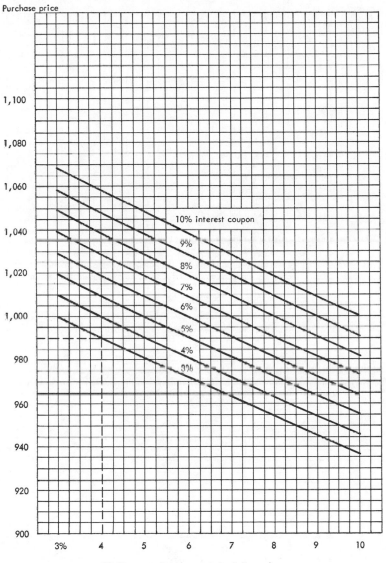

10% interest coupon
9%
8%
7%
6%
5%
4%
3%

Yield to maturity when maturity is 1 year hence

GRAPH 20

Bond yield to maturity: 2 years

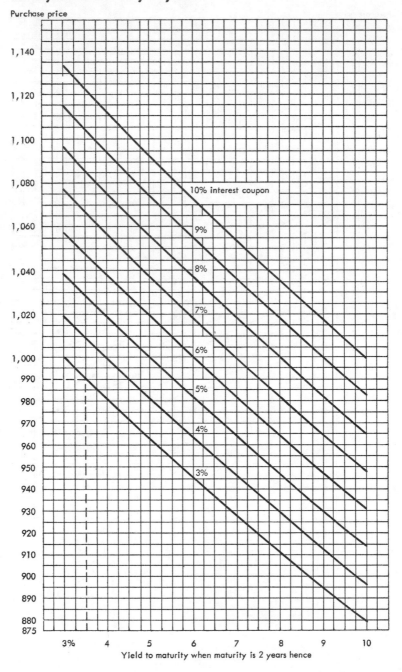

Purchase price

10% interest coupon

9%

8%

7%

6%

5%

4%

3%

Yield to maturity when maturity is 2 years hence

GRAPH   21

Bond yield to maturity: 3 years

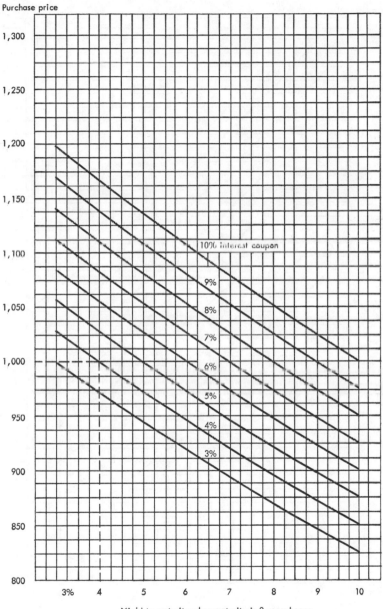

Yield to maturity when maturity is 3 years hence

GRAPH 22

Bond yield to maturity: 4 years

Purchase price

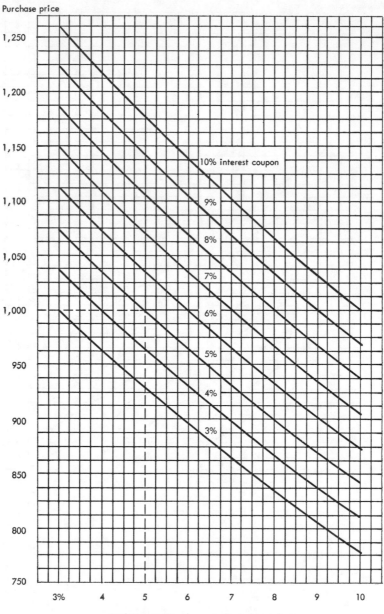

10% interest coupon

9%

8%

7%

6%

5%

4%

3%

Yield to maturity when maturity is 4 years hence

GRAPH 23

Bond yield to maturity: 5 years

Purchase price

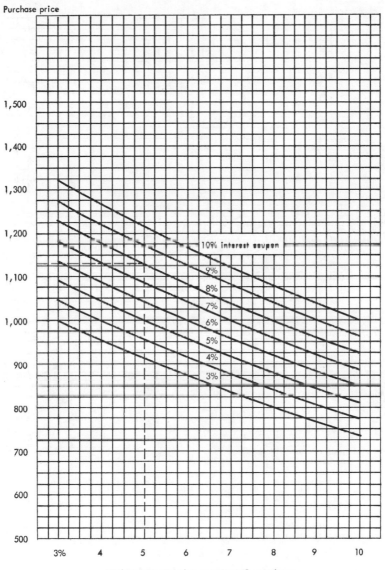

10% interest coupon
9%
8%
7%
6%
5%
4%
3%

Yield to maturity when maturity is 5 years hence

GRAPH 24

Bond yield to maturity: 6 years

Purchase price

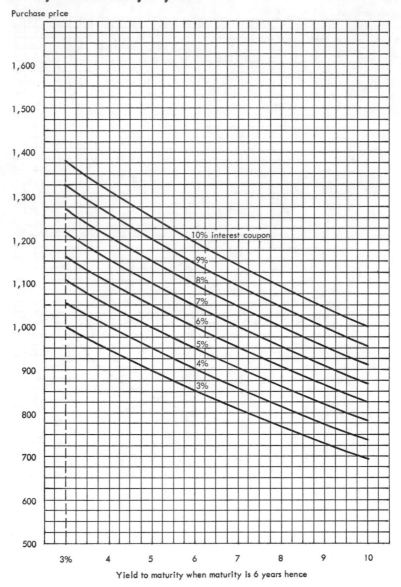

10% interest coupon

9%

8%

7%

6%

5%

4%

3%

Yield to maturity when maturity is 6 years hence

GRAPH 25

Bond yield to maturity: 7 years

Purchase price

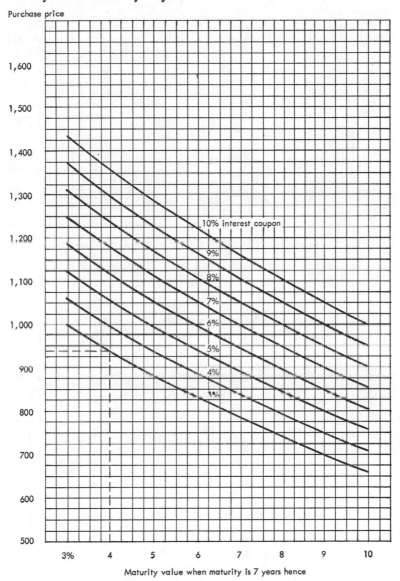

10% interest coupon

9%

8%

7%

6%

5%

4%

3%

Maturity value when maturity is 7 years hence

GRAPH 26

Bond yield to maturity: 8 years

Purchase price

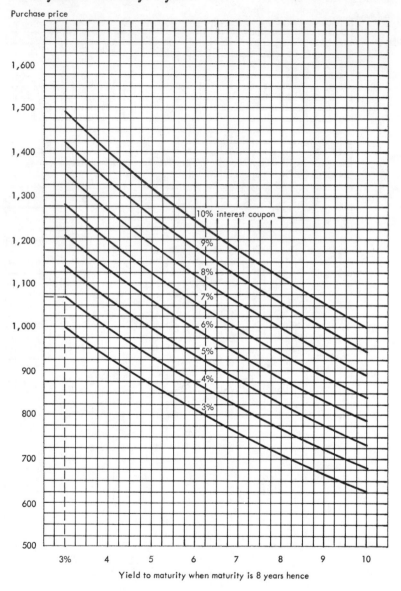

Yield to maturity when maturity is 8 years hence

53

GRAPH 27

Bond yield to maturity: 9 years

Purchase price

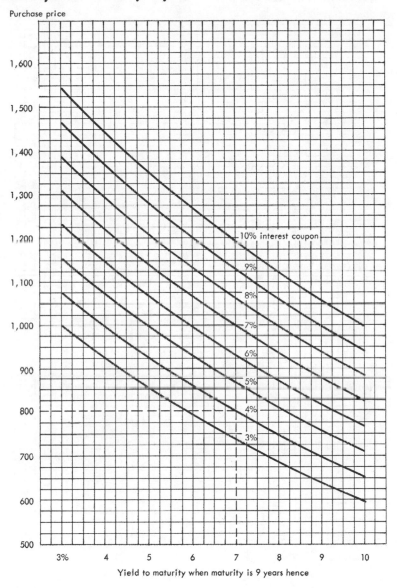

Yield to maturity when maturity is 9 years hence

GRAPH 28

Bond yield to maturity: 10 years

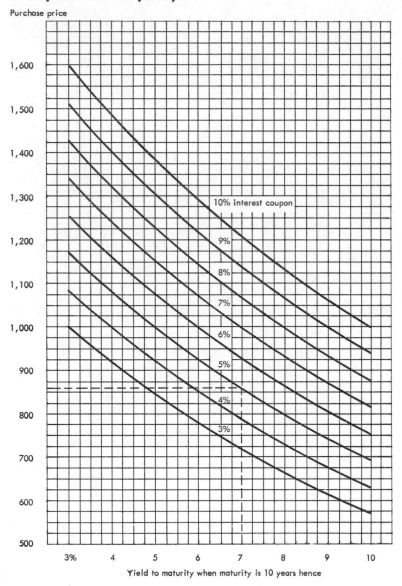

Purchase price

Yield to maturity when maturity is 10 years hence

GRAPH 29
Bond yield to maturity: 11 years

Purchase price

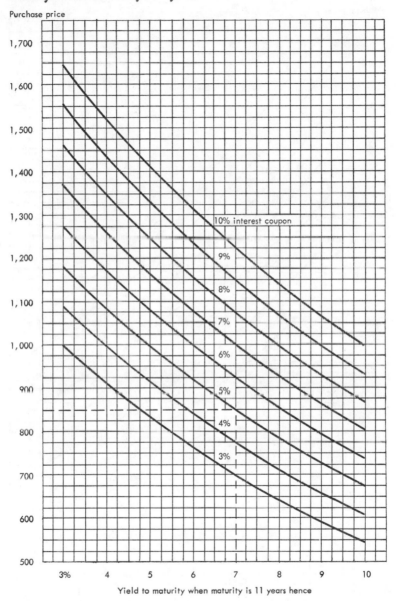

10% interest coupon

9%

8%

7%

6%

5%

4%

3%

Yield to maturity when maturity is 11 years hence

GRAPH 30

Bond yield to maturity: 12 years

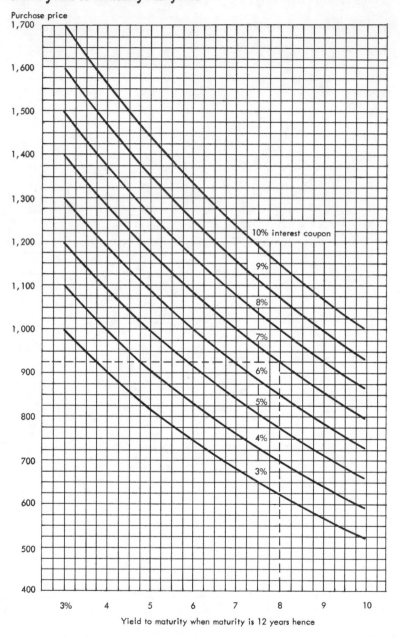

Purchase price

Yield to maturity when maturity is 12 years hence

GRAPH 31

Bond yield to maturity: 13 years

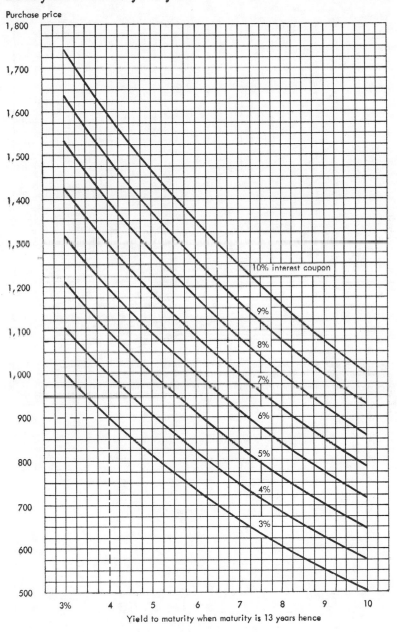

Purchase price

1,800

1,700

1,600

1,500

1,400

1,300

1,200

1,100

1,000

900

800

700

600

500

10% interest coupon

9%

8%

7%

6%

5%

4%

3%

3%   4   5   6   7   8   9   10

Yield to maturity when maturity is 13 years hence

GRAPH 32

Bond yield to maturity: 14 years

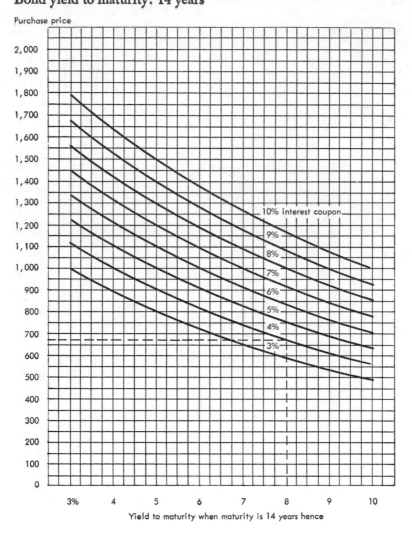

Purchase price

10% interest coupon
9%
8%
7%
6%
5%
4%
3%

Yield to maturity when maturity is 14 years hence

GRAPH 33

Bond yield to maturity: 15 years

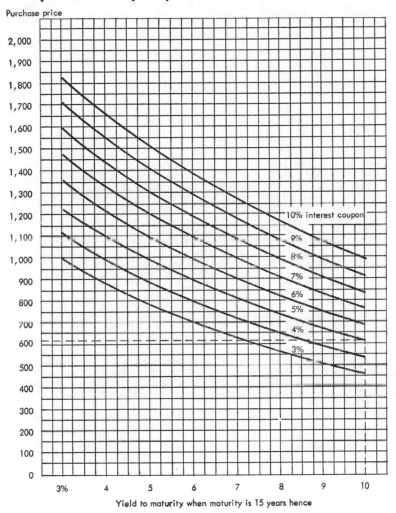

Purchase price

10% interest coupon
9%
8%
7%
6%
5%
4%
3%

Yield to maturity when maturity is 15 years hence

GRAPH 34

Bond yield to maturity: 16 years

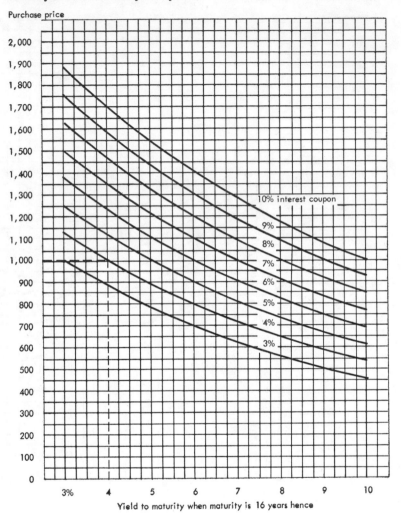

Purchase price

10% interest coupon
9%
8%
7%
6%
5%
4%
3%

Yield to maturity when maturity is 16 years hence

GRAPH 35
Bond yield to maturity: 17 years

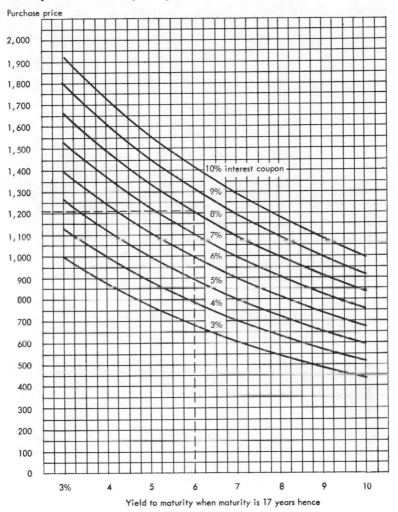

Purchase price

2,000
1,900
1,800
1,700
1,600
1,500
1,400
1,300
1,200
1,100
1,000
900
000
700
600
500
400
300
200
100
0

10% interest coupon
9%
8%
7%
6%
5%
4%
3%

3%   4   5   6   7   8   9   10

Yield to maturity when maturity is 17 years hence

GRAPH 36
Bond yield to maturity: 18 years

Purchase price

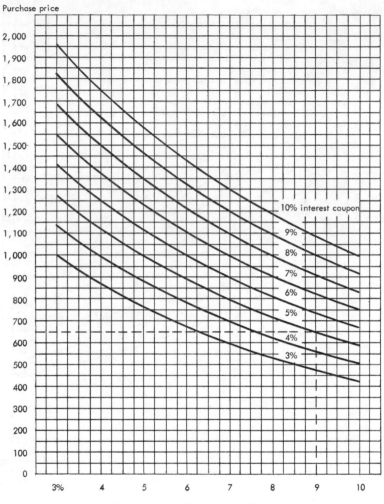

Yield to maturity when maturity is 18 years hence

GRAPH 37

Bond yield to maturity: 19 years

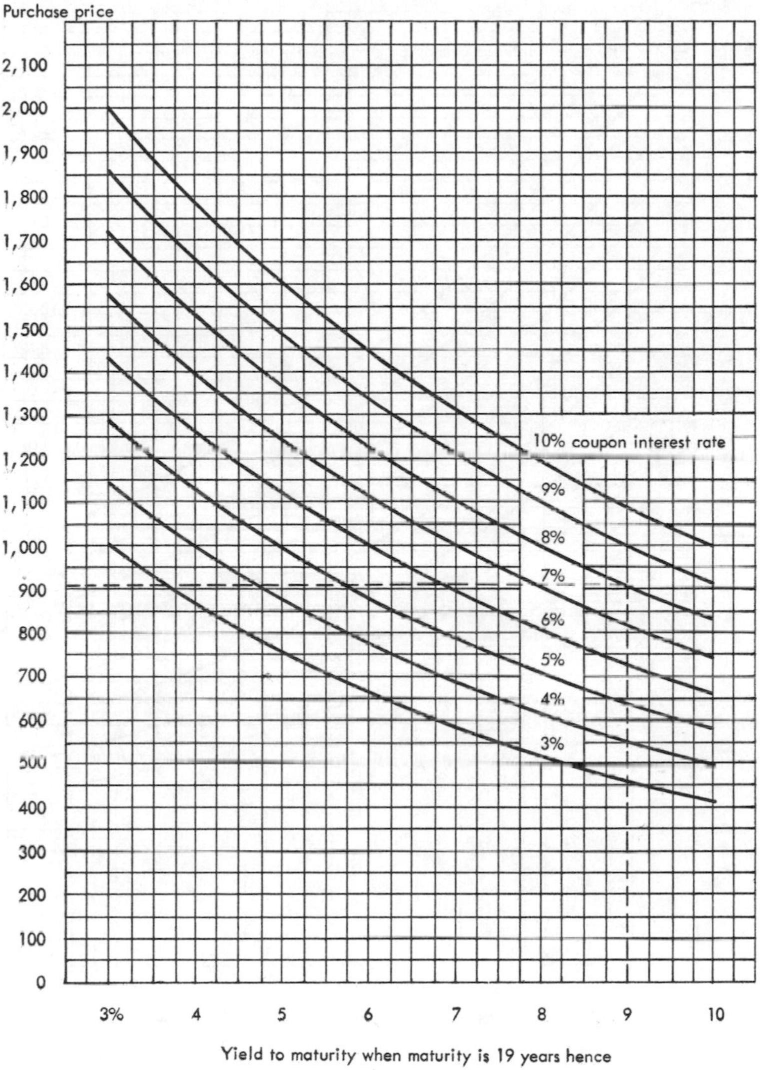

Purchase price

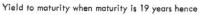

10% coupon interest rate

9%

8%

7%

6%

5%

4%

3%

3% 4 5 6 7 8 9 10

Yield to maturity when maturity is 19 years hence

GRAPH 38

Bond yield to maturity: 20 years

Purchase price

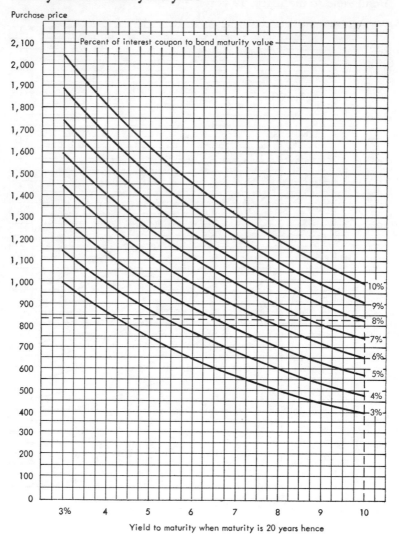

Yield to maturity when maturity is 20 years hence

GRAPH 39
Bond yield to maturity: 21 years

Purchase price

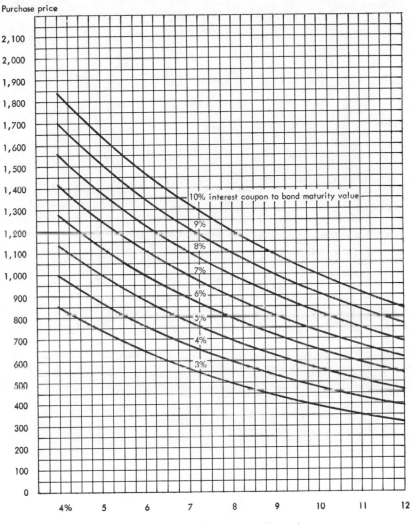

10% interest coupon to bond maturity value

9%

8%

7%

6%

5%

4%

3%

Yield to maturity when maturity is 21 years hence

GRAPH 40

Bond yield to maturity: 22 years

Purchase price

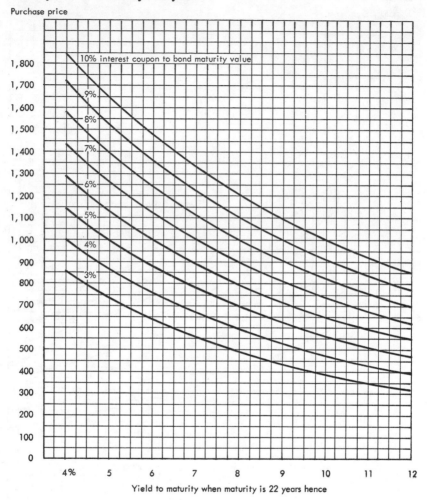

Yield to maturity when maturity is 22 years hence

GRAPH 41
Bond yield to maturity: 23 years

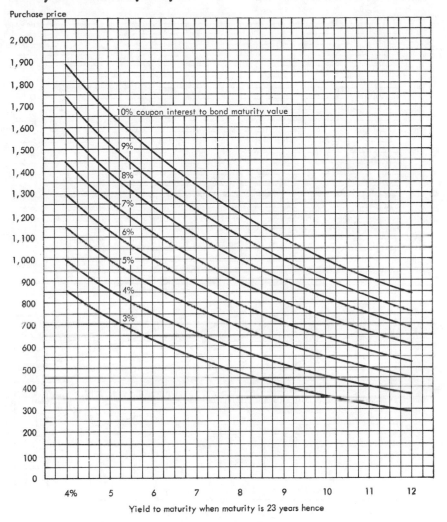

Purchase price

10% coupon interest to bond maturity value

9%
8%
7%
6%
5%
4%
3%

4% 5 6 7 8 9 10 11 12

Yield to maturity when maturity is 23 years hence

GRAPH 42

Bond yield to maturity: 24 years

Purchase price

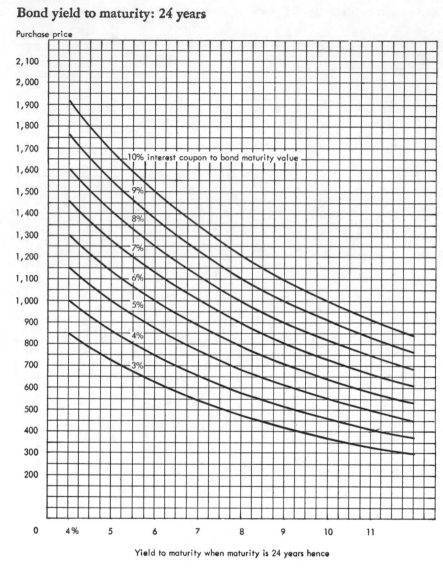

Yield to maturity when maturity is 24 years hence

GRAPH 43

Bond yield to maturity: 25 years

Purchase price

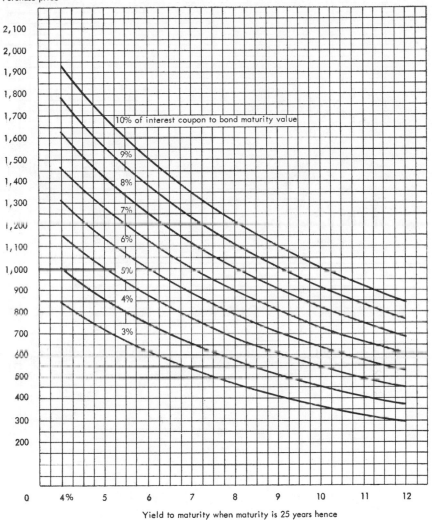

Yield to maturity when maturity is 25 years hence

70

GRAPH 44

Bond yield to maturity: 26 years

Purchase price

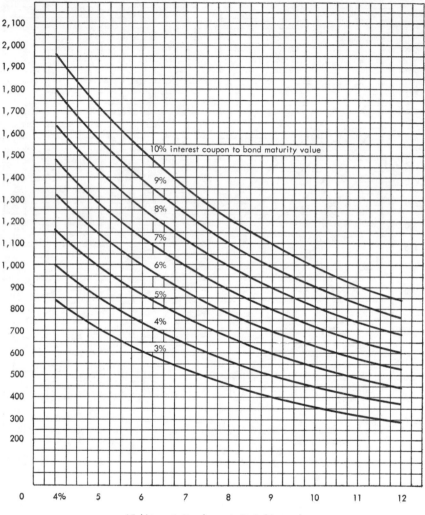

Yield to maturity when maturity is 26 years hence

GRAPH 45
Bond yield to maturity: 27 years

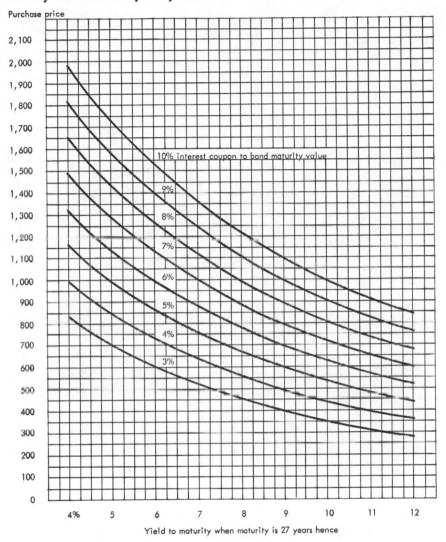

Purchase price

2,100
2,000
1,900
1,800
1,700
1,600
1,500
1,400
1,300
1,200
1,100
1,000
900
800
700
600
500
400
300
200
100
0

10% interest coupon to bond maturity value
9%
8%
7%
6%
5%
4%
3%

4%   5   6   7   8   9   10   11   12

Yield to maturity when maturity is 27 years hence

GRAPH 46

Bond yield to maturity: 28 years

Purchase price

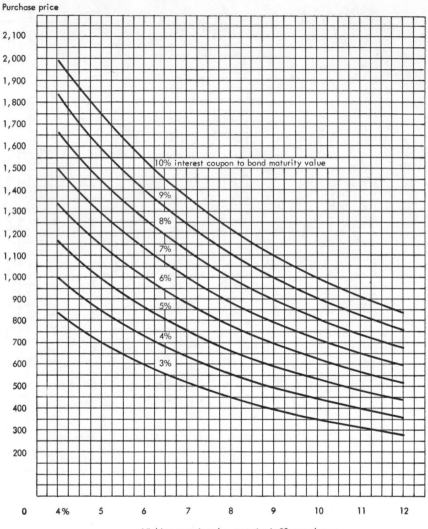

Yield to maturity when maturity is 28 years hence

GRAPH 47

Bond yield to maturity: 29 years

Purchase price

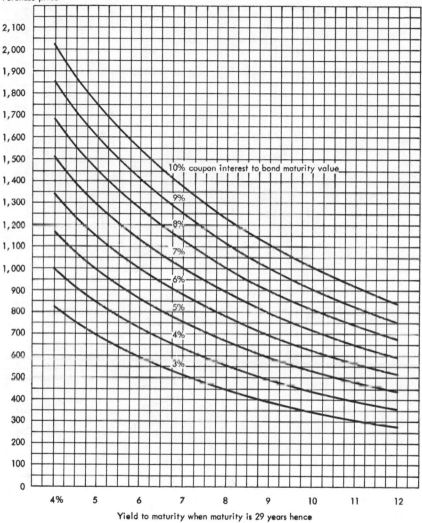

Yield to maturity when maturity is 29 years hence

GRAPH 48

Bond yield to maturity: 30 years

Purchase price

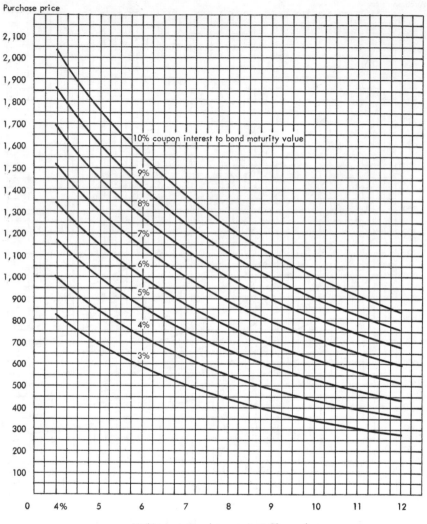

Yield to maturity when maturity is 30 years hence

7

How monthly investments
may grow:
The value of monthly
investments at various rates

The value of monthly investments after 24, 48 . . .
240 monthly investments of $100 or $1.00 per month
at various rates of compound earnings growth is shown
in the table.

Equivalent compound annual earnings	Value of the account after $100 investments each month for selected periods							
	24	48	72	96	120	150	180	240
4%..........	$2,494.20	5,196.00	8,122.30	11,292	14,725	19,421	24,609	36,677
6%..........	2,543.20	5,409.70	8,640.90	12,283	16,388	22,261	29,082	46,204
8%..........	2,593.30	5,635.00	9,202.50	13,387	18,295	25,639	34,604	58,902
10%..........	2,644.70	5,872.00	9.811.10	14,618	20,484	29,668	41,447	75,937

Value of the account after monthly investments of $1.00 per month
(multiplication factor)

	24	48	72	96	120	150	180	240
4%..........	24.942	51.960	81.223	112.92	147.25	194.21	246.09	366.77
6%..........	25.432	54.097	86.409	122.83	163.88	222.61	290.82	462.04
8%..........	25.933	56.350	92.025	133.87	182.95	256.39	346.04	589.02
10%..........	26.447	58.722	98.111	146.18	204.84	296.68	414.47	759.37

It may be seen in the table that investments in a
savings account of $100 per month at 4% interest

(compounded at ⅓ of 1% per month) would be worth, after 180 months, a total of $24,609. The same investment, at 10% earnings, would be worth $41,447.

Multiplication factor

Any amount per month (e.g., $50) may be multiplied by the *multiplication factor* in the second part of the above chart (at 8% annual growth for 180 months, the factor is 346.04) to obtain the total investment account value after completion of the specified number of monthly payments (e.g., 180). In this example—$50 per month for 180 months at 8% compound earnings per year—the value is $50 × 346.04, or $17,302.

The formula is:

$$V = R\left[\frac{(1 + i)^n - 1}{i}\right]$$

where:

V = value of the account after n monthly investments of R after the last investment is made (e.g., $17,302)

R = amount of the regular monthly investment (e.g., $50)

i = monthly compound earnings rate of the investment (e.g., .08/12)

n = number of successive monthly investments (e.g., 180 months).

The multiplication factor is the value of $\dfrac{(1 + i)^n - 1}{i}$.

To follow the examples given here, refer to Graph 49, "How monthly investments may grow." Also see Graphs 53 through 57.

GRAPH 49

How monthly investments may grow

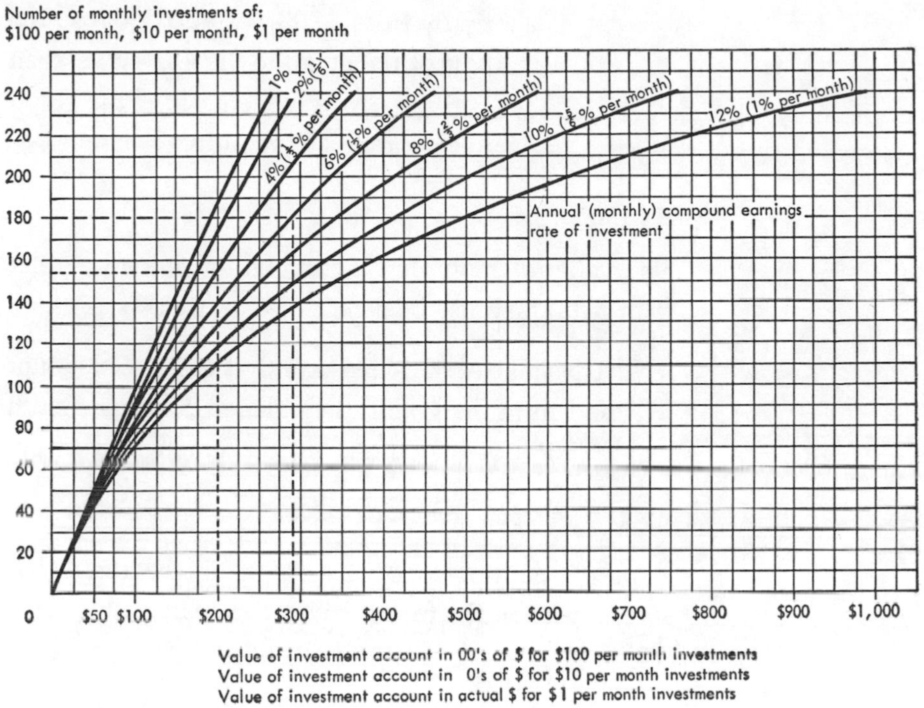

Number of monthly investments of:
$100 per month, $10 per month, $1 per month

Value of investment account in 00's of $ for $100 per month investments
Value of investment account in 0's of $ for $10 per month investments
Value of investment account in actual $ for $1 per month investments

EXAMPLE 1:

As the dashed line reveals, 180 investments on successive months of $100 each growing at 6% compound annual interest would produce an account value of about $29,082.

EXAMPLE 2:

The graphs may also be used in reverse. That is, if one wishes to have $20,000 some years from now, for how many months would one have to invest $100 per month if one can earn 4% per annum on one's investment?

Answer: About 154 months, as shown by the dotted lines on the graph: proceed vertically from $200 (or $20,000) on the base of the graph to the 4% curve, then horizontally to the left side of the graph to determine 154 months.

EXAMPLE 3:

The value of monthly investments of amounts other than $100 may also be determined, as follows:

The value of $200 per month is twice the amount shown in the graph; the value of $50 per month is 50% of that shown in the graph, and so on.

EXAMPLE 4:

A person desiring to have $30,000 in the future has several possibilities for achieving the goal:

a. At 8% earnings, 164 $100 monthly investments are required.
b. At 10% earnings, 152 $100 monthly investments are required.
c. At 6% earnings, 184 $100 monthly investments are required.
d. At 4% earnings, 206 $100 monthly investments are required.
e. At 10% earnings, 222 $50 monthly investments are required.
f. At 8% or less earnings, more than 204 $50 investments are required.

Values of the "multiplication factor" for use in the formula are given in Appendix 1.

Appendix 1

Tables of factors for future and present values of single payments and a series of payments

The tables of Appendix 1 cover the factors *under-lined* in the following formulas:

$S = P(1 + i)^n$	How P (principal) left at compound interest will grow.	Chapter 1
$P = S(1 + i)^{-n}$	What S (value of account) due in the future is worth today.	Chapters 2 and 6
$V = R\left[\dfrac{(1 + i)^n - 1}{i}\right]$	How R (regular future payments) deposited periodically will grow.	Chapter 7
$R = S\left[\dfrac{i}{(1 + i)^n - 1}\right]$	Periodic deposit that will grow into S at future date	Chapter 3
$A = R\left[\dfrac{1 - (1 + i)^{-n}}{i}\right]$	What R payable periodically is worth to-day.	Chapters 3 and 6 and Appendix 3
$R = A\left[\dfrac{i}{1 - (1 + i)^{-n}}\right]$	Periodic payment necessary to pay off an original loan of A	Appendix 3

79

The tables contain values for each of the factors identified for the following interest rates and number of periods (e.g., years, months, quarterly periods):

Interest rate %	Number of periods	Table number
½	180	1
1	180	2
1.5	180	3
2	180	4
3	180	5
4	180	6
5	180	7
6	120	8
7	120	9
8	120	10
9	120	11
10	120	12
11	60	13
12	60	14

Tables on pages 82–159 were reprinted with the permission of:

FINANCIAL PUBLISHING COMPANY
82 Brookline Avenue
Boston, Massachusetts 02215.

Readers who require more extensive information on the computation of interest will find the purchase of Financial Publishing Company's publication #376 a most valuable investment.

TABLE 1

Rate of ½%

PERIODS	AMOUNT OF 1 How $1 left at compound interest will grow.	AMOUNT OF 1 PER PERIOD How $1 deposited periodically will grow.	SINKING FUND Periodic deposit that will grow to $1 at future date.	PRESENT WORTH OF 1 What $1 due in the future is worth today.	PRESENT WORTH OF 1 PER PERIOD What $1 payable periodically is worth today.	PARTIAL PAYMENT Annuity worth $1 today. Periodic payment necessary to pay off a loan of $1.	PERIODS
1	1.005 000	1.000 000	1.000 000	.995 024	.995 024	1.005 000	1
2	1.010 025	2.005 000	.498 753	.990 074	1.985 099	.503 753	2
3	1.015 075	3.015 025	.331 672	.985 148	2.970 248	.336 672	3
4	1.020 150	4.030 100	.248 132	.980 247	3.950 495	.253 132	4
5	1.025 251	5.050 250	.198 009	.975 370	4.925 866	.203 009	5
6	1.030 377	6.075 501	.164 595	.970 518	5.896 384	.169 595	6
7	1.035 529	7.105 879	.140 728	.965 689	6.862 074	.145 728	7
8	1.040 707	8.141 408	.122 828	.960 885	7.822 959	.127 828	8
9	1.045 910	9.182 115	.108 907	.956 104	8.779 063	.113 907	9
10	1.051 140	10.228 026	.097 770	.951 347	9.730 411	.102 770	10
11	1.056 395	11.279 166	.088 659	.946 614	10.677 026	.093 659	11
12	1.061 677	12.335 562	.081 066	.941 905	11.618 932	.086 066	12
13	1.066 986	13.397 240	.074 642	.937 219	12.556 151	.079 642	13
14	1.072 321	14.464 226	.069 136	.932 556	13.488 707	.074 136	14
15	1.077 682	15.536 547	.064 364	.927 916	14.416 624	.069 364	15
16	1.083 071	16.614 230	.060 189	.923 300	15.339 925	.065 189	16
17	1.088 486	17.697 301	.056 505	.918 706	16.258 631	.061 505	17
18	1.093 928	18.785 787	.053 231	.914 136	17.172 768	.058 231	18
19	1.099 398	19.879 716	.050 302	.909 588	18.082 356	.055 302	19
20	1.104 895	20.979 115	.047 666	.905 062	18.987 419	.052 666	20
21	1.110 420	22.084 011	.045 281	.900 560	19.887 979	.050 281	21
22	1.115 972	23.194 431	.043 113	.896 079	20.784 058	.048 113	22
23	1.121 552	24.310 403	.041 134	.891 621	21.675 680	.046 134	23
24	1.127 159	25.431 955	.039 320	.887 185	22.562 866	.044 320	24
25	1.132 795	26.559 115	.037 651	.882 771	23.445 638	.042 651	25
26	1.138 459	27.691 910	.036 111	.878 379	24.324 017	.041 111	26
27	1.144 151	28.830 370	.034 685	.874 009	25.198 027	.039 685	27
28	1.149 872	29.974 521	.033 361	.869 661	26.067 689	.038 361	28
29	1.155 621	31.124 394	.032 129	.865 334	26.933 024	.037 129	29
30	1.161 400	32.280 016	.030 978	.861 029	27.794 053	.035 978	30

N	$(1+i)^N$	$\dfrac{(1+i)^N-1}{i}$	$\dfrac{i}{(1+i)^N-1}$	$(1+i)^{-N}$	$\dfrac{1-(1+i)^{-N}}{i}$	$\dfrac{i}{1-(1+i)^{-N}}$	N
31	1.167 207	33.441 416	.029 903	.856 746	28.650 799	.034 903	31
32	1.173 043	34.608 623	.028 894	.852 483	29.503 283	.033 894	32
33	1.178 908	35.781 666	.027 947	.848 242	30.351 525	.032 947	33
34	1.184 802	36.960 575	.027 055	.844 022	31.195 548	.032 055	34
35	1.190 726	38.145 378	.026 215	.839 823	32.035 371	.031 215	35
36	1.196 680	39.336 104	.025 421	.835 644	32.871 016	.030 421	36
37	1.202 663	40.532 785	.024 671	.831 487	33.702 503	.029 671	37
38	1.208 677	41.735 449	.023 960	.827 350	34.529 854	.028 960	38
39	1.214 720	42.944 126	.023 286	.823 234	35.353 089	.028 286	39
40	1.220 794	44.158 847	.022 645	.819 138	36.172 227	.027 645	40
41	1.226 898	45.379 641	.022 036	.815 063	36.987 291	.027 036	41
42	1.233 032	46.606 539	.021 456	.811 008	37.798 299	.026 456	42
43	1.239 197	47.839 572	.020 903	.806 973	38.605 273	.025 903	43
44	1.245 393	49.078 770	.020 375	.802 958	39.408 232	.025 375	44
45	1.251 620	50.324 164	.019 871	.798 964	40.207 196	.024 871	45
46	1.257 878	51.575 784	.019 388	.794 989	41.002 185	.024 388	46
47	1.264 168	52.833 663	.018 927	.791 033	41.793 219	.023 927	47
48	1.270 489	54.097 832	.018 485	.787 098	42.580 317	.023 485	48
49	1.276 841	55.368 321	.018 060	.783 182	43.363 500	.023 060	49
50	1.283 225	56.645 162	.017 653	.779 286	44.142 786	.022 653	50
51	1.289 641	57.928 388	.017 262	.775 409	44.918 195	.022 262	51
52	1.296 090	59.218 030	.016 886	.771 551	45.689 746	.021 886	52
53	1.302 570	60.514 120	.016 525	.767 712	46.457 459	.021 525	53
54	1.309 083	61.816 691	.016 176	.763 893	47.221 352	.021 176	54
55	1.315 628	63.125 774	.015 841	.760 092	47.981 445	.020 841	55
56	1.322 207	64.441 403	.015 517	.756 311	48.737 756	.020 517	56
57	1.328 818	65.763 610	.015 205	.752 548	49.490 305	.020 205	57
58	1.335 462	67.092 428	.014 904	.748 804	50.239 109	.019 904	58
59	1.342 139	68.427 891	.014 613	.745 079	50.984 188	.019 613	59
60	1.348 850	69.770 030	.014 332	.741 372	51.725 560	.019 332	60

Source: *Financial Compound Interest and Annuity Tables*, 5th ed. (Boston: Financial Publishing Co., 1970).

TABLE 1 (continued)

Rate of ½%

PERIODS	AMOUNT OF 1 — How $1 left at compound interest will grow.	AMOUNT OF 1 PER PERIOD — How $1 deposited periodically will grow.	SINKING FUND — Periodic deposit that will grow to $1 at future date.	PRESENT WORTH OF 1 — What $1 due in the future is worth today.	PRESENT WORTH OF 1 PER PERIOD — What $1 payable periodically is worth today.	PARTIAL PAYMENT — Annuity worth $1 today. Periodic payment necessary to pay off a loan of $1.	PERIODS
61	1.355 594	71.118 880	.014 060	.737 683	52.463 244	.019 060	61
62	1.362 372	72.474 475	.013 797	.734 013	53.197 258	.018 797	62
63	1.369 184	73.836 847	.013 543	.730 361	53.927 620	.018 543	63
64	1.376 030	75.206 031	.013 296	.726 728	54.654 348	.018 296	64
65	1.382 910	76.582 061	.013 057	.723 112	55.377 461	.018 057	65
66	1.389 824	77.964 972	.012 826	.719 515	56.096 976	.017 826	66
67	1.396 773	79.354 797	.012 601	.715 935	56.812 911	.017 601	67
68	1.403 757	80.751 570	.012 383	.712 373	57.525 285	.017 383	68
69	1.410 776	82.155 328	.012 172	.708 829	58.234 114	.017 172	69
70	1.417 830	83.566 105	.011 966	.705 302	58.939 417	.016 966	70
71	1.424 919	84.983 936	.011 766	.701 793	59.641 211	.016 766	71
72	1.432 044	86.408 855	.011 572	.698 302	60.339 513	.016 572	72
73	1.439 204	87.840 899	.011 384	.694 828	61.034 342	.016 384	73
74	1.446 400	89.280 104	.011 200	.691 371	61.725 713	.016 200	74
75	1.453 632	90.726 504	.011 022	.687 931	62.413 645	.016 022	75
76	1.460 900	92.180 137	.010 848	.684 509	63.098 154	.015 848	76
77	1.468 205	93.641 038	.010 679	.681 103	63.779 258	.015 679	77
78	1.475 546	95.109 243	.010 514	.677 715	64.456 973	.015 514	78
79	1.482 923	96.584 789	.010 353	.674 343	65.131 316	.015 353	79
80	1.490 338	98.067 713	.010 197	.670 988	65.802 305	.015 197	80
81	1.497 790	99.558 052	.010 044	.667 650	66.469 955	.015 044	81
82	1.505 279	101.055 842	.009 895	.664 328	67.134 284	.014 895	82
83	1.512 805	102.561 121	.009 750	.661 023	67.795 307	.014 750	83
84	1.520 369	104.073 927	.009 608	.657 734	68.453 042	.014 608	84
85	1.527 971	105.594 296	.009 470	.654 462	69.107 504	.014 470	85
86	1.535 611	107.122 268	.009 335	.651 206	69.758 711	.014 335	86
87	1.543 289	108.657 879	.009 203	.647 966	70.406 677	.014 203	87
88	1.551 005	110.201 169	.009 074	.644 742	71.051 420	.014 074	88
89	1.558 760	111.752 174	.008 948	.641 535	71.692 956	.013 948	89
90	1.566 554	113.310 935	.008 825	.638 343	72.331 299	.013 825	90

N	$(1+i)^N$	$\dfrac{(1+i)^N-1}{i}$	$\dfrac{i}{(1+i)^N-1}$	$(1+i)^{-N}$	$\dfrac{1-(1+i)^{-N}}{i}$	$\dfrac{i}{1-(1+i)^{-N}}$
91	1.574 387	114.877 490	.008 704	.635 167	72.966 467	.013 704
92	1.582 259	116.451 877	.008 587	.632 007	73.598 474	.013 587
93	1.590 170	118.034 137	.008 472	.628 863	74.227 338	.013 472
94	1.598 121	119.624 308	.008 359	.625 734	74.853 072	.013 359
95	1.606 112	121.222 429	.008 249	.622 621	75.475 694	.013 249
96	1.614 142	122.828 541	.008 141	.619 523	76.095 218	.013 141
97	1.622 213	124.442 684	.008 035	.616 441	76.711 659	.013 035
98	1.630 324	126.064 897	.007 932	.613 374	77.325 034	.012 932
99	1.638 476	127.695 222	.007 831	.610 323	77.935 357	.012 831
100	1.646 668	129.333 698	.007 731	.607 286	78.542 644	.012 731
101	1.654 901	130.980 366	.007 634	.604 265	79.146 910	.012 634
102	1.663 176	132.635 268	.007 539	.601 259	79.748 169	.012 539
103	1.671 492	134.298 445	.007 446	.598 267	80.346 437	.012 446
104	1.679 849	135.969 937	.007 354	.595 291	80.941 728	.012 354
105	1.688 248	137.649 787	.007 264	.592 329	81.534 058	.012 264
106	1.696 690	139.338 035	.007 176	.589 382	82.123 441	.012 176
107	1.705 173	141.034 726	.007 090	.586 450	82.709 891	.012 090
108	1.713 699	142.739 899	.007 005	.583 532	83.293 424	.012 005
109	1.722 267	144.453 599	.006 922	.580 629	83.874 054	.011 922
110	1.730 879	146.175 867	.006 841	.577 741	84.451 795	.011 841
111	1.739 533	147.906 746	.006 761	.574 866	85.026 661	.011 761
112	1.748 231	149.646 280	.006 682	.572 006	85.598 668	.011 682
113	1.756 972	151.394 511	.006 605	.569 160	86.167 829	.011 605
114	1.765 757	153.151 484	.006 529	.566 329	86.734 158	.011 529
115	1.774 586	154.917 241	.006 455	.563 511	87.297 670	.011 455
116	1.783 459	156.691 827	.006 381	.560 708	87.858 378	.011 381
117	1.792 376	158.475 287	.006 310	.557 918	88.416 296	.011 310
118	1.801 338	160.267 663	.006 239	.555 142	88.971 439	.011 239
119	1.810 345	162.069 001	.006 170	.552 380	89.523 820	.011 170
120	1.819 396	163.879 346	.006 102	.549 632	90.073 453	.011 102

Source: *Financial Compound Interest and Annuity Tables*, 5th ed. (Boston: Financial Publishing Co., 1970).

TABLE 1 (concluded)

Rate of ½%

PERIODS	AMOUNT OF 1 — How $1 left at compound interest will grow.	AMOUNT OF 1 PER PERIOD — How $1 deposited periodically will grow.	SINKING FUND — Periodic deposit that will grow to $1 at future due.	PRESENT WORTH OF 1 — What $1 due in the future is worth today.	PRESENT WORTH OF 1 PER PERIOD — What $1 payable periodically is worth today.	PARTIAL PAYMENT — Annuity worth $1 today. Periodic payment necessary to pay off a loan of $1.	PERIODS
121	1.828 493	165.698 743	.006 035	.546 898	90.620 351	.011 035	121
122	1.837 636	167.527 237	.005 969	.544 177	91.164 528	.010 969	122
123	1.846 824	169.364 873	.005 904	.541 470	91.705 998	.010 904	123
124	1.856 058	171.211 697	.005 840	.538 776	92.244 775	.010 840	124
125	1.865 338	173.067 756	.005 778	.536 095	92.780 870	.010 778	125
126	1.874 665	174.933 095	.005 716	.533 428	93.314 299	.010 716	126
127	1.884 038	176.807 760	.005 655	.530 774	93.845 073	.010 655	127
128	1.893 458	178.691 799	.005 596	.528 133	94.373 207	.010 596	128
129	1.902 926	180.585 258	.005 537	.525 506	94.898 714	.010 537	129
130	1.912 440	182.488 184	.005 479	.522 891	95.421 606	.010 479	130
131	1.922 003	184.400 625	.005 422	.520 290	95.941 896	.010 422	131
132	1.931 613	186.322 628	.005 367	.517 702	96.459 598	.010 367	132
133	1.941 271	188.254 241	.005 311	.515 126	96.974 725	.010 311	133
134	1.950 977	190.195 513	.005 257	.512 563	97.487 288	.010 257	134
135	1.960 732	192.146 490	.005 204	.510 013	97.997 302	.010 204	135
136	1.970 536	194.107 223	.005 151	.507 476	98.504 778	.010 151	136
137	1.980 388	196.077 759	.005 100	.504 951	99.009 729	.010 100	137
138	1.990 290	198.058 147	.005 049	.502 439	99.512 168	.010 049	138
139	2.000 242	200.048 438	.004 998	.499 939	100.012 108	.009 998	139
140	2.010 243	202.048 680	.004 949	.497 452	100.509 560	.009 949	140
141	2.020 294	204.058 924	.004 900	.494 977	101.004 537	.009 900	141
142	2.030 396	206.079 218	.004 852	.492 514	101.497 052	.009 852	142
143	2.040 548	208.109 615	.004 805	.490 064	101.987 116	.009 805	143
144	2.050 750	210.150 163	.004 758	.487 626	102.474 743	.009 758	144
145	2.061 004	212.200 913	.004 712	.485 200	102.959 943	.009 712	145
146	2.071 309	214.261 918	.004 667	.482 786	103.442 729	.009 667	146
147	2.081 666	216.333 228	.004 622	.480 384	103.923 114	.009 622	147
148	2.092 074	218.414 894	.004 578	.477 994	104.401 108	.009 578	148
149	2.102 534	220.506 968	.004 535	.475 616	104.876 725	.009 535	149
150	2.113 047	222.609 503	.004 492	.473 250	105.349 975	.009 492	150

N	$(1+i)^N$	$\dfrac{(1+i)^N - 1}{i}$	$\dfrac{i}{(1+i)^N - 1}$	$(1-i)^{-N}$	$\dfrac{1-(1+i)^{-N}}{i}$	$\dfrac{i}{1-(1+i)^{-N}}$	N
151	2.123 612	224.722 551	.004 449	.470 895	105.820 870	.009 449	151
152	2.134 230	226.846 163	.004 408	.468 552	106.289 423	.009 408	152
153	2.144 901	228.980 394	.004 367	.466 221	106.755 645	.009 367	153
154	2.155 626	231.125 296	.004 326	.463 902	107.219 547	.009 326	154
155	2.166 404	233.280 923	.004 286	.461 594	107.681 142	.009 286	155
156	2.177 236	235.447 327	.004 247	.459 297	108.140 439	.009 247	156
157	2.188 122	237.624 564	.004 208	.457 012	108.597 452	.009 208	157
158	2.199 063	239.812 687	.004 169	.454 739	109.052 191	.009 169	158
159	2.210 058	242.011 750	.004 132	.452 476	109.504 668	.009 132	159
160	2.221 109	244.221 809	.004 094	.450 225	109.954 893	.009 094	160
161	2.232 214	246.442 918	.004 057	.447 985	110.402 879	.009 057	161
162	2.243 375	248.675 132	.004 021	.445 756	110.848 636	.009 021	162
163	2.254 592	250.918 508	.003 985	.443 539	111.292 175	.008 985	163
164	2.265 865	253.173 101	.003 949	.441 332	111.733 507	.008 949	164
165	2.277 194	255.438 966	.003 914	.439 136	112.172 644	.008 914	165
166	2.288 580	257.716 161	.003 880	.435 952	112.609 596	.008 880	166
167	2.300 023	260.004 742	.003 846	.434 778	113.044 374	.008 846	167
168	2.311 523	262.304 765	.003 812	.432 615	113.476 989	.008 812	168
169	2.323 081	264.616 289	.003 779	.430 462	113.907 452	.008 779	169
170	2.334 696	266.939 371	.003 746	.428 321	114.335 773	.008 746	170
171	2.346 370	269.274 068	.003 713	.425 190	114.761 963	.008 713	171
172	2.358 102	271.620 438	.003 681	.424 069	115.186 033	.008 681	172
173	2.369 892	273.978 540	.003 649	.421 960	115.607 993	.008 649	173
174	2.381 742	276.348 433	.003 618	.419 860	116.027 854	.008 618	174
175	2.393 650	278.730 175	.003 587	.417 771	116.445 626	.008 587	175
176	2.405 619	281.123 826	.003 557	.415 693	116.861 319	.008 557	176
177	2.417 647	283.529 445	.003 526	.413 625	117.274 944	.008 526	177
178	2.429 735	285.947 092	.003 497	.411 567	117.686 512	.008 497	178
179	2.441 884	288.376 828	.003 467	.409 519	118.096 032	.008 467	179
180	2.454 093	290.818 712	.003 438	.407 482	118.503 514	.008 438	180

Source: *Financial Compound Interest and Annuity Tables*, 5th ed. (Boston: Financial Publishing Co., 1970).

TABLE 2

Rate of 1%

PERIODS	AMOUNT OF 1 — How $1 left at compound interest will grow.	AMOUNT OF 1 PER PERIOD — How $1 deposited periodically will grow.	SINKING FUND — Periodic deposit that will grow to $1 at future date.	PRESENT WORTH OF 1 — What $1 due in the future is worth today.	PRESENT WORTH OF 1 PER PERIOD — What $1 payable periodically is worth today.	PARTIAL PAYMENT — Annuity worth $1 today. Periodic payment necessary to pay off a loan of $1.	PERIODS
1	1.010 000	1.000 000	1.000 000	.990 099	.990 099	1.010 000	1
2	1.020 100	2.010 000	.497 512	.980 296	1.970 395	.507 512	2
3	1.030 301	3.030 100	.330 022	.970 590	2.940 985	.340 022	3
4	1.040 604	4.060 401	.246 281	.960 980	3.901 965	.256 281	4
5	1.051 010	5.101 005	.196 039	.951 465	4.853 431	.206 039	5
6	1.061 520	6.152 015	.162 548	.942 045	5.795 476	.172 548	6
7	1.072 135	7.213 535	.138 628	.932 718	6.728 194	.148 628	7
8	1.082 856	8.285 670	.120 690	.923 483	7.651 677	.130 690	8
9	1.093 685	9.368 527	.106 740	.914 339	8.566 017	.116 740	9
10	1.104 622	10.462 212	.095 582	.905 286	9.471 304	.105 582	10
11	1.115 668	11.566 834	.086 454	.896 323	10.367 628	.096 454	11
12	1.126 825	12.682 503	.078 848	.887 449	11.255 077	.088 848	12
13	1.138 093	13.809 328	.072 414	.878 662	12.133 740	.082 414	13
14	1.149 474	14.947 421	.066 901	.869 962	13.003 703	.076 901	14
15	1.160 968	16.096 895	.062 123	.861 349	13.865 052	.072 123	15
16	1.172 578	17.257 864	.057 944	.852 821	14.717 873	.067 944	16
17	1.184 304	18.430 443	.054 258	.844 377	15.562 251	.064 258	17
18	1.196 147	19.614 747	.050 982	.836 017	16.398 268	.060 982	18
19	1.208 108	20.810 895	.048 051	.827 739	17.226 008	.058 051	19
20	1.220 190	22.019 003	.045 415	.819 544	18.045 552	.055 415	20
21	1.232 391	23.239 194	.043 030	.811 430	18.856 983	.053 030	21
22	1.244 715	24.471 585	.040 863	.803 396	19.660 379	.050 863	22
23	1.257 163	25.716 301	.038 885	.795 441	20.455 821	.048 885	23
24	1.269 734	26.973 464	.037 073	.787 566	21.243 387	.047 073	24
25	1.282 431	28.243 199	.035 406	.779 768	22.023 155	.045 406	25
26	1.295 256	29.525 631	.033 868	.772 047	22.795 203	.043 868	26
27	1.308 208	30.820 887	.032 445	.764 403	23.559 607	.042 445	27
28	1.321 290	32.129 096	.031 124	.756 835	24.316 443	.041 124	28
29	1.334 503	33.450 387	.029 895	.749 342	25.065 785	.039 895	29
30	1.347 848	34.784 891	.028 748	.741 922	25.807 708	.038 748	30

N	$(1+i)^N$	$\dfrac{(1+i)^N-1}{i}$	$\dfrac{i}{(1+i)^N-1}$	$(1+i)^{-N}$	$\dfrac{1-(1+i)^{-N}}{i}$	$\dfrac{i}{1-(1+i)^{-N}}$	N
31	1.361 927	36.132 740	.027 675	.734 577	26.542 285	.037 675	31
32	1.374 940	37.494 067	.026 670	.727 304	27.269 589	.036 670	32
33	1.388 690	38.869 008	.025 727	.720 103	27.989 692	.035 727	33
34	1.402 576	40.257 698	.024 839	.712 973	28.702 665	.034 839	34
35	1.416 602	41.660 275	.024 003	.705 914	29.408 580	.034 003	35
36	1.430 768	43.076 878	.023 214	.698 924	30.107 505	.033 214	36
37	1.445 076	44.507 647	.022 468	.692 004	30.799 509	.032 468	37
38	1.459 527	45.952 723	.021 761	.685 153	31.484 663	.031 761	38
39	1.474 122	47.412 250	.021 091	.678 369	32.163 032	.031 091	39
40	1.488 863	48.886 373	.020 455	.671 653	32.834 686	.030 455	40
41	1.503 752	50.375 237	.019 851	.665 003	33.499 689	.029 851	41
42	1.518 789	51.878 989	.019 275	.658 418	34.158 108	.029 275	42
43	1.533 977	53.397 779	.018 727	.651 899	34.810 008	.028 727	43
44	1.549 317	54.931 757	.018 204	.645 445	35.455 453	.028 204	44
45	1.564 810	56.481 074	.017 705	.639 054	36.094 508	.027 705	45
46	1.580 458	58.045 885	.017 227	.632 727	36.727 236	.027 227	46
47	1.596 263	59.626 344	.016 771	.626 463	37.353 699	.026 771	47
48	1.612 226	61.222 607	.016 333	.620 260	37.973 959	.026 333	48
49	1.628 348	62.834 833	.015 914	.614 119	38.588 078	.025 914	49
50	1.644 631	64.463 182	.015 512	.608 038	39.196 117	.025 512	50
51	1.661 078	66.107 814	.015 126	.602 018	39.798 136	.025 126	51
52	1.677 688	67.768 892	.014 756	.596 058	40.394 194	.024 756	52
53	1.694 465	69.446 581	.014 399	.590 156	40.984 350	.024 399	53
54	1.711 410	71.141 046	.014 056	.584 313	41.568 664	.024 056	54
55	1.728 524	72.852 457	.013 726	.578 528	42.147 192	.023 726	55
56	1.745 809	74.580 981	.013 408	.572 800	42.719 992	.023 408	56
57	1.763 267	76.326 791	.013 101	.567 128	43.287 121	.023 101	57
58	1.780 900	78.090 059	.012 805	.561 513	43.848 634	.022 805	58
59	1.798 709	79.870 960	.012 520	.555 954	44.404 588	.022 520	59
60	1.816 696	81.669 669	.012 244	.550 449	44.955 038	.022 244	60

Source: *Financial Compound Interest and Annuity Tables*, 5th ed. (Boston: Financial Publishing Co., 1970).

TABLE 2 (continued)

Rate of 1%

PERIODS	AMOUNT OF 1 — How $1 left at compound interest will grow.	AMOUNT OF 1 PER PERIOD — How $1 deposited periodically will grow.	SINKING FUND — Periodic deposit that will grow to $1 at future date.	PRESENT WORTH OF 1 — What $1 due in the future is worth today.	PRESENT WORTH OF 1 PER PERIOD — What $1 payable periodically is worth today.	PARTIAL PAYMENT — Annuity worth $1 today. Periodic payment necessary to pay off a loan of $1.	PERIODS
61	1.834 863	83.486 366	.011 978	.544 999	45.500 038	.021 978	61
62	1.853 212	85.321 230	.011 720	.539 603	46.039 641	.021 720	62
63	1.871 744	87.174 442	.011 471	.534 260	46.573 902	.021 471	63
64	1.890 461	89.046 186	.011 230	.528 971	47.102 873	.021 230	64
65	1.909 366	90.936 648	.010 996	.523 733	47.626 607	.020 996	65
66	1.928 460	92.846 015	.010 770	.518 548	48.145 156	.020 770	66
67	1.947 744	94.774 475	.010 551	.513 414	48.658 570	.020 551	67
68	1.967 222	96.722 220	.010 338	.508 330	49.166 901	.020 338	68
69	1.986 894	98.689 442	.010 132	.503 298	49.670 199	.020 132	69
70	2.006 763	100.676 336	.009 932	.498 314	50.168 514	.019 932	70
71	2.026 831	102.683 100	.009 738	.493 381	50.661 895	.019 738	71
72	2.047 099	104.709 931	.009 550	.488 496	51.150 391	.019 550	72
73	2.067 570	106.757 030	.009 367	.483 659	51.634 050	.019 367	73
74	2.088 246	108.824 600	.009 189	.478 870	52.112 921	.019 189	74
75	2.109 128	110.912 846	.009 016	.474 129	52.587 051	.019 016	75
76	2.130 219	113.021 975	.008 847	.469 435	53.056 486	.018 847	76
77	2.151 521	115.152 195	.008 684	.464 787	53.521 273	.018 684	77
78	2.173 037	117.303 717	.008 524	.460 185	53.981 459	.018 524	78
79	2.194 767	119.476 754	.008 369	.455 629	54.437 088	.018 369	79
80	2.216 715	121.671 521	.008 218	.451 117	54.888 206	.018 218	80
81	2.238 882	123.888 236	.008 071	.446 651	55.334 857	.018 071	81
82	2.261 271	126.127 119	.007 928	.442 229	55.777 086	.017 928	82
83	2.283 883	128.388 390	.007 788	.437 850	56.214 937	.017 788	83
84	2.306 722	130.672 274	.007 652	.433 515	56.648 452	.017 652	84
85	2.329 789	132.978 997	.007 519	.429 223	57.077 676	.017 519	85
86	2.353 087	135.308 787	.007 390	.424 973	57.502 649	.017 390	86
87	2.376 618	137.661 874	.007 264	.420 765	57.923 415	.017 264	87
88	2.400 384	140.038 493	.007 140	.416 599	58.340 015	.017 140	88
89	2.424 388	142.438 878	.007 020	.412 475	58.752 490	.017 020	89
90	2.448 632	144.863 267	.006 903	.408 391	59.160 881	.016 903	90

6 YEARS

n	$(1+i)^N$	$\frac{(1+i)^N-1}{i}$	$\frac{i}{(1+i)^N-1}$	$(1+i)^{-N}$	$\frac{1-(1+i)^{-N}}{i}$	$\frac{i}{1-(1+i)^{-N}}$
91	2.473 119	147.311 900	.006 788	.404 347	59.555 229	.016 788
92	2.497 850	149.785 019	.006 676	.400 344	59.965 573	.016 676
93	2.522 828	152.282 869	.006 566	.396 380	60.361 953	.016 566
94	2.548 056	154.805 698	.006 459	.392 455	60.754 409	.016 459
95	2.573 537	157.353 755	.006 355	.388 570	61.142 980	.016 355
96	2.599 272	159.927 292	.006 252	.384 722	61.527 702	.016 252
97	2.625 265	162.526 565	.006 152	.380 913	61.908 616	.016 152
98	2.651 518	165.151 831	.006 055	.377 142	62.285 759	.016 055
99	2.678 033	167.803 349	.005 959	.373 408	62.659 167	.015 959
100	2.704 813	170.481 342	.005 865	.369 711	63.028 878	.015 865
101	2.731 861	173.186 196	.005 774	.366 050	63.394 929	.015 774
102	2.759 180	175.918 058	.005 684	.362 426	63.757 355	.015 684
103	2.786 772	178.677 239	.005 595	.358 838	64.116 193	.015 596
104	2.814 640	181.464 011	.005 510	.355 285	64.471 479	.015 510
105	2.842 786	184.278 651	.005 425	.351 767	64.823 246	.015 426
106	2.871 214	187.121 438	.005 344	.348 284	65.171 531	.015 344
107	2.899 926	189.992 652	.005 263	.344 836	65.516 367	.015 263
108	2.928 925	192.892 579	.005 184	.341 422	65.857 789	.015 184
109	2.958 215	195.821 505	.005 106	.338 041	66.195 831	.015 106
110	2.987 797	198.779 720	.005 030	.334 694	66.530 526	.015 030
111	3.017 675	201.767 517	.004 956	.331 380	66.861 907	.014 956
112	3.047 851	204.785 192	.004 883	.328 099	67.190 007	.014 883
113	3.078 330	207.833 044	.004 811	.324 851	67.514 858	.014 811
114	3.109 113	210.911 374	.004 741	.321 635	67.836 493	.014 741
115	3.140 204	214.020 488	.004 672	.318 450	68.154 944	.014 672
116	3.171 606	217.160 693	.004 604	.315 297	68.470 241	.014 604
117	3.203 323	220.332 300	.004 538	.312 175	68.782 417	.014 538
118	3.235 356	223.535 623	.004 473	.309 084	69.091 502	.014 473
119	3.267 709	226.770 979	.004 409	.306 024	69.397 527	.014 409
120	3.300 386	230.038 689	.004 347	.302 994	69.700 522	.014 347

Source: *Financial Compound Interest and Annuity Tables*, 5th ed. (Boston: Financial Publishing Co., 1970).

TABLE 2 (concluded)

Rate of 1%

PERIODS	AMOUNT OF 1 How $1 left at compound interest will grow.	AMOUNT OF 1 PER PERIOD How $1 deposited periodically will grow.	SINKING FUND Periodic deposit that will grow to $1 at future date.	PRESENT WORTH OF 1 What $1 due in the future is worth today.	PRESENT WORTH OF 1 PER PERIOD What $1 payable periodically is worth today.	PARTIAL PAYMENT Annuity worth $1 today. Periodic payment necessary to pay off a loan of $1.	PERIODS
121	3.333 390	233.339 076	.004 285	.299 994	70.000 516	.014 285	121
122	3.366 724	236.672 467	.004 225	.297 024	70.297 541	.014 225	122
123	3.400 391	240.039 191	.004 165	.294 083	70.591 625	.014 165	123
124	3.434 395	243.439 583	.004 107	.291 172	70.882 797	.014 107	124
125	3.468 739	246.873 979	.004 050	.288 289	71.171 086	.014 050	125
126	3.503 427	250.342 719	.003 994	.285 434	71.456 521	.013 994	126
127	3.538 461	253.846 146	.003 939	.282 608	71.739 129	.013 939	127
128	3.573 846	257.384 607	.003 885	.279 810	72.018 940	.013 885	128
129	3.609 584	260.958 454	.003 832	.277 040	72.295 980	.013 832	129
130	3.645 680	264.568 038	.003 779	.274 297	72.570 277	.013 779	130
131	3.682 137	268.213 719	.003 728	.271 581	72.841 859	.013 728	131
132	3.718 958	271.895 856	.003 677	.268 892	73.110 751	.013 677	132
133	3.756 148	275.614 814	.003 628	.266 230	73.376 981	.013 628	133
134	3.793 709	279.370 962	.003 579	.263 594	73.640 576	.013 579	134
135	3.831 646	283.164 672	.003 531	.260 984	73.901 560	.013 531	135
136	3.869 963	286.996 319	.003 484	.258 400	74.159 960	.013 484	136
137	3.908 662	290.866 282	.003 438	.255 841	74.415 802	.013 438	137
138	3.947 749	294.774 945	.003 392	.253 308	74.669 111	.013 392	138
139	3.987 226	298.722 694	.003 347	.250 800	74.919 912	.013 347	139
140	4.027 099	302.709 921	.003 303	.248 317	75.168 230	.013 303	140
141	4.067 370	306.737 020	.003 260	.245 859	75.414 089	.013 260	141
142	4.108 043	310.804 391	.003 217	.243 424	75.657 514	.013 217	142
143	4.149 124	314.912 435	.003 175	.241 014	75.898 529	.013 175	143
144	4.190 615	319.061 559	.003 134	.238 628	76.137 157	.013 134	144
145	4.232 521	323.252 174	.003 093	.236 265	76.373 423	.013 093	145
146	4.274 846	327.484 696	.003 053	.233 926	76.607 349	.013 053	146
147	4.317 595	331.759 543	.003 014	.231 610	76.838 960	.013 014	147
148	4.360 771	336.077 139	.002 975	.229 317	77.068 277	.012 975	148
149	4.404 379	340.437 910	.002 937	.227 046	77.295 324	.012 937	149
150	4.448 422	344.842 289	.002 899	.224 798	77.520 122	.012 899	150

N	$(1+i)^N$	$\dfrac{(1+i)^N-1}{i}$	$\dfrac{i}{(1+i)^N-1}$	$(1+i)^{-N}$	$\dfrac{1-(1+i)^{-N}}{i}$	$\dfrac{i}{1-(1+i)^{-N}}$	N
151	4.492 907	349.290 712	.002 862	.222 573	77.742 695	.012 862	151
152	4.537 836	353.783 619	.002 826	.220 369	77.963 065	.012 826	152
153	4.583 214	358.321 455	.002 790	.218 187	78.181 252	.012 790	153
154	4.629 046	362.904 670	.002 755	.216 027	78.397 279	.012 755	154
155	4.675 337	367.533 717	.002 720	.213 888	78.611 168	.012 720	155
156	4.722 090	372.209 054	.002 686	.211 770	78.822 938	.012 686	156
157	4.769 311	376.931 144	.002 653	.209 673	79.032 612	.012 653	157
158	4.817 004	381.700 456	.002 619	.207 597	79.240 210	.012 619	158
159	4.865 174	386.517 460	.002 587	.205 542	79.445 753	.012 587	159
160	4.913 826	391.382 635	.002 555	.203 507	79.649 260	.012 555	160
161	4.962 964	396.296 461	.002 523	.201 492	79.850 752	.012 523	161
162	5.012 594	401.259 426	.002 492	.199 497	80.050 250	.012 492	162
163	5.062 720	406.272 020	.002 461	.197 522	80.247 772	.012 461	163
164	5.113 347	411.334 740	.002 431	.195 566	80.443 339	.012 431	164
165	5.164 480	416.448 088	.002 401	.193 630	80.636 969	.012 401	165
166	5.216 125	421.612 569	.002 371	.191 713	80.828 682	.012 371	166
167	5.268 286	426.828 694	.002 342	.189 815	81.018 497	.012 342	167
168	5.320 969	432.096 981	.002 314	.187 935	81.206 433	.012 314	168
169	5.374 179	437.417 951	.002 286	.186 074	81.392 508	.012 286	169
170	5.427 921	442.792 131	.002 258	.184 232	81.576 741	.012 258	170
171	5.482 200	448.220 052	.002 231	.182 408	81.759 149	.012 231	171
172	5.537 022	453.702 252	.002 204	.180 502	81.939 752	.012 204	172
173	5.592 392	459.239 275	.002 177	.178 814	82.118 566	.012 177	173
174	5.648 316	464.831 668	.002 151	.177 043	82.295 610	.012 151	174
175	5.704 799	470.479 984	.002 125	.175 290	82.470 901	.012 125	175
176	5.761 847	476.184 784	.002 100	.173 555	82.644 456	.012 100	176
177	5.819 466	481.946 632	.002 074	.171 837	82.816 293	.012 074	177
178	5.877 660	487.766 098	.002 050	.170 135	82.986 429	.012 050	178
179	5.936 437	493.643 759	.002 025	.168 451	83.154 880	.012 025	179
180	5.995 801	499.580 197	.002 001	.166 783	83.321 663	.012 001	180

Source: *Financial Compound Interest and Annuity Tables*, 5th ed. (Boston: Financial Publishing Co., 1970).

TABLE 3

Rate of 1½%

PERIODS	AMOUNT OF 1 How $1 left at compound interest will grow.	AMOUNT OF 1 PER PERIOD How $1 deposited periodically will grow.	SINKING FUND Periodic deposit that will grow to $1 at future date.	PRESENT WORTH OF 1 What $1 due in the future is worth today.	PRESENT WORTH OF 1 PER PERIOD What $1 payable periodically is worth today.	PARTIAL PAYMENT Annuity worth $1 today. Periodic payment necessary to pay off a loan of $1.	PERIODS
1	1.015 000	1.000 000	1.000 000	.985 221	.985 221	1.015 000	1
2	1.030 225	2.015 000	.496 277	.970 661	1.955 883	.511 277	2
3	1.045 678	3.045 225	.328 982	.956 316	2.912 200	.343 382	3
4	1.061 363	4.090 903	.244 444	.942 184	3.854 384	.259 444	4
5	1.077 284	5.152 266	.194 089	.928 260	4.782 644	.209 089	5
6	1.093 443	6.229 550	.160 525	.914 542	5.697 187	.175 525	6
7	1.109 844	7.322 994	.136 556	.901 026	6.598 213	.151 556	7
8	1.126 492	8.432 839	.118 584	.887 711	7.485 925	.133 584	8
9	1.143 389	9.559 931	.104 609	.874 592	8.360 517	.119 609	9
10	1.160 540	10.702 721	.093 434	.861 667	9.222 184	.108 434	10
11	1.177 948	11.863 262	.084 293	.848 933	10.071 117	.099 293	11
12	1.195 618	13.041 211	.076 679	.836 387	10.907 505	.091 679	12
13	1.213 552	14.236 829	.070 240	.824 027	11.731 532	.085 240	13
14	1.231 755	15.450 382	.064 723	.811 849	12.543 381	.079 723	14
15	1.250 232	16.682 137	.059 944	.799 851	13.343 233	.074 944	15
16	1.268 985	17.932 369	.055 765	.788 031	14.131 264	.070 765	16
17	1.288 020	19.201 355	.052 079	.776 385	14.907 649	.067 079	17
18	1.307 340	20.489 375	.048 805	.764 911	15.672 560	.063 805	18
19	1.326 950	21.796 716	.045 878	.753 607	16.426 168	.060 878	19
20	1.346 855	23.123 667	.043 245	.742 470	17.168 638	.058 245	20
21	1.367 057	24.470 522	.040 865	.731 497	17.900 136	.055 865	21
22	1.387 563	25.857 579	.038 703	.720 687	18.620 824	.053 703	22
23	1.408 377	27.225 143	.036 730	.710 037	19.330 861	.051 730	23
24	1.429 502	28.633 520	.034 924	.699 543	20.030 405	.049 924	24
25	1.450 945	30.063 023	.033 263	.689 205	20.719 611	.048 263	25
26	1.472 709	31.513 968	.031 731	.679 020	21.398 631	.046 731	26
27	1.494 800	32.986 678	.030 315	.668 985	22.067 617	.045 315	27
28	1.517 222	34.481 478	.029 001	.659 099	22.726 716	.044 001	28
29	1.539 980	35.998 700	.027 778	.649 358	23.376 075	.042 778	29
30	1.563 080	37.538 681	.026 639	.639 762	24.015 838	.041 639	30

N	$\dfrac{i}{1-(1+i)^{-N}}$	$\dfrac{1-(1+i)^{-N}}{i}$	$(1+i)^{-N}$	$\dfrac{i}{(1+i)^N-1}$	$\dfrac{(1+i)^N-1}{i}$	$(1+i)^N$	N
31	.040 574	24.646 145	.630 307	.025 574	39.101 761	1.586 526	31
32	.039 577	25.267 138	.620 952	.024 577	40.688 288	1.610 324	32
33	.038 641	25.878 954	.611 8·5	.023 641	42.298 612	1.634 479	33
34	.037 761	26.481 728	.602 774	.022 761	43.933 091	1.658 996	34
35	.036 933	27.075 594	.593 866	.021 933	45.592 087	1.683 881	35
36	.036 152	27.660 684	.585 039	.021 152	47.275 969	1.709 139	36
37	.035 414	28.237 127	.576 443	.020 414	48.985 108	1.734 776	37
38	.034 716	28.805 051	.567 924	.019 716	50.719 885	1.760 798	38
39	.034 054	29.364 582	.559 531	.019 054	52.480 683	1.787 210	39
40	.033 427	29.915 845	.551 252	.018 427	54.267 893	1.814 018	40
41	.032 831	30.458 960	.543 115	.017 831	56.081 912	1.841 228	41
42	.032 264	30.994 050	.535 089	.017 264	57.923 141	1.868 847	42
43	.031 724	31.521 231	.527 181	.016 724	59.791 988	1.896 879	43
44	.031 210	32.040 622	.519 990	.016 210	61.688 867	1.925 333	44
45	.030 719	32.552 337	.511 714	.015 719	63.614 200	1.954 213	45
46	.030 251	33.056 489	.504 152	.015 251	65.568 413	1.983 526	46
47	.029 803	33.553 191	.496 702	.014 803	67.551 940	2.013 279	47
48	.029 374	34.042 553	.489 361	.014 374	69.565 219	2.043 478	48
49	.028 964	34.524 683	.482 129	.013 964	71.608 697	2.074 130	49
50	.028 571	34.999 688	.475 004	.013 571	73.682 828	2.105 242	50
51	.028 194	35.467 672	.467 584	.013 194	75.788 070	2.136 821	51
52	.027 832	35.928 741	.461 C68	.012 832	77.924 891	2.168 873	52
53	.027 485	36.382 996	.454 255	.012 485	80.093 764	2.201 406	53
54	.027 151	36.830 538	.447 541	.012 151	82.295 171	2.234 427	54
55	.026 830	37.271 466	.440 927	.011 830	84.529 598	2.267 943	55
56	.026 521	37.705 878	.434 411	.011 521	86.797 542	2.301 963	56
57	.026 223	38.133 870	.427 991	.011 223	89.099 506	2.336 492	57
58	.025 936	38.555 537	.421 666	.010 936	91.435 998	2.371 539	58
59	.025 660	38.970 972	.415 435	.010 660	93.807 538	2.407 113	59
60	.025 393	39.380 268	.409 295	.010 393	96.214 651	2.443 219	60

Source: *Financial Compound Interest and Annuity Tables*, 5th ed. (Boston: Financial Publishing Co., 1970).

TABLE 3 (continued)

Rate of 1½%

PERIODS	AMOUNT OF 1 How $1 left at compound interest will grow.	AMOUNT OF 1 PER PERIOD How $1 deposited periodically will grow.	SINKING FUND Periodic deposit that will grow to $1 at future date.	PRESENT WORTH OF 1 What $1 due in the future is worth today.	PRESENT WORTH OF 1 PER PERIOD What $1 payable periodically is worth today.	PARTIAL PAYMENT Annuity worth $1 today. Periodic payment necessary to pay off a loan of $1.	PERIODS
61	2.479 868	98.657 871	.010 136	.403 247	39.783 516	.025 136	61
62	2.517 066	101.137 739	.009 887	.397 287	40.180 804	.024 887	62
63	2.554 822	103.654 805	.009 647	.391 416	40.572 220	.024 647	63
64	2.593 144	106.209 627	.009 415	.385 632	40.957 852	.024 415	64
65	2.632 041	108.802 772	.009 190	.379 933	41.337 786	.024 190	65
66	2.671 522	111.434 813	.008 973	.374 318	41.712 104	.023 973	66
67	2.711 595	114.106 335	.008 763	.368 786	42.080 891	.023 763	67
68	2.752 268	116.817 930	.008 560	.363 336	42.444 227	.023 560	68
69	2.793 552	119.570 199	.008 363	.357 967	42.802 194	.023 363	69
70	2.835 456	122.363 752	.008 172	.352 676	43.154 871	.023 172	70
71	2.877 988	125.199 209	.007 987	.347 464	43.502 336	.022 987	71
72	2.921 157	128.077 197	.007 807	.342 329	43.844 666	.022 807	72
73	2.964 975	130.998 355	.007 633	.337 270	44.181 937	.022 633	73
74	3.009 449	133.963 330	.007 464	.332 286	44.514 224	.022 464	74
75	3.054 591	136.972 780	.007 300	.327 375	44.841 600	.022 300	75
76	3.100 410	140.027 372	.007 141	.322 537	45.164 138	.022 141	76
77	3.146 916	143.127 782	.006 986	.317 771	45.481 909	.021 986	77
78	3.194 120	146.274 699	.006 836	.313 075	45.794 984	.021 836	78
79	3.242 032	149.468 820	.006 690	.308 448	46.103 433	.021 690	79
80	3.290 662	152.710 852	.006 548	.303 890	46.407 323	.021 548	80
81	3.340 022	156.001 515	.006 410	.299 399	46.706 722	.021 410	81
82	3.390 123	159.341 537	.006 275	.294 974	47.001 697	.021 275	82
83	3.440 974	162.731 661	.006 145	.290 615	47.292 312	.021 145	83
84	3.492 589	166.172 635	.006 017	.286 320	47.578 633	.021 017	84
85	3.544 978	169.665 225	.005 893	.282 089	47.860 722	.020 893	85
86	3.598 153	173.210 203	.005 773	.277 920	48.138 642	.020 773	86
87	3.652 125	176.808 356	.005 655	.273 813	48.412 455	.020 655	87
88	3.706 907	180.460 482	.005 541	.269 766	48.682 222	.020 541	88
89	3.762 510	184.167 389	.005 429	.265 779	48.948 002	.020 429	89
90	3.818 948	187.929 900	.005 321	.261 852	49.209 854	.020 321	90

N	$(1+i)^N$	$\dfrac{(1+i)^N-1}{i}$	$\dfrac{i}{(1+i)^N-1}$	$(1+i)^{-N}$	$\dfrac{1-(1+i)^{-N}}{i}$	$\dfrac{i}{1-(1+i)^{-N}}$
91	3.876 232	191.748 848	.005 215	.257 982	49.467 836	.020 215
92	3.934 576	195.625 081	.005 111	.254 569	49.722 006	.020 111
93	3.993 391	199.559 457	.005 011	.250 413	49.972 420	.020 011
94	4.053 292	203.552 849	.004 912	.246 712	50.219 133	.019 912
95	4.114 092	207.606 142	.004 816	.243 065	50.462 200	.019 816
96	4.175 803	211.720 234	.004 723	.239 474	50.701 675	.019 723
97	4.238 440	215.896 038	.004 631	.235 935	50.937 611	.019 631
98	4.302 017	220.134 478	.004 542	.232 449	51.170 060	.019 542
99	4.366 547	224.436 495	.004 455	.229 013	51.399 074	.019 455
100	4.432 045	228.803 043	.004 370	.225 529	51.624 703	.019 370
101	4.498 526	233.235 088	.004 287	.222 295	51.846 998	.019 287
102	4.566 004	237.733 615	.004 206	.219 009	52.066 008	.019 206
103	4.634 494	242.299 619	.004 127	.215 773	52.281 781	.019 127
104	4.704 011	246.934 113	.004 049	.212 584	52.494 366	.019 049
105	4.774 571	251.638 125	.003 973	.209 442	52.703 809	.018 973
106	4.846 190	256.412 697	.003 899	.206 347	52.910 156	.018 899
107	4.918 883	261.258 887	.003 827	.203 298	53.113 455	.018 827
108	4.992 666	266.177 771	.003 756	.200 293	53.313 748	.018 756
109	5.067 556	271.170 437	.003 687	.197 333	53.511 082	.018 687
110	5.143 569	276.237 994	.003 620	.194 417	53.705 500	.018 620
111	5.220 723	281.381 564	.003 553	.191 544	53.897 044	.018 553
112	5.299 034	286.602 287	.003 489	.188 713	54.085 758	.018 489
113	5.378 519	291.901 322	.003 425	.185 924	54.271 682	.018 425
114	5.459 197	297.279 841	.003 363	.183 177	54.454 859	.018 363
115	5.541 085	302.739 039	.003 303	.180 470	54.635 329	.018 363
116	5.624 201	308.280 125	.003 243	.177 803	54.813 132	.018 243
117	5.708 564	313.904 326	.003 185	.175 175	54.988 308	.018 185
118	5.794 193	319.612 891	.003 128	.172 586	55.160 894	.018 128
119	5.881 106	325.407 085	.003 073	.170 036	55.330 930	.018 073
120	5.969 322	331.288 191	.003 018	.167 523	55.498 454	.018 018

Source: *Financial Compound Interest and Annuity Tables*, 5th ed. (Boston: Financial Publishing Co., 1970).

TABLE 3 (concluded)

Rate of 1½%

PERIODS	AMOUNT OF 1 How $1 left at compound interest will grow.	AMOUNT OF 1 PER PERIOD How $1 deposited periodically will grow.	SINKING FUND Periodic deposit that will grow to $1 at future date.	PRESENT WORTH OF 1 What $1 due in the future is worth today.	PRESENT WORTH OF 1 PER PERIOD What $1 payable periodically is worth today.	PARTIAL PAYMENT Annuity worth $1 today. Periodic payment necessary to pay off a loan of $1.	PERIODS
121	6.058 862	337.257 514	.002 965	.165 047	55.663 501	.017 965	121
122	6.149 745	343.916 377	.002 912	.162 608	55.826 109	.017 912	122
123	6.241 991	349.466 122	.002 861	.160 205	55.986 315	.017 861	123
124	6.335 621	355.708 114	.002 811	.157 837	56.144 152	.017 811	124
125	6.430 656	362.043 736	.002 762	.155 505	56.299 658	.017 762	125
126	6.527 115	368.474 392	.002 713	.153 207	56.452 865	.017 713	126
127	6.625 022	375.001 508	.002 666	.150 942	56.603 807	.017 666	127
128	6.724 397	381.626 530	.002 620	.148 712	56.752 520	.017 620	128
129	6.825 263	388.350 928	.002 574	.146 514	56.899 034	.017 574	129
130	6.927 642	395.176 192	.002 530	.144 349	57.043 383	.017 530	130
131	7.031 557	402.103 835	.002 486	.142 216	57.185 599	.017 486	131
132	7.137 030	409.135 393	.002 444	.140 114	57.325 714	.017 444	132
133	7.244 086	416.272 424	.002 402	.138 043	57.463 757	.017 402	133
134	7.352 747	423.516 510	.002 361	.136 003	57.599 761	.017 361	134
135	7.463 038	430.869 258	.002 320	.133 993	57.733 755	.017 320	135
136	7.574 984	438.332 296	.002 281	.132 013	57.865 768	.017 281	136
137	7.688 609	445.907 281	.002 242	.130 062	57.995 831	.017 242	137
138	7.803 938	453.595 890	.002 204	.128 140	58.123 971	.017 204	138
139	7.920 997	461.399 828	.002 167	.126 246	58.250 218	.017 167	139
140	8.039 812	469.320 826	.002 130	.124 381	58.374 599	.017 130	140
141	8.160 409	477.360 638	.002 094	.122 542	58.497 142	.017 094	141
142	8.282 815	485.521 048	.002 059	.120 731	58.617 873	.017 059	142
143	8.407 057	493.803 864	.002 025	.118 947	58.736 821	.017 025	143
144	8.533 163	502.210 922	.001 991	.117 189	58.854 011	.016 991	144
145	8.661 161	510.744 085	.001 957	.115 457	58.969 469	.016 957	145
146	8.791 078	519.405 247	.001 925	.113 751	59.083 221	.016 925	146
147	8.922 944	528.196 325	.001 893	.112 070	59.195 291	.016 893	147
148	9.056 789	537.119 270	.001 861	.110 414	59.305 706	.016 861	148
149	9.192 640	546.176 059	.001 830	.108 782	59.414 488	.016 830	149
150	9.330 530	555.368 700	.001 800	.107 175	59.521 663	.016 800	150

N	$(1+i)^N$	$\dfrac{(1+i)^N-1}{i}$	$\dfrac{i}{(1+i)^N-1}$	$(1+i)^{-N}$	$\dfrac{1-(1+i)^{-N}}{i}$	$\dfrac{i}{1-(1+i)^{-N}}$	N
151	9.470 488	564.699 231	.001 770	.105 591	59.627 255	.016 770	151
152	9.612 545	574.169 719	.001 741	.104 030	59.731 285	.016 741	152
153	9.756 733	583.782 265	.001 712	.102 493	59.833 779	.016 712	153
154	9.903 084	593.538 999	.001 684	.100 978	59.934 757	.016 684	154
155	10.051 631	603.442 084	.001 657	.099 486	60.034 244	.016 657	155
156	10.202 405	613.493 715	.001 630	.098 016	60.132 260	.016 630	156
157	10.355 441	623.696 121	.001 603	.096 567	60.228 827	.016 603	157
158	10.510 773	634.051 563	.001 577	.095 140	60.323 968	.016 577	158
159	10.668 435	644.562 336	.001 551	.093 734	60.417 702	.016 551	159
160	10.828 461	655.230 771	.001 526	.092 349	60.510 051	.016 526	160
161	10.990 888	666.059 233	.001 501	.090 984	60.601 036	.016 501	161
162	11.155 751	677.050 121	.001 476	.089 639	60.690 676	.016 476	162
163	11.323 088	688.205 873	.001 453	.088 315	60.778 991	.016 453	163
164	11.492 934	699.528 961	.001 429	.087 009	60.866 001	.016 429	164
165	11.665 328	711.021 896	.001 406	.085 724	60.951 725	.016 406	165
166	11.840 308	722.687 224	.001 383	.084 457	61.036 182	.016 383	166
167	12.017 912	734.527 533	.001 361	.083 209	61.119 391	.016 361	167
168	12.198 181	746.545 446	.001 339	.081 979	61.201 371	.016 339	168
169	12.381 154	758.743 627	.001 317	.080 757	61.282 139	.016 317	169
170	12.566 871	771.124 782	.001 296	.079 574	61.361 713	.016 296	170
171	12.755 374	783.691 653	.001 276	.078 398	61.440 111	.016 276	171
172	12.946 705	796.447 028	.001 255	.077 239	61.517 351	.016 255	172
173	13.140 906	809.393 734	.001 235	.076 098	61.593 449	.016 235	173
174	13.338 019	822.534 640	.001 215	.074 973	61.668 423	.016 215	174
175	13.538 089	835.872 659	.001 196	.073 865	61.742 289	.016 196	175
176	13.741 161	849.410 749	.001 177	.072 774	61.815 063	.016 177	176
177	13.947 278	863.151 910	.001 158	.071 698	61.886 761	.016 158	177
178	14.156 487	877.099 189	.001 140	.070 638	61.957 400	.016 140	178
179	14.368 835	891.255 677	.001 122	.069 595	62.026 995	.016 122	179
180	14.584 367	905.624 512	.001 104	.068 566	62.095 562	.016 104	180

Source: *Financial Compound Interest and Annuity Tables*, 5th ed. (Boston: Financial Publishing Co., 1970).

TABLE 4

Rate of 2%

PERIODS	AMOUNT OF 1 — How $1 left at compound interest will grow.	AMOUNT OF 1 PER PERIOD — How $1 deposited periodically will grow.	SINKING FUND — Periodic deposit that will grow to $1 at future date.	PRESENT WORTH OF 1 — What $1 due in the future is worth today.	PRESENT WORTH OF 1 PER PERIOD — What $1 payable periodically is worth today.	PARTIAL PAYMENT — Annuity worth $1 today. Periodic payment necessary to pay off a loan of $1.	PERIODS
1	1.020 000	1.000 000	1.000 000	.980 392	.980 392	1.020 000	1
2	1.040 400	2.020 000	.495 049	.961 168	1.941 560	.515 049	2
3	1.061 208	3.060 400	.326 754	.942 322	2.883 883	.346 754	3
4	1.082 432	4.121 608	.242 623	.923 845	3.807 728	.262 623	4
5	1.104 080	5.204 040	.192 158	.905 730	4.713 459	.212 158	5
6	1.126 162	6.308 120	.158 525	.887 971	5.601 430	.178 525	6
7	1.148 685	7.434 283	.134 511	.870 560	6.471 991	.154 511	7
8	1.171 659	8.582 969	.116 509	.853 490	7.325 481	.136 509	8
9	1.195 092	9.754 628	.102 515	.836 755	8.162 236	.122 515	9
10	1.218 994	10.949 720	.091 326	.820 348	8.982 585	.111 326	10
11	1.243 374	12.168 715	.082 177	.804 263	9.786 848	.102 177	11
12	1.268 241	13.412 089	.074 559	.788 493	10.575 341	.094 559	12
13	1.293 606	14.680 331	.068 118	.773 032	11.348 373	.088 118	13
14	1.319 478	15.973 938	.062 601	.757 875	12.106 248	.082 601	14
15	1.345 868	17.293 416	.057 825	.743 014	12.849 263	.077 825	15
16	1.372 785	18.639 285	.053 650	.728 445	13.577 709	.073 650	16
17	1.400 241	20.012 070	.049 969	.714 162	14.291 871	.069 969	17
18	1.428 246	21.412 312	.046 702	.700 159	14.992 031	.066 702	18
19	1.456 811	22.840 558	.043 781	.686 430	15.678 462	.063 781	19
20	1.485 947	24.297 369	.041 156	.672 971	16.351 433	.061 156	20
21	1.515 666	25.783 317	.038 784	.659 775	17.011 209	.058 784	21
22	1.545 979	27.298 983	.036 631	.646 839	17.658 048	.056 631	22
23	1.576 899	28.844 963	.034 668	.634 155	18.292 204	.054 668	23
24	1.608 437	30.421 862	.032 871	.621 721	18.913 925	.052 871	24
25	1.640 605	32.030 299	.031 220	.609 530	19.523 456	.051 220	25
26	1.673 418	33.670 905	.029 699	.597 579	20.121 035	.049 699	26
27	1.706 886	35.344 323	.028 293	.585 862	20.706 897	.048 293	27
28	1.741 024	37.051 210	.026 989	.574 374	21.281 272	.046 989	28
29	1.775 844	38.792 214	.025 778	.563 112	21.844 384	.045 778	29
30	1.811 361	40.568 079	.024 649	.552 070	22.396 455	.044 649	30

N	$(1+i)^N$	$\dfrac{(1+i)^N-1}{i}$	$\dfrac{i}{(1+i)^N-1}$	$(1+i)^{-N}$	$\dfrac{1-(1+i)^{-N}}{i}$	$\dfrac{i}{1-(1+i)^{-N}}$	N
31	1.847 588	42.379 440	.023 596	.541 245	22.937 701	.043 596	31
32	1.884 540	44.227 029	.022 610	.530 633	23.468 334	.042 610	32
33	1.922 231	46.111 570	.021 686	.520 228	23.988 563	.041 686	33
34	1.960 676	48.033 801	.020 818	.510 028	24.498 591	.040 818	34
35	1.999 889	49.994 477	.020 002	.500 027	24.998 619	.040 002	35
36	2.039 887	51.994 367	.019 232	.490 223	25.488 842	.039 232	36
37	2.080 685	54.034 254	.018 506	.480 650	25.969 453	.038 506	37
38	2.122 298	56.114 939	.017 820	.471 187	26.440 640	.037 820	38
39	2.164 744	58.237 238	.017 171	.461 948	26.902 588	.037 171	39
40	2.208 039	60.401 983	.016 555	.452 890	27.355 479	.036 555	40
41	2.252 200	62.610 022	.015 971	.444 010	27.799 489	.035 971	41
42	2.297 244	64.862 223	.015 417	.435 304	28.234 793	.035 417	42
43	2.343 189	67.159 467	.014 889	.426 768	28.661 562	.034 889	43
44	2.390 053	69.502 657	.014 387	.418 400	29.079 963	.034 387	44
45	2.437 854	71.892 710	.013 909	.410 196	29.490 159	.033 909	45
46	2.486 611	74.330 564	.013 453	.402 153	29.892 313	.033 453	46
47	2.536 343	76.817 175	.013 017	.394 258	30.286 581	.033 017	47
48	2.587 070	79.353 519	.012 601	.385 537	30.673 119	.032 601	48
49	2.638 811	81.940 589	.012 203	.378 958	31.052 078	.032 203	49
50	2.691 588	84.579 401	.011 823	.371 527	31.423 605	.031 823	50
51	2.745 419	87.270 989	.011 458	.364 243	31.787 848	.031 458	51
52	2.800 328	90.016 409	.011 109	.357 101	32.144 949	.031 109	52
53	2.856 334	92.816 737	.010 773	.350 099	32.495 048	.030 773	53
54	2.913 461	95.673 072	.010 452	.343 234	32.838 283	.030 452	54
55	2.971 730	98.586 533	.010 143	.336 504	33.174 787	.030 143	55
56	3.031 165	101.558 264	.009 846	.329 906	33.504 693	.029 846	56
57	3.091 788	104.589 429	.009 561	.323 437	33.828 131	.029 561	57
58	3.153 624	107.681 218	.009 286	.317 095	34.145 226	.029 286	58
59	3.216 696	110.834 842	.009 022	.310 877	34.456 104	.029 022	59
60	3.281 030	114.051 539	.008 767	.304 782	34.760 886	.028 767	60

Source: *Financial Compound Interest and Annuity Tables*, 5th ed. (Boston: Financial Publishing Co., 1970).

TABLE 4 (continued)

Rate of 2%

PERIODS	AMOUNT OF 1 — How $1 left at compound interest will grow.	AMOUNT OF 1 PER PERIOD — How $1 deposited periodically will grow.	SINKING FUND — Periodic deposit that will grow to $1 at future date.	PRESENT WORTH OF 1 — What $1 due in the future is worth today.	PRESENT WORTH OF 1 PER PERIOD — What $1 payable periodically is worth today.	PARTIAL PAYMENT — Annuity worth $1 today. Periodic payment necessary to pay off a loan of $1.	PERIODS
61	3.346 651	117.332 570	.008 522	.298 806	35.059 692	.028 522	61
62	3.413 584	120.679 221	.008 286	.292 947	35.352 640	.028 286	62
63	3.481 856	124.092 806	.008 058	.287 203	35.639 843	.028 058	63
64	3.551 493	127.574 662	.007 838	.281 571	35.921 414	.027 838	64
65	3.622 523	131.126 155	.007 626	.276 050	36.197 465	.027 626	65
66	3.694 973	134.748 678	.007 421	.270 637	36.468 103	.027 421	66
67	3.768 873	138.443 652	.007 223	.265 331	36.733 434	.027 223	67
68	3.844 250	142.212 525	.007 031	.260 128	36.993 563	.027 031	68
69	3.921 135	146.056 775	.006 846	.255 028	37.248 591	.026 846	69
70	3.999 558	149.977 911	.006 667	.250 027	37.498 619	.026 667	70
71	4.079 549	153.977 469	.006 494	.245 125	37.743 744	.026 494	71
72	4.161 140	158.057 018	.006 326	.240 318	37.984 063	.026 326	72
73	4.244 363	162.218 159	.006 164	.235 606	38.219 669	.026 164	73
74	4.329 250	166.462 522	.006 007	.230 986	38.450 656	.026 007	74
75	4.415 835	170.791 772	.005 855	.226 457	38.677 114	.025 855	75
76	4.504 152	175.207 608	.005 707	.222 017	38.899 131	.025 707	76
77	4.594 235	179.711 760	.005 564	.217 664	39.116 795	.025 564	77
78	4.686 119	184.305 995	.005 425	.213 396	39.330 191	.025 425	78
79	4.779 842	188.992 115	.005 291	.209 211	39.539 403	.025 291	79
80	4.875 439	193.771 957	.005 160	.205 109	39.744 513	.025 160	80
81	4.972 947	198.647 396	.005 034	.201 087	39.945 601	.025 034	81
82	5.072 406	203.620 344	.004 911	.197 145	40.142 746	.024 911	82
83	5.173 855	208.692 751	.004 791	.193 279	40.336 026	.024 791	83
84	5.277 332	213.866 606	.004 675	.189 489	40.525 515	.024 675	84
85	5.382 878	219.143 938	.004 563	.185 774	40.711 289	.024 563	85
86	5.490 536	224.526 817	.004 453	.182 131	40.893 421	.024 453	86
87	5.600 347	230.017 354	.004 347	.178 560	41.071 981	.024 347	87
88	5.712 354	235.617 701	.004 244	.175 059	41.247 041	.024 244	88
89	5.826 601	241.330 055	.004 143	.171 626	41.418 667	.024 143	89
90	5.943 133	247.156 656	.004 046	.168 261	41.586 929	.024 046	90

103

N	$(1+i)^N$	$\dfrac{(1+i)^N-1}{i}$	$\dfrac{i}{(1+i)^N-1}$	$(1+i)^{-N}$	$\dfrac{1-(1+i)^{-N}}{i}$	$\dfrac{i}{1-(1+i)^{-N}}$
91	6.061 995	253.099 789	.003 951	.164 962	41.751 891	.023 951
92	6.183 235	259.161 785	.003 858	.161 727	41.913 618	.023 858
93	6.306 900	265.345 020	.003 768	.158 556	42.072 175	.023 768
94	6.433 038	271.651 921	.003 681	.155 447	42.227 622	.023 681
95	6.561 699	278.084 959	.003 596	.152 399	42.380 022	.023 596
96	6.692 933	284.646 658	.003 513	.149 421	42.529 433	.023 513
97	6.826 791	291.339 592	.003 432	.146 481	42.675 915	.023 432
98	6.963 327	298.166 383	.003 353	.143 609	42.819 525	.023 353
99	7.102 594	305.129 711	.003 277	.140 793	42.960 318	.023 277
100	7.244 646	312.232 905	.003 202	.138 032	43.098 351	.023 202
101	7.389 539	319.476 952	.003 130	.135 326	43.233 678	.023 130
102	7.537 329	326.866 491	.003 059	.132 672	43.366 351	.023 059
103	7.688 076	334.403 820	.002 990	.130 071	43.496 422	.022 990
104	7.841 837	342.091 897	.002 923	.127 521	43.623 943	.022 923
105	7.998 674	349.933 735	.002 857	.125 020	43.748 964	.022 857
106	8.158 648	357.932 409	.002 793	.122 559	43.871 533	.022 793
107	8.321 821	366.091 058	.002 731	.120 156	43.991 699	.022 731
108	8.488 257	374.412 879	.002 670	.117 809	44.109 509	.022 670
109	8.658 022	382.901 136	.002 611	.115 499	44.225 009	.022 611
110	8.831 183	391.559 159	.002 553	.113 235	44.338 244	.022 553
111	9.007 806	400.390 342	.002 497	.111 014	44.449 259	.022 497
112	9.187 962	409.398 149	.002 442	.108 838	44.558 097	.022 442
113	9.371 722	418.586 112	.002 388	.106 801	44.664 801	.022 388
114	9.559 156	427.957 834	.002 336	.104 611	44.769 413	.022 336
115	9.750 339	437.516 991	.002 285	.102 550	44.871 973	.022 285
116	9.945 346	447.267 331	.002 235	.100 549	44.972 523	.022 235
117	10.144 253	457.212 678	.002 187	.098 577	45.071 101	.022 187
118	10.347 138	467.356 931	.002 139	.096 645	45.167 746	.022 139
119	10.554 081	477.704 070	.002 093	.094 750	45.262 496	.022 093
120	10.765 163	488.258 151	.002 048	.092 892	45.355 388	.022 048

Source: *Financial Compound Interest and Annuity Tables*, 5th ed. (Boston: Financial Publishing Co., 1970).

TABLE 4 (concluded)

Rate of 2%

PERIODS	AMOUNT OF 1 — How $1 left at compound interest will grow.	AMOUNT OF 1 PER PERIOD — How $1 deposited periodically will grow.	SINKING FUND — Periodic deposit that will grow to $1 at future date.	PRESENT WORTH OF 1 — What $1 due in the future is worth today.	PRESENT WORTH OF 1 PER PERIOD — What $1 payable periodically is worth today.	PARTIAL PAYMENT — Annuity worth $1 today. Periodic payment necessary to pay off a loan of $1.	PERIODS
121	10.980 466	499.023 314	.002 003	.091 070	45.446 459	.022 003	121
122	11.200 075	510.003 781	.001 960	.089 285	45.535 744	.021 960	122
123	11.424 077	521.203 856	.001 918	.087 534	45.623 278	.021 918	123
124	11.652 558	532.627 933	.001 877	.085 818	45.709 096	.021 877	124
125	11.885 609	544.280 492	.001 837	.084 135	45.793 232	.021 837	125
126	12.123 322	556.166 102	.001 798	.082 485	45.875 717	.021 798	126
127	12.365 788	568.289 424	.001 759	.080 868	45.956 586	.021 759	127
128	12.613 104	580.655 212	.001 722	.079 282	46.035 868	.021 722	128
129	12.865 366	593.268 317	.001 685	.077 728	46.113 596	.021 685	129
130	13.122 673	606.133 683	.001 649	.076 203	46.189 800	.021 649	130
131	13.385 127	619.256 357	.001 614	.074 709	46.264 510	.021 614	131
132	13.652 829	632.641 484	.001 580	.073 244	46.337 755	.021 580	132
133	13.925 886	646.294 313	.001 547	.071 808	46.409 564	.021 547	133
134	14.204 404	660.220 200	.001 514	.070 400	46.479 964	.021 514	134
135	14.488 492	674.424 604	.001 482	.069 020	46.548 985	.021 482	135
136	14.778 261	688.913 096	.001 451	.067 666	46.616 652	.021 451	136
137	15.073 827	703.691 358	.001 421	.066 340	46.682 992	.021 421	137
138	15.375 303	718.765 185	.001 391	.065 039	46.748 031	.021 391	138
139	15.682 809	734.140 489	.001 362	.063 764	46.811 795	.021 362	139
140	15.996 465	749.823 298	.001 333	.062 513	46.874 309	.021 333	140
141	16.316 395	765.819 764	.001 305	.061 288	46.935 597	.021 305	141
142	16.642 723	782.136 160	.001 278	.060 086	46.995 683	.021 278	142
143	16.975 577	798.778 883	.001 251	.058 908	47.054 592	.021 251	143
144	17.315 089	815.754 461	.001 225	.057 753	47.112 345	.021 225	144
145	17.661 391	833.069 550	.001 200	.056 620	47.168 965	.021 200	145
146	18.014 618	850.730 941	.001 175	.055 510	47.224 476	.021 175	146
147	18.374 911	868.745 560	.001 151	.054 422	47.278 898	.021 151	147
148	18.742 409	887.120 471	.001 127	.053 354	47.332 253	.021 127	148
149	19.117 257	905.862 880	.001 103	.052 308	47.384 562	.021 103	149
150	19.499 602	924.980 138	.001 081	.051 283	47.435 845	.021 081	150

N	$\dfrac{i}{1-(1+i)^{-N}}$	$\dfrac{1-(1+i)^{-N}}{i}$	$(1+i)^{-N}$	$\dfrac{i}{(1+i)^{N}-1}$	$\dfrac{(1+i)^{N}-1}{i}$	$(1+i)^{N}$	N
151	.021 058	47.486 122	.050 277	.001 058	944.479 741	19.889 594	151
152	.021 036	47.535 414	.049 291	.001 036	964.369 535	20.287 386	152
153	.021 015	47.583 739	.048 325	.001 015	984.656 722	20.693 134	153
154	.020 994	47.631 117	.047 377	.000 994	1005.349 857	21.106 997	154
155	.020 974	47.677 565	.046 448	.000 974	1026.456 854	21.529 137	155
156	.020 954	47.723 103	.045 537	.000 954	1047.985 991	21.959 719	156
157	.020 934	47.767 748	.044 645	.000 934	1069.945 711	22.398 914	157
158	.020 915	47.811 518	.043 769	.000 915	1092.344 625	22.846 892	158
159	.020 896	47.854 429	.042 911	.000 896	1115.191 517	23.303 830	159
160	.020 878	47.896 499	.042 070	.000 878	1138.495 348	23.769 906	160
161	.020 860	47.937 745	.041 245	.000 860	1162.265 255	24.245 305	161
162	.020 842	47.978 181	.040 436	.000 842	1186.510 560	24.730 211	162
163	.020 825	48.017 824	.039 643	.000 825	1211.240 771	25.224 815	163
164	.020 808	48.056 691	.038 866	.000 808	1236.465 586	25.729 311	164
165	.020 792	48.094 795	.038 104	.000 792	1262.194 898	26.243 897	165
166	.020 776	48.132 152	.037 356	.000 776	1288.438 796	26.768 775	166
167	.020 760	48.168 776	.036 624	.000 760	1315.207 572	27.304 151	167
168	.020 744	48.204 682	.035 906	.000 744	1342.511 724	27.850 234	168
169	.020 729	48.239 885	.035 202	.000 729	1370.361 958	28.407 239	169
170	.020 714	48.274 397	.034 512	.000 714	1398.769 197	28.975 383	170
171	.020 700	48.308 232	.033 835	.000 700	1427.744 581	29.554 891	171
172	.020 686	48.341 404	.033 171	.000 636	1457.299 473	30.145 989	172
173	.020 672	48.373 926	.032 521	.000 672	1487.445 462	30.748 909	173
174	.020 658	48.405 809	.031 383	.000 658	1518.194 372	31.363 887	174
175	.020 645	48.437 068	.031 258	.000 645	1549.558 259	31.991 165	175
176	.020 632	48.467 714	.030 545	.000 632	1581.549 424	32.630 988	176
177	.020 619	48.497 759	.030 344	.000 619	1614.180 413	33.283 608	177
178	.020 606	48.527 214	.029 455	.000 606	1647.464 021	33.949 280	178
179	.020 594	48.556 092	.028 378	.000 594	1681.413 301	34.628 266	179
180	.020 582	48.584 404	.028 511	.000 582	1716.041 567	35.320 831	180

Source: *Financial Compound Interest and Annuity Tables*, 5th ed. (Boston: Financial Publishing Co., 1970).

TABLE 5

Rate of 3%

PERIODS	AMOUNT OF 1 — How $1 left at compound interest will grow.	AMOUNT OF 1 PER PERIOD — How $1 deposited periodically will grow.	SINKING FUND — Periodic deposit that will grow to $1 at future date.	PRESENT WORTH OF 1 — What $1 due in the future is worth today.	PRESENT WORTH OF 1 PER PERIOD — What $1 payable periodically is worth today.	PARTIAL PAYMENT — Annuity worth $1 today. Periodic payment necessary to pay off a loan of $1.	PERIODS
1	1.030 000	1.000 000	1.000 000	.970 873	.970 873	1.030 000	1
2	1.060 900	2.030 000	.492 610	.942 595	1.913 469	.522 610	2
3	1.092 727	3.090 900	.323 530	.915 141	2.828 611	.353 530	3
4	1.125 508	4.183 627	.239 027	.888 487	3.717 098	.269 027	4
5	1.159 274	5.309 135	.188 354	.862 608	4.579 707	.218 354	5
6	1.194 052	6.468 409	.154 597	.837 484	5.417 191	.184 597	6
7	1.229 873	7.662 462	.130 506	.813 091	6.230 282	.160 506	7
8	1.266 770	8.892 336	.112 456	.789 409	7.019 692	.142 456	8
9	1.304 773	10.159 106	.098 433	.766 416	7.786 108	.128 433	9
10	1.343 916	11.463 879	.087 230	.744 093	8.530 202	.117 230	10
11	1.384 233	12.807 795	.078 077	.722 421	9.252 624	.108 077	11
12	1.425 760	14.192 029	.070 462	.701 379	9.954 003	.100 462	12
13	1.468 533	15.617 790	.064 029	.680 951	10.634 955	.094 029	13
14	1.512 589	17.086 324	.058 526	.661 117	11.296 073	.088 526	14
15	1.557 967	18.598 913	.053 766	.641 861	11.937 935	.083 766	15
16	1.604 706	20.156 881	.049 610	.623 166	12.561 102	.079 610	16
17	1.652 847	21.761 587	.045 952	.605 016	13.166 118	.075 952	17
18	1.702 433	23.414 435	.042 708	.587 394	13.753 513	.072 708	18
19	1.753 506	25.116 868	.039 813	.570 286	14.323 799	.069 813	19
20	1.806 111	26.870 374	.037 215	.553 675	14.877 474	.067 215	20
21	1.860 294	28.676 485	.034 871	.537 549	15.415 024	.064 871	21
22	1.916 103	30.536 780	.032 747	.521 892	15.936 916	.062 747	22
23	1.973 586	32.452 883	.030 813	.506 691	16.443 608	.060 813	23
24	2.032 794	34.426 470	.029 047	.491 933	16.935 542	.059 047	24
25	2.093 777	36.459 264	.027 427	.477 605	17.413 147	.057 427	25
26	2.156 591	38.553 042	.025 938	.463 694	17.876 842	.055 938	26
27	2.221 289	40.709 633	.024 564	.450 189	18.327 031	.054 564	27
28	2.287 927	42.930 922	.023 293	.437 076	18.764 108	.053 293	28
29	2.356 565	45.218 850	.022 114	.424 346	19.188 454	.052 114	29
30	2.427 262	47.575 415	.021 019	.411 986	19.600 441	.051 019	30

N	$\dfrac{i}{1-(1+i)^{-N}}$	$\dfrac{1-(1+i)^{-N}}{i}$	$(1+i)^{-N}$	$\dfrac{i}{(1+i)^N-1}$	$\dfrac{(1+i)^N-1}{i}$	$(1+i)^N$	N
31	.049 998	20.000 428	.399 987	.019 998	50.002 678	2.500 080	31
32	.049 046	20.388 765	.388 337	.019 046	52.502 758	2.575 082	32
33	.048 156	20.765 791	.377 026	.018 156	55.077 841	2.652 535	33
34	.047 321	21.131 836	.366 044	.017 321	57.730 176	2.731 905	34
35	.046 539	21.487 220	.355 383	.016 539	60.462 081	2.813 862	35
36	.045 803	21.832 252	.345 032	.015 803	63.275 944	2.898 278	36
37	.045 111	22.167 235	.334 932	.015 111	66.174 222	2.985 226	37
38	.044 459	22.492 461	.325 226	.014 459	69.159 449	3.074 783	38
39	.043 843	22.808 215	.315 753	.013 843	72.234 232	3.167 026	39
40	.043 262	23.114 771	.306 556	.013 262	75.401 259	3.262 037	40
41	.042 712	23.412 399	.297 628	.012 712	78.663 297	3.359 898	41
42	.042 191	23.701 359	.288 959	.012 191	82.023 196	3.460 695	42
43	.041 698	23.981 902	.280 542	.011 698	85.483 892	3.564 516	43
44	.041 229	24.254 273	.272 371	.011 229	89.048 409	3.671 452	44
45	.040 785	24.518 712	.264 438	.010 785	92.719 861	3.781 595	45
46	.040 362	24.775 449	.256 736	.010 362	96.501 457	3.895 043	46
47	.039 960	25.024 707	.249 258	.009 960	100.396 500	4.011 895	47
48	.039 577	25.266 706	.241 998	.009 577	104.408 395	4.132 251	48
49	.039 213	25.501 656	.234 950	.009 213	108.540 647	4.256 219	49
50	.038 865	25.729 764	.228 107	.008 865	112.796 867	4.383 906	50
51	.038 533	25.951 227	.221 463	.008 533	117.180 773	4.515 423	51
52	.038 217	26.166 239	.215 012	.008 217	121.696 196	4.650 885	52
53	.037 914	26.374 990	.208 750	.007 914	126.347 082	4.790 412	53
54	.037 625	26.577 660	.202 670	.007 625	131.137 494	4.934 124	54
55	.037 349	26.774 427	.196 767	.007 349	136.071 619	5.082 148	55
56	.037 084	26.965 463	.191 036	.007 084	141.153 768	5.234 613	56
57	.036 831	27.150 935	.185 471	.006 831	146.388 381	5.391 651	57
58	.036 588	27.331 005	.180 069	.006 588	151.780 032	5.553 400	58
59	.036 355	27.505 830	.174 825	.006 355	157.333 433	5.720 003	59
60	.036 132	27.675 563	.169 733	.006 132	163.053 436	5.891 603	60

Source: *Financial Compound Interest and Annuity Tables*, 5th ed. (Boston: Financial Publishing Co., 1970).

TABLE 5 (continued)

Rate of 3%

PERIODS	AMOUNT OF 1 How $1 left at compound interest will grow.	AMOUNT OF 1 PER PERIOD How $1 deposited periodically will grow.	SINKING FUND Periodic deposit that will grow to $1 at future date.	PRESENT WORTH OF 1 What $1 due in the future is worth today.	PRESENT WORTH OF 1 PER PERIOD What $1 payable periodically is worth today.	PARTIAL PAYMENT Annuity worth $1 today. Periodic payment necessary to pay off a loan of $1.	PERIODS
61	6.068 351	168.945 039	.005 919	.164 789	27.840 353	.035 919	61
62	6.250 401	175.013 391	.005 713	.159 989	28.000 342	.035 713	62
63	6.437 913	181.263 792	.005 516	.155 329	28.155 672	.035 516	63
64	6.631 051	187.701 706	.005 327	.150 805	28.306 478	.035 327	64
65	6.829 982	194.332 757	.005 145	.146 413	28.452 891	.035 145	65
66	7.034 882	201.162 740	.004 971	.142 148	28.595 040	.034 971	66
67	7.245 928	208.197 622	.004 803	.138 008	28.733 048	.034 803	67
68	7.463 306	215.443 551	.004 641	.133 988	28.867 037	.034 641	68
69	7.687 205	222.906 857	.004 486	.130 086	28.997 123	.034 486	69
70	7.917 821	230.594 063	.004 336	.126 297	29.123 421	.034 336	70
71	8.155 356	238.511 885	.004 192	.122 618	29.246 040	.034 192	71
72	8.400 017	246.667 242	.004 054	.119 047	29.365 087	.034 054	72
73	8.652 017	255.067 259	.003 920	.115 579	29.480 667	.033 920	73
74	8.911 578	263.719 277	.003 791	.112 213	29.592 881	.033 791	74
75	9.178 925	272.630 855	.003 667	.108 945	29.701 826	.033 667	75
76	9.454 293	281.809 781	.003 548	.105 772	29.807 598	.033 548	76
77	9.737 922	291.264 074	.003 433	.102 691	29.910 289	.033 433	77
78	10.030 059	301.001 996	.003 322	.099 700	30.009 989	.033 322	78
79	10.330 961	311.032 056	.003 215	.096 796	30.106 786	.033 215	79
80	10.640 890	321.363 018	.003 111	.093 977	30.200 763	.033 111	80
81	10.960 117	332.003 909	.003 012	.091 239	30.292 003	.033 012	81
82	11.288 920	342.964 026	.002 915	.088 582	30.380 585	.032 915	82
83	11.627 588	354.252 947	.002 822	.086 002	30.466 588	.032 822	83
84	11.976 416	365.880 535	.002 733	.083 497	30.550 085	.032 733	84
85	12.335 708	377.856 951	.002 646	.081 065	30.631 151	.032 646	85
86	12.705 779	390.192 660	.002 562	.078 704	30.709 855	.032 562	86
87	13.086 953	402.898 440	.002 482	.076 411	30.786 267	.032 482	87
88	13.479 561	415.985 393	.002 403	.074 186	30.860 453	.032 403	88
89	13.883 948	429.464 955	.002 328	.072 025	30.932 479	.032 328	89
90	14.300 467	443.348 903	.002 255	.069 927	31.002 407	.032 255	90

N	$(1+i)^N$	$\dfrac{(1+i)^N - 1}{i}$	$\dfrac{i}{(1+i)^N - 1}$	$(1+i)^{-N}$	$\dfrac{1-(1+i)^{-N}}{i}$	$\dfrac{i}{1-(1+i)^{-N}}$
91	14.729 481	457.649 370	.002 185	.067 891	31.070 298	.032 185
92	15.171 365	472.378 851	.002 116	.065 913	31.136 211	.032 116
93	15.626 506	487.550 217	.002 051	.063 993	31.200 205	.032 051
94	16.095 301	503.176 729	.001 987	.062 129	31.262 334	.031 987
95	16.578 160	519.272 025	.001 925	.060 320	31.322 655	.031 925
96	17.075 505	535.850 186	.001 866	.058 563	31.381 219	.031 866
97	17.587 770	552.925 692	.001 808	.056 857	31.438 077	.031 808
98	18.115 403	570.513 462	.001 752	.055 201	31.493 278	.031 752
99	18.658 866	588.628 866	.001 698	.053 593	31.546 872	.031 698
100	19.218 631	607.287 732	.001 646	.052 032	31.598 905	.031 646
101	19.795 190	626.506 364	.001 596	.050 517	31.649 422	.031 596
102	20.389 046	646.301 555	.001 547	.049 045	31.698 468	.031 547
103	21.000 718	666.690 602	.001 499	.047 617	31.746 086	.031 499
104	21.630 739	687.691 320	.001 454	.046 230	31.792 316	.031 454
105	22.279 661	709.322 059	.001 409	.044 833	31.837 200	.031 409
106	22.948 051	731.601 721	.001 366	.043 576	31.880 777	.031 366
107	23.636 493	754.549 773	.001 325	.042 307	31.923 084	.031 325
108	24.345 587	778.186 266	.001 285	.041 075	31.964 159	.031 285
109	25.075 955	802.531 854	.001 246	.039 878	32.004 038	.031 246
110	25.828 234	827.607 810	.001 208	.038 717	32.042 756	.031 208
111	26.603 081	853.436 044	.001 171	.037 589	32.080 345	.031 171
112	27.401 173	880.039 125	.001 136	.036 494	32.116 840	.031 136
113	28.223 208	907.440 299	.001 102	.035 431	32.152 272	.031 102
114	29.069 905	935.663 508	.001 068	.034 399	32.186 672	.031 068
115	29.942 002	964.733 413	.001 036	.033 397	32.220 070	.031 036
116	30.840 262	994.675 416	.001 005	.032 425	32.252 495	.031 005
117	31.765 470	1025.515 678	.000 975	.031 480	32.283 975	.030 975
118	32.718 434	1057.281 149	.000 945	.030 563	32.314 539	.030 945
119	33.699 987	1089.999 583	.000 917	.029 573	32.344 213	.030 917
120	34.710 987	1123.699 571	.000 889	.028 809	32.373 022	.030 889

Source: *Financial Compound Interest and Annuity Tables*, 5th ed. (Boston: Financial Publishing Co., 1970).

TABLE 5 (concluded)

Rate of 3%

PERIODS	AMOUNT OF 1 — How $1 left at compound interest will grow.	AMOUNT OF 1 PER PERIOD — How $1 deposited periodically will grow.	SINKING FUND — Periodic deposit that will grow to $1 at future date.	PRESENT WORTH OF 1 — What $1 due in the future is worth today.	PRESENT WORTH OF 1 PER PERIOD — What $1 payable periodically is worth today.	PARTIAL PAYMENT — Annuity worth $1 today. Periodic payment necessary to pay off a loan of $1.	PERIODS
121	35.752 316	1158.410 558	.000 863	.027 970	32.400 992	.030 863	121
122	36.824 886	1194.162 875	.000 837	.027 155	32.428 148	.030 837	122
123	37.929 632	1230.987 761	.000 812	.026 364	32.454 512	.030 812	123
124	39.067 521	1268.917 394	.000 788	.025 596	32.480 109	.030 788	124
125	40.239 547	1307.984 915	.000 764	.024 851	32.504 960	.030 764	125
126	41.446 733	1348.224 463	.000 741	.024 127	32.529 088	.030 741	126
127	42.690 135	1389.671 197	.000 719	.023 424	32.552 512	.030 719	127
128	43.970 839	1432.361 333	.000 698	.022 742	32.575 255	.030 698	128
129	45.289 965	1476.332 173	.000 677	.022 079	32.597 335	.030 677	129
130	46.648 664	1521.622 138	.000 657	.021 436	32.618 771	.030 657	130
131	48.048 124	1568.270 802	.000 637	.020 812	32.639 584	.030 637	131
132	49.489 567	1616.318 926	.000 618	.020 206	32.659 790	.030 618	132
133	50.974 254	1665.808 494	.000 600	.019 617	32.679 408	.030 600	133
134	52.503 482	1716.782 749	.000 582	.019 046	32.698 454	.030 582	134
135	54.078 586	1769.286 231	.000 565	.018 491	32.716 946	.030 565	135
136	55.700 944	1823.364 818	.000 548	.017 953	32.734 899	.030 548	136
137	57.371 972	1879.065 763	.000 532	.017 430	32.752 329	.030 532	137
138	59.093 132	1936.437 736	.000 516	.016 922	32.769 251	.030 516	138
139	60.865 926	1995.530 868	.000 501	.016 429	32.785 681	.030 501	139
140	62.691 903	2056.396 794	.000 486	.015 951	32.801 632	.030 486	140
141	64.572 660	2119.088 698	.000 471	.015 486	32.817 118	.030 471	141
142	66.509 840	2183.661 359	.000 457	.015 035	32.832 154	.030 457	142
143	68.505 135	2250.171 199	.000 444	.014 597	32.846 751	.030 444	143
144	70.560 290	2318.676 335	.000 431	.014 172	32.860 924	.030 431	144
145	72.677 098	2389.236 626	.000 418	.013 759	32.874 683	.030 418	145
146	74.857 411	2461.913 724	.000 406	.013 358	32.888 042	.030 406	146
147	77.103 134	2536.771 136	.000 394	.012 969	32.901 011	.030 394	147
148	79.416 228	2613.874 270	.000 382	.012 591	32.913 603	.030 382	148
149	81.798 714	2693.290 498	.000 371	.012 225	32.925 828	.030 371	149
150	84.252 676	2775.089 213	.000 360	.011 869	32.937 698	.030 360	150

N	$\dfrac{i}{1-(1+i)^{-N}}$	$\dfrac{1-(1+i)^{-N}}{i}$	$(1+i)^{-N}$	$\dfrac{i}{(1+i)^{N}-1}$	$\dfrac{(1+i)^{N}-1}{i}$	$(1+i)^{N}$	N
151	.030 349	32.949 221	.011 523	.000 349	2859.341 890	86.780 256	151
152	.030 339	32.960 409	.011 187	.000 339	2946.122 146	89.383 664	152
153	.030 329	32.971 861	.010 861	.000 329	3035.505 811	92.065 174	153
154	.030 319	32.981 816	.010 545	.000 319	3127.570 985	94.827 129	154
155	.030 310	32.992 054	.010 238	.000 310	3222.398 115	97.671 943	155
156	.030 301	33.001 994	.009 940	.000 301	3320.070 058	100.602 101	156
157	.030 292	33.011 645	.009 650	.000 292	3420.672 160	103.620 164	157
158	.030 283	33.021 015	.009 369	.000 283	3524.292 325	106.728 769	158
159	.030 275	33.030 111	.009 096	.000 275	3631.021 094	109.930 632	159
160	.030 267	33.038 943	.008 831	.000 267	3740.951 727	113.228 551	160
161	.030 259	33.047 517	.008 574	.000 259	3854.180 279	116.625 408	161
162	.030 251	33.055 842	.008 324	.000 251	3970.805 688	120.124 170	162
163	.030 244	33.063 924	.008 082	.000 244	4090.929 858	123.727 895	163
164	.030 237	33.071 771	.007 846	.000 237	4214.657 754	127.439 732	164
165	.030 230	33.079 390	.007 618	.000 230	4342.097 487	131.262 924	165
166	.030 223	33.086 786	.007 396	.000 223	4473.360 411	135.200 812	166
167	.030 216	33.093 967	.007 180	.000 216	4608.561 224	139.256 836	167
168	.030 210	33.100 939	.006 971	.000 210	4747.818 060	143.434 541	168
169	.030 204	33.107 708	.006 768	.000 204	4891.252 602	147.737 578	169
170	.030 198	33.114 279	.006 571	.000 198	5038.990 180	152.169 705	170
171	.030 192	33.120 659	.006 380	.000 192	5191.159 886	156.734 796	171
172	.030 186	33.126 854	.006 194	.000 186	5347.894 682	161.436 840	172
173	.030 181	33.132 868	.006 013	.000 181	5509.331 523	166.279 945	173
174	.030 176	33.138 706	.005 838	.000 176	5675.611 468	171.268 344	174
175	.030 171	33.144 375	.005 568	.000 171	5846.879 812	176.406 394	175
176	.030 166	33.149 879	.005 503	.000 166	6023.286 207	181.698 586	176
177	.030 161	33.155 222	.005 343	.000 161	6204.984 793	187.149 543	177
178	.030 156	33.160 410	.005 187	.000 156	6392.134 337	192.764 030	178
179	.030 151	33.165 446	.005 036	.000 151	6584.898 367	198.546 951	179
180	.030 147	33.170 336	.004 889	.000 147	6783.445 318	204.503 359	180

Source: *Financial Compound Interest and Annuity Tables*, 5th ed. (Boston: Financial Publishing Co., 1970).

TABLE 6

Rate of 4%

PERIODS	AMOUNT OF 1 How $1 left at compound interest will grow.	AMOUNT OF 1 PER PERIOD How $1 deposited periodically will grow.	SINKING FUND Periodic deposit that will grow to $1 at future date.	PRESENT WORTH OF 1 What $1 due in the future is worth today.	PRESENT WORTH OF 1 PER PERIOD What $1 payable periodically is worth today.	PARTIAL PAYMENT Annuity worth $1 today. Periodic payment necessary to pay off a loan of $1.	PERIODS
1	1.040 000	1.000 000	1.000 000	.961 538	.961 538	1.040 000	1
2	1.081 600	2.040 000	.490 196	.924 556	1.886 094	.530 196	2
3	1.124 864	3.121 600	.320 348	.888 996	2.775 091	.360 348	3
4	1.169 858	4.246 464	.235 490	.854 804	3.629 895	.275 490	4
5	1.216 652	5.416 322	.184 627	.821 927	4.451 822	.224 627	5
6	1.265 319	6.632 975	.150 761	.790 314	5.242 136	.190 761	6
7	1.315 931	7.898 294	.126 609	.759 917	6.002 054	.166 609	7
8	1.368 569	9.214 226	.108 527	.730 690	6.732 744	.148 527	8
9	1.423 311	10.582 795	.094 492	.702 586	7.435 331	.134 492	9
10	1.480 244	12.006 107	.083 290	.675 564	8.110 895	.123 290	10
11	1.539 454	13.486 351	.074 149	.649 580	8.760 476	.114 149	11
12	1.601 032	15.025 805	.066 552	.624 597	9.385 073	.106 552	12
13	1.665 073	16.626 837	.060 143	.600 574	9.985 647	.100 143	13
14	1.731 676	18.291 911	.054 668	.577 475	10.563 122	.094 668	14
15	1.800 943	20.023 587	.049 941	.555 264	11.118 387	.089 941	15
16	1.872 981	21.824 531	.045 819	.533 908	11.652 295	.085 819	16
17	1.947 900	23.697 512	.042 198	.513 373	12.165 668	.082 198	17
18	2.025 816	25.645 412	.038 993	.493 628	12.659 296	.078 993	18
19	2.106 849	27.671 229	.036 138	.474 642	13.133 939	.076 138	19
20	2.191 123	29.778 078	.033 581	.456 386	13.590 326	.073 581	20
21	2.278 768	31.969 201	.031 280	.438 833	14.029 159	.071 280	21
22	2.369 918	34.247 969	.029 198	.421 955	14.451 115	.069 198	22
23	2.464 715	36.617 888	.027 309	.405 726	14.856 841	.067 309	23
24	2.563 304	39.082 604	.025 586	.390 121	15.246 963	.065 586	24
25	2.665 836	41.645 908	.024 011	.375 116	15.622 079	.064 011	25
26	2.772 469	44.311 744	.022 567	.360 689	15.982 769	.062 567	26
27	2.883 368	47.084 214	.021 238	.346 816	16.329 585	.061 238	27
28	2.998 703	49.967 582	.020 012	.333 477	16.663 063	.060 012	28
29	3.118 651	52.966 286	.018 879	.320 651	16.983 714	.058 879	29
30	3.243 397	56.084 937	.017 830	.308 318	17.292 033	.057 830	30

N	$(1+i)^N$	$\dfrac{(1+i)^N-1}{i}$	$\dfrac{i}{(1+i)^N-1}$	$(1+i)^{-N}$	$\dfrac{1-(1+i)^{-N}}{i}$	$\dfrac{i}{1-(1+i)^{-N}}$
31	3.373 133	59.328 335	.016 855	.296 460	17.588 493	.056 855
32	3.508 058	62.701 468	.015 948	.285 057	17.873 551	.055 948
33	3.648 381	66.209 527	.015 103	.274 094	18.147 645	.055 103
34	3.794 316	69.857 908	.014 314	.263 552	18.411 197	.054 314
35	3.946 088	73.652 224	.013 577	.253 415	18.664 613	.053 577
36	4.103 932	77.598 913	.012 886	.243 668	18.908 281	.052 886
37	4.268 089	81.702 246	.012 239	.234 296	19.142 578	.052 239
38	4.438 813	85.970 336	.011 631	.225 285	19.367 864	.051 631
39	4.616 365	90.409 149	.011 050	.216 620	19.584 484	.051 060
40	4.801 020	95.025 515	.010 523	.208 289	19.792 773	.050 523
41	4.993 061	99.826 536	.010 017	.200 277	19.993 051	.050 017
42	5.192 783	104.819 597	.009 540	.192 574	20.185 626	.049 540
43	5.400 495	110.012 381	.009 039	.185 168	20.370 794	.049 089
44	5.616 515	115.412 876	.008 654	.178 046	20.548 841	.048 654
45	5.841 175	121.029 392	.008 262	.171 198	20.720 039	.048 262
46	6.074 822	126.870 567	.007 882	.164 613	20.884 653	.047 882
47	6.317 815	132.945 390	.007 521	.158 282	21.042 936	.047 521
48	6.570 528	139.263 206	.007 180	.152 194	21.195 130	.047 180
49	6.833 349	145.833 734	.006 857	.146 341	21.341 472	.046 857
50	7.106 683	152.667 083	.006 550	.140 712	21.482 184	.046 550
51	7.390 950	159.773 767	.006 258	.135 300	21.617 485	.046 258
52	7.686 588	167.164 717	.005 982	.130 096	21.747 581	.045 982
53	7.994 052	174.851 306	.005 719	.125 093	21.872 674	.045 719
54	8.313 814	182.845 358	.005 469	.120 281	21.992 956	.045 469
55	8.646 366	191.159 172	.005 231	.115 655	22.108 612	.045 231
56	8.992 221	199.805 539	.005 004	.111 207	22.219 819	.045 004
57	9.351 910	208.797 761	.004 789	.106 930	22.326 749	.044 789
58	9.725 986	218.149 671	.004 584	.102 817	22.429 566	.044 584
59	10.115 026	227.875 658	.004 388	.098 862	22.528 429	.044 388
60	10.519 627	237.990 685	.004 201	.095 060	22.623 489	.044 201

Source: *Financial Compound Interest and Annuity Tables*, 5th ed. (Boston: Financial Publishing Co., 1970).

TABLE 6 (continued)

Rate of 4%

PERIODS	AMOUNT OF 1 How $1 left at compound interest will grow.	AMOUNT OF 1 PER PERIOD How $1 deposited periodically will grow.	SINKING FUND Periodic deposit that will grow to $1 at future date.	PRESENT WORTH OF 1 What $1 due in the future is worth today.	PRESENT WORTH OF 1 PER PERIOD What $1 payable periodically is worth today.	PARTIAL PAYMENT Annuity worth $1 today. Periodic payment necessary to pay off a loan of $1.	PERIODS
61	10.940 412	248.510 312	.004 023	.091 404	22.714 894	.044 023	61
62	11.378 029	259.450 725	.003 854	.087 888	22.802 782	.043 854	62
63	11.833 150	270.828 754	.003 692	.084 508	22.887 291	.043 692	63
64	12.306 476	282.661 904	.003 537	.081 258	22.968 549	.043 537	64
65	12.798 735	294.968 380	.003 390	.078 132	23.046 681	.043 390	65
66	13.310 684	307.767 115	.003 249	.075 127	23.121 809	.043 249	66
67	13.843 112	321.077 800	.003 114	.072 238	23.194 047	.043 114	67
68	14.396 836	334.920 912	.002 985	.069 459	23.263 507	.042 985	68
69	14.972 709	349.317 748	.002 862	.066 788	23.330 295	.042 862	69
70	15.571 618	364.290 458	.002 745	.064 219	23.394 514	.042 745	70
71	16.194 483	379.862 077	.002 632	.061 749	23.456 264	.042 632	71
72	16.842 262	396.056 560	.002 524	.059 374	23.515 638	.042 524	72
73	17.515 952	412.898 822	.002 421	.057 090	23.572 729	.042 421	73
74	18.216 591	430.414 775	.002 323	.054 895	23.627 624	.042 323	74
75	18.945 254	448.631 366	.002 229	.052 783	23.680 408	.042 229	75
76	19.703 064	467.576 621	.002 138	.050 753	23.731 161	.042 138	76
77	20.491 187	487.279 686	.002 052	.048 801	23.779 963	.042 052	77
78	21.310 834	507.770 873	.001 969	.046 924	23.826 887	.041 969	78
79	22.163 268	529.081 708	.001 890	.045 119	23.872 007	.041 890	79
80	23.049 799	551.244 976	.001 814	.043 384	23.915 391	.041 814	80
81	23.971 791	574.294 775	.001 741	.041 715	23.957 107	.041 741	81
82	24.930 662	598.266 566	.001 671	.040 111	23.997 218	.041 671	82
83	25.927 889	623.197 229	.001 604	.038 568	24.035 787	.041 604	83
84	26.965 004	649.125 118	.001 540	.037 085	24.072 872	.041 540	84
85	28.043 604	676.090 123	.001 479	.035 658	24.108 531	.041 479	85
86	29.165 349	704.133 728	.001 420	.034 287	24.142 818	.041 420	86
87	30.331 963	733.299 077	.001 363	.032 968	24.175 786	.041 363	87
88	31.545 241	763.631 040	.001 309	.031 700	24.207 487	.041 309	88
89	32.807 051	795.176 282	.001 257	.030 481	24.237 968	.041 257	89
90	34.119 333	827.983 333	.001 207	.029 308	24.267 277	.041 207	90

N	$(1+i)^N$	$\dfrac{(1+i)^N - 1}{i}$	$\dfrac{i}{(1+i)^N - 1}$	$(1+i)^{-N}$	$\dfrac{1-(1+i)^{-N}}{i}$	$\dfrac{i}{1-(1+i)^{-N}}$	N
91	35.484 106	862.102 656	.001 159	.028 131	24.295 459	.041 159	91
92	36.903 470	897.586 773	.001 114	.027 097	24.322 556	.041 114	92
93	38.379 609	934.490 244	.001 070	.026 055	24.348 612	.041 070	93
94	39.914 794	972.869 854	.001 027	.025 053	24.373 665	.041 027	94
95	41.511 385	1012.784 648	.000 987	.024 089	24.397 755	.040 987	95
96	43.171 841	1054.296 034	.000 948	.023 163	24.420 918	.040 948	96
97	44.898 715	1097.467 875	.000 911	.022 272	24.443 191	.040 911	97
98	46.694 663	1142.366 590	.000 875	.021 415	24.464 606	.040 875	98
99	48.562 450	1189.061 254	.000 840	.020 592	24.485 198	.040 840	99
100	50.504 948	1237.623 704	.000 808	.019 800	24.504 998	.040 808	100
101	52.525 146	1288.128 652	.000 776	.019 038	24.524 037	.040 776	101
102	54.626 151	1340.653 798	.000 745	.018 306	24.542 343	.040 745	102
103	56.811 198	1395.279 950	.000 716	.017 602	24.559 945	.040 716	103
104	59.083 645	1452.091 148	.000 688	.016 925	24.576 871	.040 688	104
105	61.446 991	1511.174 794	.000 661	.016 274	24.593 145	.040 661	105
106	63.904 871	1572.621 786	.000 635	.015 648	24.608 793	.040 635	106
107	66.461 066	1636.526 658	.000 611	.015 046	24.623 839	.040 611	107
108	69.119 508	1702.987 724	.000 587	.014 467	24.638 307	.040 587	108
109	71.884 289	1772.107 233	.000 564	.013 511	24.652 218	.040 564	109
110	74.759 660	1843.991 522	.000 542	.013 376	24.665 595	.040 542	110
111	77.750 047	1918.751 183	.000 521	.012 861	24.678 456	.040 521	111
112	80.860 049	1996.501 231	.000 500	.012 367	24.690 823	.040 500	112
113	84.094 451	2077.361 280	.000 481	.011 891	24.702 715	.040 481	113
114	87.458 229	2161.455 731	.000 462	.011 434	24.714 149	.040 462	114
115	90.956 558	2248.913 960	.000 444	.010 994	24.725 143	.040 444	115
116	94.594 820	2339.870 519	.000 427	.010 571	24.735 714	.040 427	116
117	98.378 613	2434.465 339	.000 410	.010 164	24.745 879	.040 410	117
118	102.313 758	2532.843 953	.000 394	.009 773	24.755 653	.040 394	118
119	106.406 308	2635.157 711	.000 379	.009 397	24.765 051	.040 379	119
120	110.662 560	2741.564 020	.000 364	.009 036	24.774 088	.040 364	120

Source: *Financial Compound Interest and Annuity Tables*, 5th ed. (Boston: Financial Publishing Co., 1970).

TABLE 6 (concluded)

Rate of 4%

PERIODS	AMOUNT OF 1. How $1 left at compound interest will grow.	AMOUNT OF 1 PER PERIOD. How $1 deposited periodically will grow.	SINKING FUND. Periodic deposit that will grow to $1 at future date.	PRESENT WORTH OF 1. What $1 due in the future is worth today.	PRESENT WORTH OF 1 PER PERIOD. What $1 payable periodically is worth today.	PARTIAL PAYMENT. Annuity worth $1 today. Periodic payment necessary to pay off a loan of $1.	PERIODS
121	115.089 063	2852.226 580	.000 350	.008 688	24.782 776	.040 350	121
122	119.692 625	2967.315 644	.000 337	.008 354	24.791 131	.040 337	122
123	124.480 330	3087.008 269	.000 323	.008 033	24.799 165	.040 323	123
124	129.459 544	3211.488 600	.000 311	.007 724	24.806 889	.040 311	124
125	134.637 925	3340.948 144	.000 299	.007 427	24.814 316	.040 299	125
126	140.023 442	3475.586 070	.000 287	.007 141	24.821 458	.040 287	126
127	145.624 380	3615.609 513	.000 276	.006 866	24.828 325	.040 276	127
128	151.449 355	3761.233 893	.000 265	.006 602	24.834 928	.040 265	128
129	157.507 329	3912.683 249	.000 255	.006 348	24.841 277	.040 255	129
130	163.807 623	4070.190 579	.000 245	.006 104	24.847 381	.040 245	130
131	170.359 928	4233.998 202	.000 236	.005 869	24.853 251	.040 236	131
132	177.174 325	4404.358 130	.000 227	.005 644	24.858 896	.040 227	132
133	184.261 298	4581.532 456	.000 218	.005 427	24.864 323	.040 218	133
134	191.631 750	4765.793 754	.000 209	.005 218	24.869 541	.040 209	134
135	199.297 020	4957.425 504	.000 201	.005 017	24.874 559	.040 201	135
136	207.268 900	5156.722 524	.000 193	.004 824	24.879 383	.040 193	136
137	215.559 657	5363.991 425	.000 186	.004 639	24.884 022	.040 186	137
138	224.182 043	5579.551 082	.000 179	.004 460	24.888 483	.040 179	138
139	233.149 325	5803.733 126	.000 172	.004 289	24.892 772	.040 172	139
140	242.475 298	6036.882 451	.000 165	.004 124	24.896 896	.040 165	140
141	252.174 309	6279.357 749	.000 159	.003 965	24.900 862	.040 159	141
142	262.261 282	6531.532 059	.000 153	.003 812	24.904 675	.040 153	142
143	272.751 733	6793.793 341	.000 147	.003 666	24.908 341	.040 147	143
144	283.661 803	7066.545 075	.000 141	.003 525	24.911 866	.040 141	144
145	295.008 275	7350.206 878	.000 136	.003 389	24.915 256	.040 136	145
146	306.808 606	7645.215 153	.000 130	.003 259	24.918 515	.040 130	146
147	319.080 950	7952.023 759	.000 125	.003 134	24.921 649	.040 125	147
148	331.844 188	8271.104 709	.000 120	.003 013	24.924 663	.040 120	148
149	345.117 955	8602.948 898	.000 116	.002 897	24.927 560	.040 116	149
150	358.922 674	8948.066 854	.000 111	.002 786	24.930 347	.040 111	150

N	$(1+i)^N$	$\dfrac{(1+i)^N-1}{i}$	$\dfrac{i}{(1+i)^N-1}$	$(1+i)^{-N}$	$\dfrac{1-(1+i)^{-N}}{i}$	$\dfrac{i}{1-(1+i)^{-N}}$	N
151	373.279 581	9306.989 528	.000 107	.002 678	24.933 026	.040 107	151
152	388.210 764	9680.269 109	.000 103	.002 575	24.935 601	.040 103	152
153	403.739 194	10068.479 873	.000 099	.002 476	24.938 078	.040 099	153
154	419.888 762	10472.219 068	.000 095	.002 381	24.940 460	.040 095	154
155	436.684 313	10892.107 831	.000 091	.002 289	24.942 750	.040 091	155
156	454.151 685	11328.792 144	.000 088	.002 201	24.944 952	.040 088	156
157	472.317 753	11782.943 830	.000 084	.002 117	24.947 069	.040 084	157
158	491.210 463	12255.261 583	.000 081	.002 035	24.949 105	.040 081	158
159	510.858 881	12746.472 047	.000 078	.001 957	24.951 062	.040 078	159
160	531.293 237	13257.330 929	.000 075	.001 882	24.952 945	.040 075	160
161	552.544 966	13788.624 166	.000 072	.001 809	24.954 754	.040 072	161
162	574.646 765	14341.169 132	.000 069	.001 740	24.956 495	.040 069	162
163	597.632 635	14915.815 898	.000 067	.001 673	24.958 168	.040 067	163
164	621.537 941	15513.448 534	.000 064	.001 608	24.959 777	.040 064	164
165	646.399 459	16134.986 475	.000 061	.001 547	24.961 324	.040 061	165
166	672.255 437	16781.385 934	.000 059	.001 487	24.962 811	.040 059	166
167	699.145 654	17453.641 371	.000 057	.001 430	24.964 242	.040 057	167
168	727.111 481	18152.787 026	.000 055	.001 375	24.965 617	.040 055	168
169	756.195 940	18879.898 507	.000 052	.001 322	24.966 939	.040 052	169
170	786.443 777	19636.094 448	.000 050	.001 271	24.968 211	.040 050	170
171	817.901 529	20422.538 226	.000 048	.001 222	24.969 433	.040 048	171
172	850.617 590	21240.439 755	.000 047	.001 175	24.970 609	.040 047	172
173	884.642 293	22091.057 345	.000 045	.001 130	24.971 739	.040 045	173
174	920.027 985	22975.699 639	.000 043	.001 086	24.972 826	.040 043	174
175	956.829 104	23895.727 624	.000 041	.001 045	24.973 872	.040 041	175
176	995.102 269	24852.556 729	.000 040	.001 004	24.974 876	.040 040	176
177	1034.906 359	25847.658 998	.000 038	.000 966	24.975 843	.040 038	177
178	1076.302 614	26882.565 358	.000 037	.000 929	24.976 772	.040 037	178
179	1119.354 718	27958.867 973	.000 035	.000 893	24.977 665	.040 035	179
180	1164.128 907	29078.222 692	.000 034	.000 859	24.978 524	.040 034	180

Source: *Financial Compound Interest and Annuity Tables*, 5th ed. (Boston: Financial Publishing Co., 1970).

118

TABLE 7

Rate of 5%

PERIODS	AMOUNT OF 1 — How $1 left at compound interest will grow.	AMOUNT OF 1 PER PERIOD — How $1 deposited periodically will grow.	SINKING FUND — Periodic deposit that will grow to $1 at future date.	PRESENT WORTH OF 1 — What $1 due in the future is worth today.	PRESENT WORTH OF 1 PER PERIOD — What $1 payable periodically is worth today.	PARTIAL PAYMENT — Annuity worth $1 today. Periodic payment necessary to pay off a loan of $1.	PERIODS
1	1.050 000	1.000 000	1.000 000	.952 380	.952 380	1.050 000	1
2	1.102 500	2.050 000	.487 804	.907 029	1.859 410	.537 804	2
3	1.157 625	3.152 500	.317 208	.863 837	2.723 248	.367 208	3
4	1.215 506	4.310 125	.232 011	.822 702	3.545 950	.282 011	4
5	1.276 281	5.525 631	.180 974	.783 526	4.329 476	.230 974	5
6	1.340 095	6.801 912	.147 017	.746 215	5.075 692	.197 017	6
7	1.407 100	8.142 008	.122 819	.710 681	5.786 373	.172 819	7
8	1.477 455	9.549 108	.104 721	.676 839	6.463 212	.154 721	8
9	1.551 328	11.026 564	.090 690	.644 608	7.107 821	.140 690	9
10	1.628 894	12.577 892	.079 504	.613 913	7.721 734	.129 504	10
11	1.710 339	14.206 787	.070 388	.584 679	8.306 414	.120 388	11
12	1.795 856	15.917 126	.062 825	.556 837	8.863 251	.112 825	12
13	1.885 649	17.712 982	.056 455	.530 321	9.393 572	.106 455	13
14	1.979 931	19.598 631	.051 023	.505 067	9.898 640	.101 023	14
15	2.078 928	21.578 563	.046 342	.481 017	10.379 658	.096 342	15
16	2.182 874	23.657 491	.042 269	.458 111	10.837 769	.092 269	16
17	2.292 018	25.840 366	.038 699	.436 296	11.274 066	.088 699	17
18	2.406 619	28.132 384	.035 546	.415 520	11.689 586	.085 546	18
19	2.526 950	30.539 003	.032 745	.395 733	12.085 320	.082 745	19
20	2.653 297	33.065 954	.030 242	.376 889	12.462 210	.080 242	20
21	2.785 962	35.719 251	.027 996	.358 942	12.821 152	.077 996	21
22	2.925 260	38.505 214	.025 970	.341 849	13.163 002	.075 970	22
23	3.071 523	41.430 475	.024 136	.325 571	13.488 573	.074 136	23
24	3.225 099	44.501 998	.022 470	.310 067	13.798 641	.072 470	24
25	3.386 354	47.727 098	.020 952	.295 302	14.093 944	.070 952	25
26	3.555 672	51.113 453	.019 564	.281 240	14.375 185	.069 564	26
27	3.733 456	54.669 126	.018 291	.267 848	14.643 033	.068 291	27
28	3.920 129	58.402 582	.017 122	.255 093	14.898 127	.067 122	28
29	4.116 135	62.322 711	.016 045	.242 946	15.141 073	.066 045	29
30	4.321 942	66.438 847	.015 051	.231 377	15.372 451	.065 051	30

N	$(1+i)^N$	$\frac{(1+i)^N - 1}{i}$	$\frac{i}{(1+i)^N - 1}$	$(1+i)^{-N}$	$\frac{1-(1+i)^{-N}}{i}$	$\frac{i}{1-(1+i)^{-N}}$	N
31	4.538 039	70.760 789	.014 132	.220 359	15.592 810	.064 132	31
32	4.764 941	75.298 829	.013 280	.209 856	15.802 676	.063 280	32
33	5.003 188	80.063 770	.012 490	.199 872	16.002 549	.062 490	33
34	5.253 347	85.066 959	.011 755	.190 354	16.192 904	.061 755	34
35	5.516 015	90.320 307	.011 071	.181 290	16.374 194	.061 071	35
36	5.791 816	95.836 322	.010 434	.172 657	16.546 851	.060 434	36
37	6.081 406	101.628 138	.009 839	.164 435	16.711 287	.059 839	37
38	6.385 477	107.709 545	.009 284	.156 605	16.867 892	.058 284	38
39	6.704 751	114.095 023	.008 764	.149 147	17.017 040	.058 764	39
40	7.039 988	120.799 774	.008 278	.142 045	17.159 086	.058 278	40
41	7.391 988	127.839 762	.007 822	.135 281	17.294 367	.057 822	41
42	7.761 587	135.231 751	.007 394	.128 839	17.423 207	.057 394	42
43	8.149 666	142.993 338	.006 993	.122 704	17.545 911	.056 993	43
44	8.557 150	151.143 005	.006 616	.116 861	17.662 773	.056 616	44
45	8.985 007	159.700 155	.006 261	.111 296	17.774 069	.056 261	45
46	9.434 258	168.685 163	.005 928	.105 996	17.880 066	.055 928	46
47	9.905 971	178.119 421	.005 614	.100 949	17.981 015	.055 614	47
48	10.401 269	188.025 392	.005 318	.096 142	18.077 157	.055 318	48
49	10.921 333	198.426 662	.005 039	.091 563	18.168 721	.055 039	49
50	11.467 399	209.347 995	.004 776	.087 203	18.255 925	.054 776	50
51	12.040 769	220.815 395	.004 528	.083 051	18.338 976	.054 528	51
52	12.642 808	232.856 165	.004 294	.079 096	18.418 072	.054 294	52
53	13.274 948	245.498 973	.004 073	.075 329	18.493 402	.054 073	53
54	13.938 696	258.773 922	.003 864	.071 742	18.565 145	.053 864	54
55	14.635 630	272.712 618	.003 666	.068 326	18.633 471	.053 666	55
56	15.367 412	287.348 249	.003 480	.065 072	18.698 544	.053 480	56
57	16.135 783	302.715 661	.003 303	.061 974	18.760 518	.053 303	57
58	16.942 572	318.851 444	.003 136	.059 022	18.819 541	.053 136	58
59	17.789 700	335.794 017	.002 978	.056 212	18.875 754	.052 978	59
60	18.679 185	353.583 717	.002 828	.053 535	18.929 289	.052 828	60

Source: *Financial Compound Interest and Annuity Tables*, 5th ed. (Boston: Financial Publishing Co., 1970).

TABLE 7 (continued)

Rate of 5%

PERIODS	AMOUNT OF 1 How $1 left at compound interest will grow.	AMOUNT OF 1 PER PERIOD How $1 deposited periodically will grow.	SINKING FUND Periodic deposit that will grow to $1 at future date.	PRESENT WORTH OF 1 What $1 due in the future is worth today.	PRESENT WORTH OF 1 PER PERIOD What $1 payable periodically is worth today.	PARTIAL PAYMENT Annuity worth $1 today. Periodic payment necessary to pay off a loan of $1.	PERIODS
61	19.613 145	372.262 903	.002 686	.050 986	18.980 275	.052 686	61
62	20.593 802	391.876 048	.002 551	.048 558	19.028 834	.052 551	62
63	21.623 492	412.469 851	.002 424	.046 245	19.075 080	.052 424	63
64	22.704 657	434.093 343	.002 303	.044 043	19.119 123	.052 303	64
65	23.839 900	456.798 011	.002 189	.041 946	19.161 070	.052 189	65
66	25.031 895	480.637 911	.002 080	.039 949	19.201 019	.052 080	66
67	26.283 490	505.669 807	.001 977	.038 046	19.239 066	.051 977	67
68	27.597 664	531.953 297	.001 879	.036 234	19.275 301	.051 879	68
69	28.977 548	559.550 962	.001 787	.034 509	19.309 810	.051 787	69
70	30.426 425	588.528 510	.001 699	.032 866	19.342 676	.051 699	70
71	31.947 746	618.954 936	.001 615	.031 301	19.373 977	.051 615	71
72	33.545 134	650.902 683	.001 536	.029 810	19.403 788	.051 536	72
73	35.222 390	684.447 817	.001 461	.028 391	19.432 179	.051 461	73
74	36.983 510	719.670 208	.001 389	.027 039	19.459 218	.051 389	74
75	38.832 685	756.653 718	.001 321	.025 751	19.484 969	.051 321	75
76	40.774 320	795.486 404	.001 257	.024 525	19.509 495	.051 257	76
77	42.813 036	836.260 724	.001 195	.023 357	19.532 852	.051 195	77
78	44.953 688	879.073 760	.001 137	.022 245	19.555 097	.051 137	78
79	47.201 372	924.027 448	.001 082	.021 185	19.576 283	.051 082	79
80	49.561 441	971.228 821	.001 029	.020 176	19.596 460	.051 029	80
81	52.039 513	1020.790 262	.000 979	.019 216	19.615 676	.050 979	81
82	54.641 488	1072.829 775	.000 932	.018 301	19.633 977	.050 932	82
83	57.373 563	1127.471 264	.000 886	.017 429	19.651 407	.050 886	83
84	60.242 241	1184.844 827	.000 843	.016 599	19.668 007	.050 843	84
85	63.254 353	1245.087 068	.000 803	.015 809	19.683 816	.050 803	85
86	66.417 071	1308.341 422	.000 764	.015 056	19.698 872	.050 764	86
87	69.737 924	1374.758 493	.000 727	.014 339	19.713 211	.050 727	87
88	73.224 820	1444.496 418	.000 692	.013 656	19.726 868	.050 692	88
89	76.886 061	1517.721 239	.000 658	.013 006	19.739 874	.050 658	89
90	80.730 365	1594.607 300	.000 627	.012 386	19.752 261	.050 627	90

N	$(1+i)^N$	$\dfrac{(1+i)^N-1}{i}$	$\dfrac{i}{(1+i)^N-1}$	$(1+i)^{-N}$	$\dfrac{1-(1+i)^{-N}}{i}$	$\dfrac{i}{1-(1+i)^{-N}}$	N
91	84.766 883	1675.337 666	.000 596	.011 797	19.764 058	.050 596	91
92	89.005 227	1760.104 549	.000 568	.011 235	19.775 294	.050 568	92
93	93.455 488	1849.109 776	.000 540	.010 700	19.785 994	.050 540	93
94	98.128 263	1942.565 265	.000 514	.010 190	19.796 185	.050 514	94
95	103.034 676	2040.693 528	.000 490	.009 705	19.805 890	.050 490	95
96	108.186 410	2143.728 205	.000 466	.009 243	19.815 133	.050 466	96
97	113.595 730	2251.914 615	.000 444	.008 803	19.823 937	.050 444	97
98	119.275 517	2365.510 346	.000 422	.008 333	19.832 320	.050 422	98
99	125.239 293	2484.785 863	.000 402	.007 934	19.840 305	.050 402	99
100	131.501 257	2610.025 156	.000 383	.007 634	19.847 910	.050 383	100
101	138.076 320	2741.526 414	.000 364	.007 242	19.855 152	.050 364	101
102	144.980 136	2879.602 735	.000 347	.006 897	19.862 050	.050 347	102
103	152.229 143	3024.582 872	.000 330	.006 559	19.868 619	.050 330	103
104	159.840 600	3176.812 015	.000 314	.006 256	19.874 875	.050 314	104
105	167.832 630	3336.652 616	.000 299	.005 958	19.880 833	.050 299	105
106	176.224 262	3504.485 247	.000 285	.005 674	19.886 508	.050 285	106
107	185.035 475	3680.709 509	.000 271	.005 434	19.891 912	.050 271	107
108	194.287 249	3865.744 985	.000 258	.005 147	19.897 059	.050 258	108
109	204.001 611	4060.032 234	.000 246	.004 901	19.901 961	.050 246	109
110	214.201 692	4264.033 846	.000 234	.004 658	19.906 630	.050 234	110
111	224.911 776	4478.235 538	.000 223	.004 446	19.911 076	.050 223	111
112	236.157 365	4703.147 315	.000 212	.004 234	19.915 310	.050 212	112
113	247.965 234	4939.304 681	.000 202	.004 032	19.919 343	.050 202	113
114	260.363 495	5187.269 915	.000 192	.003 840	19.923 184	.050 192	114
115	273.381 670	5447.633 411	.000 183	.003 657	19.926 842	.050 183	115
116	287.050 754	5721.015 081	.000 174	.003 483	19.930 325	.050 174	116
117	301.403 291	6008.065 835	.000 166	.003 317	19.933 643	.050 166	117
118	316.473 456	6309.469 127	.000 158	.003 159	19.936 803	.050 158	118
119	332.297 129	6625.942 584	.000 150	.003 009	19.939 812	.050 150	119
120	348.911 985	6958.239 713	.000 143	.002 866	19.942 678	.050 143	120

Source: *Financial Compound Interest and Annuity Tables*, 5th ed. (Boston: Financial Publishing Co., 1970).

TABLE 7 (concluded)

Rate of 5%

PERIODS	AMOUNT OF 1 How $1 left at compound interest will grow.	AMOUNT OF 1 PER PERIOD How $1 deposited periodically will grow.	SINKING FUND Periodic deposit that will grow to $1 at future date.	PRESENT WORTH OF 1 What $1 due in the future is worth today.	PRESENT WORTH OF 1 PER PERIOD What $1 payable periodically is worth today.	PARTIAL PAYMENT Annuity worth $1 today. Periodic payment necessary to pay off a loan of $1.	PERIODS
121	366.357 584	7307.151 699	.000 136	.002 729	19.945 408	.050 136	121
122	384.675 464	7673.509 283	.000 130	.002 599	19.948 008	.050 130	122
123	403.909 237	8058.184 748	.000 124	.002 475	19.950 483	.050 124	123
124	424.104 699	8462.093 985	.000 118	.002 357	19.952 841	.050 118	124
125	445.309 934	8886.198 684	.000 112	.002 245	19.955 087	.050 112	125
126	467.575 430	9331.508 619	.000 107	.002 138	19.957 226	.050 107	126
127	490.954 202	9799.084 050	.000 102	.002 036	19.959 263	.050 102	127
128	515.501 912	10290.038 252	.000 097	.001 939	19.961 202	.050 097	128
129	541.277 008	10805.540 165	.000 092	.001 847	19.963 050	.050 092	129
130	568.340 858	11346.817 173	.000 088	.001 759	19.964 809	.050 088	130
131	596.757 901	11915.158 032	.000 083	.001 675	19.966 485	.050 083	131
132	626.595 796	12511.915 933	.000 079	.001 595	19.968 081	.050 079	132
133	657.925 586	13138.511 730	.000 076	.001 519	19.969 601	.050 076	133
134	690.821 865	13796.437 316	.000 072	.001 447	19.971 048	.050 072	134
135	725.362 959	14487.259 182	.000 069	.001 378	19.972 427	.050 069	135
136	761.631 107	15212.622 141	.000 065	.001 312	19.973 740	.050 065	136
137	799.712 662	15974.253 248	.000 062	.001 250	19.974 991	.050 062	137
138	839.698 295	16773.965 911	.000 059	.001 190	19.976 181	.050 059	138
139	881.683 210	17613.664 207	.000 056	.001 134	19.977 316	.050 056	139
140	925.767 370	18495.347 417	.000 054	.001 080	19.978 396	.050 054	140
141	972.055 739	19421.114 788	.000 051	.001 028	19.979 425	.050 051	141
142	1020.658 526	20393.170 527	.000 049	.000 979	19.980 404	.050 049	142
143	1071.691 452	21413.829 054	.000 046	.000 933	19.981 337	.050 046	143
144	1125.276 025	22485.520 506	.000 044	.000 888	19.982 226	.050 044	144
145	1181.539 826	23610.796 532	.000 042	.000 846	19.983 072	.050 042	145
146	1240.616 817	24792.336 958	.000 040	.000 806	19.983 878	.050 040	146
147	1302.647 658	26032.953 176	.000 038	.000 767	19.984 646	.050 038	147
148	1367.780 041	27335.600 835	.000 036	.000 731	19.985 377	.050 036	148
149	1436.169 043	28703.380 877	.000 034	.000 696	19.986 074	.050 034	149
150	1507.977 496	30139.549 921	.000 033	.000 663	19.986 737	.050 033	150

N	$(1+i)^N$	$\dfrac{(1+i)^N-1}{i}$	$\dfrac{i}{(1+i)^N-1}$	$(1+i)^{-N}$	$\dfrac{1-(1+i)^{-N}}{i}$	$\dfrac{i}{1-(1+i)^{-N}}$	N
151	1583.376 970	31647.527 417	.000 031	.000 631	19.987 368	.050 031	151
152	1662.545 189	33230.903 787	.000 030	.000 602	19.987 970	.050 030	152
153	1745.672 448	34893.448 977	.000 028	.000 572	19.988 543	.050 028	153
154	1832.956 071	36639.121 426	.000 027	.000 545	19.989 088	.050 027	154
155	1924.603 874	38472.077 497	.000 025	.000 519	19.989 608	.050 025	155
156	2020.834 068	40396.681 372	.000 024	.000 494	19.990 103	.050 024	156
157	2121.875 772	42417.515 441	.000 023	.000 471	19.990 574	.050 023	157
158	2227.969 560	44539.391 213	.000 022	.000 443	19.991 023	.050 022	158
159	2339.368 038	46767.360 773	.000 021	.000 427	19.991 450	.050 021	159
160	2456.336 440	49106.728 812	.000 020	.000 407	19.991 857	.050 020	160
161	2579.153 262	51563.065 253	.000 019	.000 387	19.992 245	.050 019	161
162	2708.110 925	54142.218 515	.000 018	.000 369	19.992 614	.050 018	162
163	2843.516 472	56850.329 441	.000 017	.000 351	19.992 966	.050 017	163
164	2985.692 295	59693.845 913	.000 016	.000 334	19.993 301	.050 016	164
165	3134.976 910	62679.538 209	.000 015	.000 318	19.993 620	.050 015	165
166	3291.725 755	65814.515 119	.000 015	.000 303	19.993 924	.050 015	166
167	3456.312 043	69106.240 875	.000 014	.000 289	19.994 213	.050 014	167
168	3629.127 645	72562.552 919	.000 013	.000 275	19.994 489	.050 013	168
169	3810.584 028	76191.680 565	.000 013	.000 262	19.994 751	.050 013	169
170	4001.113 229	80002.264 593	.000 012	.000 249	19.995 001	.050 012	170
171	4201.168 891	84003.377 823	.000 011	.000 238	19.995 239	.050 011	171
172	4411.227 335	88204.546 714	.000 011	.000 226	19.995 466	.050 011	172
173	4631.788 702	92615.774 050	.000 010	.000 215	19.995 682	.050 010	173
174	4863.378 137	97247.562 752	.000 010	.000 205	19.995 887	.050 010	174
175	5106.547 044	102110.940 890	.000 009	.000 195	19.996 083	.050 009	175
176	5361.874 396	107217.487 935	.000 009	.000 186	19.996 269	.050 009	176
177	5629.968 116	112579.362 331	.000 008	.000 177	19.996 447	.050 008	177
178	5911.466 522	118209.330 448	.000 008	.000 169	19.996 616	.050 008	178
179	6207.039 848	124120.796 970	.000 008	.000 161	19.996 777	.050 008	179
180	6517.391 840	130327.836 819	.000 007	.000 153	19.996 931	.050 007	180

Source: *Financial Compound Interest and Annuity Tables*, 5th ed. (Boston: Financial Publishing Co., 1970).

TABLE 8

Rate of 6%

PERIODS	AMOUNT OF 1 — How $1 left at compound interest will grow.	AMOUNT OF 1 PER PERIOD — How $1 deposited periodically will grow.	SINKING FUND — Periodic deposit that will grow to $1 at future date.	PRESENT WORTH OF 1 — What $1 due in the future is worth today.	PRESENT WORTH OF 1 PER PERIOD — What $1 payable periodically is worth today.	PARTIAL PAYMENT — Annuity worth $1 today. Periodic payment necessary to pay off a loan of $1.
1	1.060 000	1.000 000	1.000 000	.943 396	.943 392	1.060 000
2	1.123 600	2.060 000	.485 436	.889 996	1.833 392	.545 436
3	1.191 016	3.183 600	.314 109	.839 619	2.673 011	.374 109
4	1.262 476	4.374 616	.228 591	.792 093	3.465 105	.288 591
5	1.338 225	5.637 092	.177 396	.747 258	4.212 363	.237 396
6	1.418 519	6.975 318	.143 362	.704 960	4.917 324	.203 362
7	1.503 630	8.393 837	.119 135	.665 057	5.582 381	.179 135
8	1.593 848	9.897 467	.101 035	.627 412	6.209 793	.161 035
9	1.689 478	11.491 315	.087 022	.591 898	6.801 692	.147 022
10	1.790 847	13.180 794	.075 867	.558 394	7.360 087	.135 867
11	1.898 298	14.971 642	.066 792	.526 787	7.886 874	.126 792
12	2.012 196	16.869 941	.059 277	.496 969	8.383 843	.119 277
13	2.132 928	18.882 137	.052 960	.468 839	8.852 682	.112 960
14	2.260 903	21.015 065	.047 584	.442 300	9.294 983	.107 584
15	2.396 558	23.275 969	.042 962	.417 265	9.712 248	.102 962
16	2.540 351	25.672 528	.038 952	.393 646	10.105 895	.098 952
17	2.692 772	28.212 879	.035 444	.371 364	10.477 259	.095 444
18	2.854 339	30.905 652	.032 356	.350 343	10.827 603	.092 356
19	3.025 599	33.759 991	.029 620	.330 513	11.158 116	.089 620
20	3.207 135	36.785 591	.027 184	.311 804	11.469 921	.087 184
21	3.399 563	39.992 726	.025 004	.294 155	11.764 076	.085 004
22	3.603 537	43.392 290	.023 045	.277 505	12.041 581	.083 045
23	3.819 749	46.995 827	.021 278	.261 797	12.303 378	.081 278
24	4.048 934	50.815 577	.019 679	.246 978	12.550 357	.079 679
25	4.291 870	54.864 511	.018 226	.232 998	12.783 356	.078 226
26	4.549 382	59.156 382	.016 904	.219 810	13.003 166	.076 904
27	4.822 345	63.705 765	.015 697	.207 367	13.210 534	.075 697
28	5.111 686	68.528 111	.014 592	.195 630	13.406 164	.074 592
29	5.418 387	73.639 798	.013 579	.184 556	13.590 721	.073 579
30	5.743 491	79.058 186	.012 648	.174 110	13.764 831	.072 648

N	$(1+i)^N$	$\dfrac{(1+i)^N - 1}{i}$	$\dfrac{i}{(1+i)^N - 1}$	$(1+i)^{-N}$	$\dfrac{1-(1+i)^{-N}}{i}$	$\dfrac{i}{1-(1+i)^{-N}}$	N
31	6.088 100	84.801 677	.011 792	.164 254	13.929 085	.071 792	31
32	6.453 386	90.889 778	.011 002	.154 957	14.084 043	.071 002	32
33	6.840 589	97.343 164	.010 272	.146 185	14.230 229	.070 272	33
34	7.251 025	104.183 754	.009 598	.137 911	14.368 141	.069 598	34
35	7.686 086	111.434 779	.008 973	.130 105	14.498 246	.068 973	35
36	8.147 251	119.120 866	.008 394	.122 740	14.620 987	.068 394	36
37	8.636 087	127.268 118	.007 857	.115 793	14.736 780	.067 857	37
38	9.154 252	135.904 205	.007 358	.109 238	14.846 019	.067 358	38
39	9.703 507	145.058 458	.006 893	.103 055	14.949 074	.066 893	39
40	10.285 717	154.761 965	.006 461	.097 222	15.046 296	.066 461	40
41	10.902 861	165.047 683	.006 058	.091 719	15.138 015	.066 058	41
42	11.557 032	175.950 544	.005 683	.086 527	15.224 543	.065 683	42
43	12.250 454	187.507 577	.005 333	.081 629	15.306 172	.065 333	43
44	12.985 481	199.758 031	.005 006	.077 009	15.383 182	.065 006	44
45	13.764 610	212.743 513	.004 700	.072 650	15.455 832	.064 700	45
46	14.590 487	226.508 124	.004 414	.068 557	15.524 369	.064 414	46
47	15.465 916	241.098 612	.004 147	.064 658	15.589 028	.064 147	47
48	16.393 871	256.564 528	.003 897	.060 998	15.650 026	.063 897	48
49	17.377 504	272.958 400	.003 663	.057 545	15.707 572	.063 663	49
50	18.420 154	290.335 904	.003 444	.054 288	15.761 860	.063 444	50
51	19.525 363	308.756 058	.003 238	.051 215	15.813 076	.063 238	51
52	20.696 885	328.281 422	.003 046	.048 316	15.861 392	.063 046	52
53	21.938 698	348.978 307	.002 865	.045 581	15.906 974	.062 865	53
54	23.255 020	370.917 006	.002 696	.043 001	15.949 975	.062 696	54
55	24.650 321	394.172 026	.002 536	.040 557	15.990 542	.062 536	55
56	26.129 340	418.822 348	.002 387	.038 271	16.028 814	.062 387	56
57	27.697 101	444.951 689	.002 247	.036 134	16.064 918	.062 247	57
58	29.358 927	472.648 790	.002 115	.034 051	16.098 980	.062 115	58
59	31.120 463	502.007 717	.001 992	.032 133	16.131 113	.061 992	59
60	32.987 690	533.128 180	.001 875	.030 314	16.161 427	.061 875	60

Source: *Financial Compound Interest and Annuity Tables*, 5th ed. (Boston: Financial Publishing Co., 1970).

TABLE 8 (continued)

Rate of 6%

PERIODS	AMOUNT OF 1 How $1 left at compound interest will grow.	AMOUNT OF 1 PER PERIOD How $1 deposited periodically will grow.	SINKING FUND Periodic deposit that will grow to $1 at future date.	PRESENT WORTH OF 1 What $1 due in the future is worth today.	PRESENT WORTH OF 1 PER PERIOD What $1 payable periodically is worth today.	PARTIAL PAYMENT Annuity worth $1 today. Periodic payment necessary to pay off a loan of $1.	PERIODS
61	34.966 952	566.115 871	.001 766	.028 598	16.190 026	.061 766	61
62	37.064 969	601.082 824	.001 663	.026 979	16.217 005	.061 663	62
63	39.288 867	638.147 793	.001 567	.025 452	16.242 458	.061 567	63
64	41.646 199	677.436 661	.001 476	.024 011	16.266 470	.061 476	64
65	44.144 971	719.082 860	.001 390	.022 652	16.289 122	.061 390	65
66	46.793 669	763.227 832	.001 310	.021 370	16.310 493	.061 310	66
67	49.601 290	810.021 502	.001 234	.020 160	16.330 653	.061 234	67
68	52.577 367	859.622 792	.001 163	.019 019	16.349 673	.061 163	68
69	55.732 009	912.200 160	.001 096	.017 943	16.367 616	.061 096	69
70	59.075 930	967.932 169	.001 033	.016 927	16.384 543	.061 033	70
71	62.620 485	1027.008 099	.000 973	.015 969	16.400 513	.060 973	71
72	66.377 715	1089.628 585	.000 917	.015 065	16.415 578	.060 917	72
73	70.360 378	1156.006 300	.000 865	.014 212	16.429 790	.060 865	73
74	74.582 000	1226.366 679	.000 815	.013 408	16.443 198	.060 815	74
75	79.056 920	1300.948 679	.000 768	.012 649	16.455 848	.060 768	75
76	83.800 336	1380.005 600	.000 724	.011 933	16.467 781	.060 724	76
77	88.828 356	1463.805 936	.000 683	.011 257	16.479 038	.060 683	77
78	94.158 057	1552.634 292	.000 644	.010 620	16.489 659	.060 644	78
79	99.807 541	1646.792 350	.000 607	.010 019	16.499 678	.060 607	79
80	105.795 993	1746.599 891	.000 572	.009 452	16.509 130	.060 572	80
81	112.143 753	1852.395 884	.000 539	.008 917	16.518 047	.060 539	81
82	118.872 378	1964.539 637	.000 509	.008 412	16.526 460	.060 509	82
83	126.004 720	2083.412 016	.000 479	.007 936	16.534 396	.060 479	83
84	133.565 004	2209.416 737	.000 452	.007 486	16.541 883	.060 452	84
85	141.578 904	2342.981 741	.000 426	.007 063	16.548 946	.060 426	85
86	150.073 638	2484.560 645	.000 402	.006 663	16.555 610	.060 402	86
87	159.078 057	2634.634 284	.000 379	.006 286	16.561 896	.060 379	87
88	168.622 740	2793.712 341	.000 357	.005 930	16.567 826	.060 357	88
89	178.740 104	2962.335 082	.000 337	.005 594	16.573 421	.060 337	89
90	189.464 511	3141.075 187	.000 318	.005 278	16.578 699	.060 318	90

N	$(1+i)^N$	$\dfrac{(1+i)^N - 1}{i}$	$\dfrac{i}{(1+i)^N - 1}$	$(1+i)^{-N}$	$\dfrac{1-(1+i)^{-N}}{i}$	$\dfrac{i}{1-(1+i)^{-N}}$	N
91	200.832 381	3330.539 698	.000 300	.004 979	16.583 678	.060 300	91
92	212.882 324	3531.372 080	.000 283	.004 697	16.588 376	.060 283	92
93	225.655 264	3744.254 405	.000 267	.004 431	16.592 807	.060 267	93
94	239.194 580	3969.909 669	.000 251	.004 180	16.596 988	.060 251	94
95	253.546 254	4209.104 249	.000 237	.003 944	16.600 932	.060 237	95
96	268.759 030	4462.650 504	.000 224	.003 720	16.604 653	.060 224	96
97	284.884 572	4731.409 534	.000 211	.003 510	16.608 163	.060 211	97
98	301.977 646	5016.294 106	.000 199	.003 311	16.611 474	.060 199	98
99	320.096 305	5318.271 753	.000 188	.003 124	16.614 599	.060 188	99
100	339.302 083	5638.368 058	.000 177	.002 947	16.617 546	.060 177	100
101	359.660 208	5977.670 142	.000 167	.002 780	16.620 326	.060 167	101
102	381.239 821	6337.330 350	.000 157	.002 623	16.622 949	.060 157	102
103	404.114 210	6718.570 171	.000 148	.002 474	16.625 424	.060 148	103
104	428.361 062	7122.684 381	.000 140	.002 334	16.627 758	.060 140	104
105	454.062 726	7551.045 444	.000 132	.002 202	16.629 961	.060 132	105
106	481.306 490	8005.108 171	.000 124	.002 077	16.632 038	.060 124	106
107	510.184 879	8486.414 661	.000 117	.001 960	16.633 998	.060 117	107
108	540.795 972	8996.599 541	.000 111	.001 849	16.635 847	.060 111	108
109	573.243 730	9537.395 514	.000 104	.001 744	16.637 592	.060 104	109
110	607.638 354	10110.639 244	.000 098	.001 645	16.639 238	.060 098	110
111	644.096 655	10718.277 599	.000 093	.001 552	16.640 790	.060 093	111
112	682.742 455	11362.374 255	.000 088	.001 464	16.642 255	.060 088	112
113	723.707 002	12045.116 710	.000 083	.001 381	16.643 637	.060 083	113
114	767.129 422	12768.823 713	.000 078	.001 303	16.644 940	.060 078	114
115	813.157 188	13535.953 136	.000 073	.001 229	16.646 170	.060 073	115
116	861.946 619	14349.110 324	.000 069	.001 160	16.647 330	.060 069	116
117	913.663 416	15211.056 944	.000 065	.001 094	16.648 425	.060 065	117
118	968.483 221	16124.720 360	.000 062	.001 032	16.649 457	.060 062	118
119	1026.592 214	17093.203 582	.000 058	.000 974	16.650 431	.060 058	119
120	1088.187 747	18119.795 797	.000 055	.000 918	16.651 350	.060 055	120

Source: *Financial Compound Interest and Annuity Tables*, 5th ed. (Boston: Financial Publishing Co., 1970).

TABLE 9

Rate of 7%

PERIODS	AMOUNT OF 1 How $1 left at compound interest will grow.	AMOUNT OF 1 PER PERIOD How $1 deposited periodically will grow.	SINKING FUND Periodic deposit that will grow to $1 at future date.	PRESENT WORTH OF 1 What $1 due in the future is worth today.	PRESENT WORTH OF 1 PER PERIOD What $1 payable periodically is worth today.	PARTIAL PAYMENT Annuity worth $1 today. Periodic payment necessary to pay off a loan of $1.	PERIODS
1	1.070 000	1.000 000	1.000 000	.934 579	.934 579	1.070 000	1
2	1.144 900	2.070 000	.483 091	.873 438	1.808 018	.553 091	2
3	1.225 043	3.214 900	.311 051	.816 297	2.624 316	.381 051	3
4	1.310 796	4.439 943	.225 228	.762 895	3.387 211	.295 228	4
5	1.402 551	5.750 739	.173 890	.712 986	4.100 197	.243 890	5
6	1.500 730	7.153 290	.139 795	.666 342	4.766 539	.209 795	6
7	1.605 781	8.654 021	.115 553	.622 749	5.389 289	.185 553	7
8	1.718 186	10.259 802	.097 467	.582 009	5.971 298	.167 467	8
9	1.838 459	11.977 988	.083 486	.543 933	6.515 232	.153 486	9
10	1.967 151	13.816 447	.072 377	.508 349	7.023 581	.142 377	10
11	2.104 851	15.783 599	.063 356	.475 092	7.498 674	.133 356	11
12	2.252 191	17.888 451	.055 901	.444 011	7.942 686	.125 901	12
13	2.409 845	20.140 642	.049 650	.414 964	8.357 650	.119 650	13
14	2.578 534	22.550 487	.044 344	.387 817	8.745 467	.114 344	14
15	2.759 031	25.129 022	.039 794	.362 446	9.107 914	.109 794	15
16	2.952 163	27.888 053	.035 857	.338 734	9.446 648	.105 857	16
17	3.158 815	30.840 217	.032 425	.316 574	9.763 222	.102 425	17
18	3.379 932	33.999 032	.029 412	.295 863	10.059 086	.099 412	18
19	3.616 527	37.378 964	.026 753	.276 508	10.335 595	.096 753	19
20	3.869 684	40.995 492	.024 392	.258 419	10.594 014	.094 392	20
21	4.140 562	44.865 176	.022 289	.241 513	10.835 527	.092 289	21
22	4.430 401	49.005 739	.020 405	.225 713	11.061 240	.090 405	22
23	4.740 529	53.436 140	.018 713	.210 946	11.272 187	.088 713	23
24	5.072 366	58.176 670	.017 189	.197 146	11.469 334	.087 189	24
25	5.427 432	63.249 037	.015 810	.184 249	11.653 583	.085 810	25
26	5.807 352	68.676 470	.014 561	.172 195	11.825 778	.084 561	26
27	6.213 867	74.483 823	.013 425	.160 930	11.986 709	.083 425	27
28	6.648 838	80.697 690	.012 391	.150 402	12.137 111	.082 391	28
29	7.114 257	87.346 529	.011 448	.140 562	12.277 674	.081 448	29
30	7.612 255	94.460 786	.010 586	.131 367	12.409 041	.080 586	30

N	$(1+i)^N$	$\dfrac{(1+i)^N-1}{i}$	$\dfrac{i}{(1+i)^N-1}$	$(1+i)^{-N}$	$\dfrac{1-(1+i)^{-N}}{i}$	$\dfrac{i}{1-(1+i)^{-N}}$
31	8.145 112	102.073 041	.009 796	.122 773	12.531 814	.079 796
32	8.715 270	110.218 154	.009 072	.114 741	12.646 555	.079 072
33	9.325 339	118.933 425	.008 408	.107 234	12.753 790	.078 408
34	9.978 113	128.258 764	.007 796	.100 219	12.854 009	.077 796
35	10.676 581	138.236 878	.007 233	.093 652	12.947 672	.077 233
36	11.423 942	148.913 459	.006 715	.087 535	13.035 207	.076 715
37	12.223 618	160.337 402	.006 236	.081 808	13.117 016	.076 236
38	13.079 271	172.561 020	.005 795	.076 456	13.193 473	.075 795
39	13.994 820	185.640 291	.005 386	.071 455	13.264 928	.075 386
40	14.974 457	199.635 111	.005 009	.066 780	13.331 708	.075 009
41	16.022 669	214.609 569	.004 659	.062 411	13.394 120	.074 659
42	17.144 256	230.632 239	.004 335	.058 328	13.452 448	.074 335
43	18.344 354	247.776 496	.004 035	.054 512	13.506 961	.074 035
44	19.628 459	266.120 851	.003 757	.050 946	13.557 908	.073 757
45	21.002 451	285.749 310	.003 499	.047 613	13.605 521	.073 499
46	22.472 623	306.751 762	.003 259	.044 498	13.650 020	.073 259
47	24.045 707	329.224 385	.003 037	.041 587	13.691 607	.073 037
48	25.728 906	353.270 092	.002 830	.038 866	13.730 474	.072 830
49	27.529 929	378.998 999	.002 638	.036 524	13.766 798	.072 638
50	29.457 025	406.528 929	.002 459	.033 947	13.800 746	.072 459
51	31.519 016	435.985 954	.002 293	.031 726	13.832 473	.072 293
52	33.725 347	467.504 971	.002 139	.029 651	13.862 124	.072 139
53	36.086 122	501.230 319	.001 995	.027 711	13.889 835	.071 995
54	38.612 150	537.316 441	.001 861	.025 898	13.915 734	.071 861
55	41.315 001	575.928 592	.001 736	.024 204	13.939 938	.071 736
56	44.207 051	617.243 594	.001 620	.022 620	13.962 559	.071 620
57	47.301 545	661.450 645	.001 511	.021 140	13.983 700	.071 511
58	50.612 653	708.752 190	.001 410	.019 757	14.003 458	.071 410
59	54.155 539	759.364 844	.001 316	.018 465	14.021 923	.071 316
60	57.946 426	813.520 383	.001 229	.017 257	14.039 181	.071 229

Source: *Financial Compound Interest and Annuity Tables*, 5th ed. (Boston: Financial Publishing Co., 1970).

TABLE 9 (continued)

Rate of 7%

PERIODS	AMOUNT OF 1 How $1 left at compound interest will grow.	AMOUNT OF 1 PER PERIOD How $1 deposited periodically will grow.	SINKING FUND Periodic deposit that will grow to $1 at future date.	PRESENT WORTH OF 1 What $1 due in the future is worth today.	PRESENT WORTH OF 1 PER PERIOD What $1 payable periodically is worth today.	PARTIAL PAYMENT Annuity worth $1 today. Periodic payment necessary to pay off a loan of $1.	PERIODS
61	62.002 676	871.466 810	.001 147	.016 128	14.055 309	.071 147	61
62	66.342 864	933.469 486	.001 071	.015 073	14.070 382	.071 071	62
63	70.986 864	999.812 350	.001 000	.014 087	14.084 469	.071 000	63
64	75.955 945	1070.799 215	.000 933	.013 165	14.097 635	.070 933	64
65	81.272 861	1146.755 160	.000 872	.012 304	14.109 939	.070 872	65
66	86.961 961	1228.028 021	.000 814	.011 499	14.121 438	.070 814	66
67	93.049 298	1314.989 983	.000 760	.010 746	14.132 185	.070 760	67
68	99.562 749	1408.039 282	.000 710	.010 043	14.142 229	.070 710	68
69	106.532 142	1507.602 032	.000 663	.009 386	14.151 616	.070 663	69
70	113.989 392	1614.134 174	.000 619	.008 772	14.160 389	.070 619	70
71	121.968 649	1728.123 566	.000 578	.008 198	14.168 588	.070 578	71
72	130.506 455	1850.092 216	.000 540	.007 662	14.176 250	.070 540	72
73	139.641 906	1980.598 671	.000 504	.007 161	14.183 411	.070 504	73
74	149.416 840	2120.240 578	.000 471	.006 692	14.190 104	.070 471	74
75	159.876 019	2269.657 418	.000 440	.006 254	14.196 359	.070 440	75
76	171.067 340	2429.533 437	.000 411	.005 845	14.202 204	.070 411	76
77	183.042 054	2600.600 778	.000 384	.005 463	14.207 668	.070 384	77
78	195.854 998	2783.642 833	.000 359	.005 105	14.212 774	.070 359	78
79	209.564 848	2979.497 831	.000 335	.004 771	14.217 545	.070 335	79
80	224.234 387	3189.062 679	.000 313	.004 459	14.222 005	.070 313	80
81	239.930 794	3413.297 067	.000 292	.004 167	14.226 173	.070 292	81
82	256.725 950	3653.227 861	.000 273	.003 895	14.230 068	.070 273	82
83	274.696 766	3909.953 812	.000 255	.003 640	14.233 708	.070 255	83
84	293.925 540	4184.650 579	.000 238	.003 402	14.237 111	.070 238	84
85	314.500 328	4478.576 119	.000 223	.003 179	14.240 290	.070 223	85
86	336.515 351	4793.076 448	.000 208	.002 971	14.243 262	.070 208	86
87	360.071 425	5129.591 799	.000 194	.002 777	14.246 039	.070 194	87
88	385.276 425	5489.663 225	.000 182	.002 595	14.248 635	.070 182	88
89	412.245 775	5874.939 651	.000 170	.002 425	14.251 060	.070 170	89
90	441.102 979	6287.185 426	.000 159	.002 267	14.253 327	.070 159	90

N	$(1+i)^N$	$\dfrac{(1+i)^N-1}{i}$	$\dfrac{i}{(1+i)^N-1}$	$(1+i)^{-N}$	$\dfrac{1-(1+i)^{-N}}{i}$	$\dfrac{i}{1-(1+i)^{-N}}$	N
91	471.980 188	6728.288 406	.000 148	.002 118	14.255 446	.070 148	91
92	505.018 801	7200.268 595	.000 138	.001 980	14.257 426	.070 138	92
93	540.370 117	7705.287 396	.000 129	.001 850	14.259 277	.070 129	93
94	578.196 026	8245.657 514	.000 121	.001 729	14.261 006	.070 121	94
95	618.669 747	8823.853 540	.000 113	.001 616	14.262 623	.070 113	95
96	661.976 630	9442.523 288	.000 105	.001 510	14.264 133	.070 105	96
97	708.314 994	10104.499 918	.000 098	.001 411	14.265 545	.070 098	97
98	757.897 043	10812.814 912	.000 092	.001 319	14.266 865	.070 092	98
99	810.949 836	11570.711 956	.000 086	.001 233	14.268 098	.070 086	99
100	867.716 325	12381.661 793	.000 080	.001 152	14.269 250	.070 080	100
101	928.456 468	13249.378 119	.000 075	.001 077	14.270 327	.070 075	101
102	993.448 421	14177.834 587	.000 070	.001 006	14.271 334	.070 070	102
103	1062.989 810	15171.283 008	.000 065	.000 940	14.272 275	.070 065	103
104	1137.399 097	16234.272 819	.000 061	.000 879	14.273 154	.070 061	104
105	1217.017 034	17371.671 916	.000 057	.000 821	14.273 975	.070 057	105
106	1302.208 226	18588.688 951	.000 053	.000 767	14.274 743	.070 053	106
107	1393.362 802	19890.897 177	.000 050	.000 717	14.275 461	.070 050	107
108	1490.898 198	21284.259 980	.000 046	.000 670	14.276 132	.070 046	108
109	1595.261 072	22775.158 178	.000 043	.000 625	14.276 759	.070 043	109
110	1706.929 347	24370.419 251	.000 041	.000 585	14.277 345	.070 041	110
111	1826.414 401	26077.348 598	.000 038	.000 547	14.277 892	.070 038	111
112	1954.263 410	27903.763 000	.000 035	.000 511	14.278 404	.070 035	112
113	2091.061 848	29858.026 410	.000 033	.000 478	14.278 882	.070 033	113
114	2237.436 178	31949.088 259	.000 031	.000 445	14.279 329	.070 031	114
115	2394.056 710	34186.524 437	.000 029	.000 417	14.279 747	.070 029	115
116	2561.640 680	36580.581 148	.000 027	.000 390	14.280 137	.070 027	116
117	2740.955 528	39142.221 828	.000 025	.000 364	14.280 502	.070 025	117
118	2932.822 414	41883.177 356	.000 023	.000 340	14.280 843	.070 023	118
119	3138.119 984	44815.999 771	.000 022	.000 318	14.281 161	.070 022	119
120	3357.788 382	47954.119 755	.000 020	.000 297	14.281 459	.070 020	120

Source: *Financial Compound Interest and Annuity Tables*, 5th ed. (Boston: Financial Publishing Co., 1970).

TABLE 10

Rate of 8%

PERIODS	AMOUNT OF 1 How $1 left at compound interest will grow.	AMOUNT OF 1 PER PERIOD How $1 deposited periodically will grow.	SINKING FUND Periodic deposit that will grow to $1 at future date.	PRESENT WORTH OF 1 What $1 due in the future is worth today.	PRESENT WORTH OF 1 PER PERIOD What $1 payable periodically is worth today.	PARTIAL PAYMENT Annuity worth $1 today. Periodic payment necessary to pay off a loan of $1.	PERIODS
1	1.080 000	1.000 000	1.000 000	.925 925	.925 925	1.080 000	1
2	1.166 400	2.080 000	.480 769	.857 338	1.783 264	.560 769	2
3	1.259 712	3.246 400	.308 033	.793 832	2.577 096	.388 033	3
4	1.360 488	4.506 112	.221 920	.735 029	3.312 126	.301 920	4
5	1.469 328	5.866 600	.170 456	.680 583	3.992 710	.250 456	5
6	1.586 874	7.335 929	.136 315	.630 169	4.622 879	.216 315	6
7	1.713 824	8.922 803	.112 072	.583 490	5.206 370	.192 072	7
8	1.850 930	10.636 627	.094 014	.540 268	5.746 638	.174 014	8
9	1.999 004	12.487 557	.080 079	.500 248	6.246 887	.160 079	9
10	2.158 924	14.486 562	.069 029	.463 193	6.710 081	.149 029	10
11	2.331 638	16.645 487	.060 076	.428 882	7.138 964	.140 076	11
12	2.518 170	18.977 126	.052 695	.397 113	7.536 078	.132 695	12
13	2.719 623	21.495 296	.046 521	.367 697	7.903 775	.126 521	13
14	2.937 193	24.214 920	.041 296	.340 461	8.244 236	.121 296	14
15	3.172 169	27.152 113	.036 829	.315 241	8.559 478	.116 829	15
16	3.425 942	30.324 283	.032 976	.291 890	8.851 369	.112 976	16
17	3.700 018	33.750 225	.029 629	.270 268	9.121 638	.109 629	17
18	3.996 019	37.450 243	.026 702	.250 249	9.371 887	.106 702	18
19	4.315 701	41.446 263	.024 127	.231 712	9.603 599	.104 127	19
20	4.660 957	45.761 964	.021 852	.214 548	9.818 147	.101 852	20
21	5.033 833	50.422 921	.019 832	.198 655	10.016 803	.099 832	21
22	5.436 540	55.456 755	.018 032	.183 940	10.200 743	.098 032	22
23	5.871 463	60.893 295	.016 422	.170 315	10.371 058	.096 422	23
24	6.341 180	66.764 759	.014 977	.157 699	10.528 758	.094 977	24
25	6.848 475	73.105 939	.013 678	.146 017	10.674 776	.093 678	25
26	7.396 353	79.954 415	.012 507	.135 201	10.809 977	.092 507	26
27	7.988 061	87.350 768	.011 448	.125 186	10.935 164	.091 448	27
28	8.627 106	95.338 829	.010 488	.115 913	11.051 078	.090 488	28
29	9.317 274	103.965 936	.009 618	.107 327	11.158 406	.089 618	29
30	10.062 656	113.283 211	.008 827	.099 377	11.257 783	.088 827	30

N	$\dfrac{i}{1-(1+i)^{-N}}$	$\dfrac{1-(1+i)^{-N}}{i}$	$(1+i)^{-N}$	$\dfrac{i}{(1+i)^N-1}$	$\dfrac{(1+i)^N-1}{i}$	$(1+i)^N$	N
31	.088 107	11.349 799	.092 016	.008 107	123.345 868	10.867 669	31
32	.087 450	11.434 999	.085 200	.007 450	134.213 537	11.737 082	32
33	.086 851	11.513 888	.078 888	.006 851	145.950 620	12.676 049	33
34	.086 304	11.586 933	.073 045	.006 304	158.626 670	13.690 133	34
35	.085 803	11.654 568	.067 634	.005 803	172.316 803	14.785 344	35
36	.085 344	11.717 192	.062 624	.005 344	187.102 147	15.968 171	36
37	.084 924	11.775 178	.057 985	.004 924	203.070 319	17.245 625	37
38	.084 538	11.828 868	.053 690	.004 538	220.315 945	18.625 275	38
39	.084 185	11.878 582	.049 713	.004 185	238.941 221	20.115 297	39
40	.083 860	11.924 613	.046 030	.003 860	259.056 518	21.724 521	40
41	.083 561	11.967 234	.042 621	.003 561	280.781 040	23.462 483	41
42	.083 286	12.006 698	.039 464	.003 286	304.243 523	25.339 481	42
43	.083 034	12.043 239	.036 540	.003 034	329.583 005	27.366 640	43
44	.082 801	12.077 073	.033 834	.002 801	356.949 645	29.555 971	44
45	.082 587	12.108 401	.031 327	.002 587	386.505 617	31.920 449	45
46	.082 389	12.137 408	.029 007	.002 389	418.426 066	34.474 085	46
47	.082 207	12.164 267	.026 858	.002 207	452.900 152	37.232 012	47
48	.082 040	12.189 136	.024 869	.002 040	490.132 164	40.210 573	48
49	.081 885	12.212 163	.023 026	.001 885	530.342 737	43.427 418	49
50	.081 742	12.233 484	.021 321	.001 742	573.770 156	46.901 612	50
51	.081 611	12.253 226	.019 741	.001 611	620.671 768	50.653 741	51
52	.081 489	12.271 506	.018 279	.001 489	671.325 510	54.706 040	52
53	.081 377	12.288 431	.016 925	.001 377	726.031 551	59.082 524	53
54	.081 273	12.304 103	.015 671	.001 273	785.114 075	63.809 126	54
55	.081 177	12.318 614	.014 510	.001 177	848.923 201	68.913 856	55
56	.081 089	12.332 050	.013 435	.001 089	917.837 057	74.426 964	56
57	.081 007	12.344 490	.012 440	.001 007	992.264 022	80.381 121	57
58	.080 932	12.356 010	.011 519	.000 932	1072.645 143	86.811 611	58
59	.080 862	12.366 675	.010 665	.000 862	1159.456 755	93.756 540	59
60	.080 797	12.376 551	.009 875	.000 797	1253.213 295	101.257 063	60

Source: *Financial Compound Interest and Annuity Tables*, 5th ed. (Boston: Financial Publishing Co., 1970).

TABLE 10 (continued)

Rate of 8%

PERIODS	AMOUNT OF 1 How $1 left at compound interest will grow.	AMOUNT OF 1 PER PERIOD How $1 deposited periodically will grow.	SINKING FUND Periodic deposit that will grow to $1 at future date.	PRESENT WORTH OF 1 What $1 due in the future is worth today.	PRESENT WORTH OF 1 PER PERIOD What $1 payable periodically is worth today.	PARTIAL PAYMENT Annuity worth $1 today. Periodic payment necessary to pay off a loan of $1.	PERIODS
61	109.357 628	1354.470 359	.000 738	.009 144	12.385 696	.080 738	61
62	118.106 239	1463.827 988	.000 683	.008 466	12.394 163	.080 683	62
63	127.554 738	1581.934 227	.000 632	.007 839	12.402 002	.080 632	63
64	137.759 117	1709.488 965	.000 584	.007 259	12.409 261	.080 584	64
65	148.779 846	1847.248 082	.000 541	.006 721	12.415 983	.080 541	65
66	160.682 234	1996.027 929	.000 500	.006 223	12.422 206	.080 500	66
67	173.536 813	2156.710 163	.000 463	.005 762	12.427 969	.080 463	67
68	187.419 758	2330.246 976	.000 429	.005 335	12.433 304	.080 429	68
69	202.413 338	2517.666 734	.000 397	.004 940	12.438 245	.080 397	69
70	218.606 405	2720.080 073	.000 367	.004 574	12.442 819	.080 367	70
71	236.094 918	2938.686 479	.000 340	.004 235	12.447 055	.080 340	71
72	254.982 511	3174.781 398	.000 314	.003 921	12.450 977	.080 314	72
73	275.381 112	3429.763 909	.000 291	.003 631	12.454 608	.080 291	73
74	297.411 601	3705.145 022	.000 269	.003 362	12.457 970	.080 269	74
75	321.204 529	4002.556 624	.000 249	.003 113	12.461 083	.080 249	75
76	346.900 892	4323.761 154	.000 231	.002 882	12.463 966	.080 231	76
77	374.652 963	4670.662 046	.000 214	.002 669	12.466 635	.080 214	77
78	404.625 200	5045.315 010	.000 198	.002 471	12.469 107	.080 198	78
79	436.995 216	5449.940 211	.000 183	.002 288	12.471 395	.080 183	79
80	471.954 834	5886.935 428	.000 169	.002 118	12.473 514	.080 169	80
81	509.711 221	6358.890 262	.000 157	.001 961	12.475 476	.080 157	81
82	550.488 118	6868.601 483	.000 145	.001 816	12.477 292	.080 145	82
83	594.527 168	7419.089 602	.000 134	.001 682	12.478 974	.080 134	83
84	642.089 341	8013.616 770	.000 124	.001 557	12.480 532	.080 124	84
85	693.456 488	8655.706 112	.000 115	.001 442	12.481 974	.080 115	85
86	748.933 008	9349.162 601	.000 106	.001 335	12.483 309	.080 106	86
87	808.847 648	10098.095 609	.000 099	.001 236	12.484 545	.080 099	87
88	873.555 460	10906.943 257	.000 091	.001 144	12.485 690	.080 091	88
89	943.439 897	11780.498 718	.000 084	.001 059	12.486 750	.080 084	89
90	1018.915 089	12723.938 615	.000 078	.000 981	12.487 732	.080 078	90

N	$(1+i)^N$	$\dfrac{(1+i)^N-1}{i}$	$\dfrac{i}{(1+i)^N-1}$	$(1+i)^{-N}$	$\dfrac{1-(1+i)^{-N}}{i}$	$\dfrac{i}{1-(1+i)^{-N}}$
91	1100.428 296	13742.853 705	.000 072	.000 908	12.488 640	.080 072
92	1188.462 560	14843.282 001	.000 067	.000 841	12.489 482	.080 067
93	1283.539 564	16031.744 561	.000 062	.000 779	12.490 261	.080 062
94	1386.222 730	17315.284 126	.000 057	.000 721	12.490 982	.080 057
95	1497.120 548	18701.506 856	.000 053	.000 667	12.491 650	.080 053
96	1616.890 192	20198.627 405	.000 049	.000 618	12.492 269	.080 049
97	1746.241 407	21815.517 597	.000 045	.000 572	12.492 841	.080 045
98	1885.940 720	23561.759 005	.000 042	.000 530	12.493 372	.080 042
99	2036.815 978	25447.699 726	.000 039	.000 490	12.493 862	.080 039
100	2199.761 256	27484.515 704	.000 036	.000 454	12.494 317	.080 036
101	2375.742 156	29684.276 960	.000 033	.000 420	12.494 738	.080 033
102	2565.801 529	32060.019 117	.000 031	.000 389	12.495 128	.080 031
103	2771.065 651	34625.820 646	.000 028	.000 360	12.495 489	.080 028
104	2992.750 903	37396.886 298	.000 026	.000 334	12.495 823	.080 026
105	3232.170 976	40389.637 202	.000 024	.000 309	12.496 132	.080 024
106	3490.744 654	43621.808 178	.000 022	.000 286	12.496 419	.080 022
107	3770.004 226	47112.552 832	.000 021	.000 265	12.496 684	.080 021
108	4071.604 564	50882.557 059	.000 019	.000 245	12.496 929	.080 019
109	4397.332 929	54954.161 624	.000 018	.000 227	12.497 157	.080 018
110	4749.119 564	59351.494 554	.000 016	.000 210	12.497 367	.080 016
111	5129.049 129	64100.614 118	.000 015	.000 194	12.497 562	.080 015
112	5539.373 059	69229.663 248	.000 014	.000 180	12.497 743	.080 014
113	5982.522 904	74769.036 308	.000 013	.000 167	12.497 910	.080 013
114	6461.124 737	80751.559 212	.000 012	.000 154	12.498 065	.080 012
115	6978.014 715	87212.683 949	.000 011	.000 143	12.498 208	.080 011
116	7536.255 893	94190.698 665	.000 010	.000 132	12.498 341	.080 010
117	8139.156 364	101726.954 558	.000 009	.000 122	12.498 464	.080 009
118	8790.288 873	109866.110 923	.000 009	.000 113	12.498 577	.080 009
119	9493.511 983	118656.399 797	.000 008	.000 105	12.498 683	.080 008
120	10252.992 942	128149.911 781	.000 007	.000 097	12.498 780	.080 007

Source: *Financial Compound Interest and Annuity Tables*, 5th ed. (Boston: Financial Publishing Co., 1970).

TABLE 11

Rate of 9%

PERIODS	AMOUNT OF 1 How $1 left at compound interest will grow.	AMOUNT OF 1 PER PERIOD How $1 deposited periodically will grow.	SINKING FUND Periodic deposit that will grow to $1 at future date.	PRESENT WORTH OF 1 What $1 due in the future is worth today.	PRESENT WORTH OF 1 PER PERIOD What $1 payable periodically is worth today.	PARTIAL PAYMENT Annuity worth $1 today. Periodic payment necessary to pay off a loan of $1.
1	1.090 000	1.000 000	1.000 000	.917 431	.917 431	1.090 000
2	1.188 100	2.090 000	.478 468	.841 679	1.759 111	.568 468
3	1.295 029	3.278 100	.305 054	.772 183	2.531 294	.395 054
4	1.411 581	4.573 129	.218 668	.708 425	3.239 719	.308 668
5	1.538 623	5.984 710	.167 092	.649 931	3.889 651	.257 092
6	1.677 100	7.523 334	.132 919	.596 267	4.485 918	.222 919
7	1.828 039	9.200 434	.108 690	.547 034	5.032 952	.198 690
8	1.992 562	11.028 473	.090 674	.501 866	5.534 819	.180 674
9	2.171 893	13.021 036	.076 798	.460 427	5.995 246	.166 798
10	2.357 363	15.192 929	.065 820	.422 410	6.417 657	.155 820
11	2.580 426	17.560 293	.056 946	.387 532	6.805 190	.146 946
12	2.812 664	20.140 719	.049 650	.355 534	7.160 725	.139 650
13	3.065 804	22.953 384	.043 566	.326 178	7.486 903	.133 566
14	3.341 727	26.019 189	.038 433	.299 246	7.786 150	.128 433
15	3.642 482	29.360 916	.034 058	.274 538	8.060 688	.124 058
16	3.970 305	33.003 398	.030 299	.251 869	8.312 558	.120 299
17	4.327 633	36.973 704	.027 046	.231 073	8.543 631	.117 046
18	4.717 120	41.301 337	.024 212	.211 993	8.755 625	.114 212
19	5.141 661	46.018 458	.021 730	.194 489	8.950 114	.111 730
20	5.604 410	51.160 119	.019 546	.178 430	9.128 545	.109 546
21	6.108 807	56.764 530	.017 616	.163 698	9.292 243	.107 616
22	6.658 600	62.873 338	.015 904	.150 181	9.442 425	.105 904
23	7.257 874	69.531 938	.014 381	.137 781	9.580 206	.104 381
24	7.911 083	76.789 813	.013 022	.126 404	9.706 611	.103 022
25	8.623 080	84.700 896	.011 806	.115 967	9.822 579	.101 806
26	9.399 157	93.323 976	.010 715	.106 392	9.928 972	.100 715
27	10.245 082	102.723 134	.009 734	.097 607	10.026 579	.099 734
28	11.167 139	112.968 216	.008 852	.089 548	10.116 128	.098 852
29	12.172 182	124.135 356	.008 055	.082 154	10.198 282	.098 055
30	13.267 678	136.307 538	.007 336	.075 371	10.273 654	.097 336

N	$(1+i)^N$	$\dfrac{(1+i)^N-1}{i}$	$\dfrac{i}{(1+i)^N-1}$	$(1+i)^{-N}$	$\dfrac{1-(1+i)^{-N}}{i}$	$\dfrac{i}{1-(1+i)^{-N}}$
31	14.461 769	149.575 217	.006 685	.069 147	10.342 801	.096 685
32	15.763 328	164.036 986	.006 096	.063 438	10.406 240	.096 096
33	17.182 028	179.800 315	.005 561	.058 200	10.464 440	.095 561
34	18.728 410	196.982 343	.005 076	.053 394	10.517 835	.095 076
35	20.413 967	215.710 754	.004 635	.048 986	10.566 821	.094 635
36	22.251 225	236.124 722	.004 235	.044 941	10.611 762	.094 235
37	24.253 835	258.375 947	.003 870	.041 230	10.652 993	.093 870
38	26.436 680	282.629 782	.003 538	.037 826	10.690 819	.093 538
39	28.815 981	309.066 463	.003 235	.034 702	10.725 522	.093 235
40	31.409 420	337.882 445	.002 959	.031 837	10.757 360	.092 959
41	34.236 267	369.291 865	.002 707	.029 208	10.786 568	.092 707
42	37.317 531	403.528 132	.002 478	.026 797	10.813 366	.092 478
43	40.676 109	440.845 664	.002 268	.024 584	10.837 950	.092 268
44	44.336 959	481.521 774	.002 076	.022 554	10.860 505	.092 076
45	48.327 286	525.858 734	.001 901	.020 692	10.881 197	.091 901
46	52.676 741	574.186 020	.001 741	.018 983	10.900 180	.091 741
47	57.417 648	626.862 762	.001 595	.017 416	10.917 597	.091 595
48	62.585 236	684.280 411	.001 461	.015 978	10.933 575	.091 461
49	68.217 908	746.865 648	.001 338	.014 658	10.948 234	.091 338
50	74.357 520	815.083 556	.001 226	.013 448	10.961 682	.091 226
51	81.049 696	889.441 076	.001 124	.012 338	10.974 021	.091 124
52	88.344 169	970.490 773	.001 030	.011 319	10.985 340	.091 030
53	96.295 144	1058.834 942	.000 944	.010 384	10.995 725	.090 944
54	104.961 707	1155.130 087	.000 865	.009 527	11.005 252	.090 865
55	114.408 261	1260.091 795	.000 793	.008 740	11.013 993	.090 793
56	124.705 005	1374.500 057	.000 727	.008 018	11.022 011	.090 727
57	135.928 455	1499.205 062	.000 667	.007 356	11.029 368	.090 667
58	148.162 016	1635.133 518	.000 611	.006 749	11.036 118	.090 611
59	161.496 598	1783.295 534	.000 560	.006 192	11.042 310	.090 560
60	176.031 291	1944.792 132	.000 514	.005 680	11.047 991	.090 514

Source: *Financial Compound Interest and Annuity Tables*, 5th ed. (Boston: Financial Publishing Co., 1970).

TABLE 11 (continued)

Rate of 9%

PERIODS	AMOUNT OF 1 — How $1 left at compound interest will grow.	AMOUNT OF 1 PER PERIOD — How $1 deposited periodically will grow.	SINKING FUND — Periodic deposit that will grow to $1 at future date.	PRESENT WORTH OF 1 — What $1 due in the future is worth today.	PRESENT WORTH OF 1 PER PERIOD — What $1 payable periodically is worth today.	PARTIAL PAYMENT — Annuity worth $1 today. Periodic payment necessary to pay off a loan of $1.	PERIODS
61	191.874 108	2120.823 424	.000 471	.005 211	11.053 202	.090 471	61
62	209.142 777	2312.697 533	.000 432	.004 781	11.057 984	.090 432	62
63	227.965 627	2521.840 311	.000 396	.004 386	11.062 370	.090 396	63
64	248.482 534	2749.805 939	.000 363	.004 024	11.066 395	.090 363	64
65	270.845 962	2998.288 473	.000 333	.003 692	11.070 087	.090 333	65
66	295.222 099	3269.134 436	.000 305	.003 387	11.073 474	.090 305	66
67	321.792 088	3564.356 535	.000 280	.003 107	11.076 582	.090 280	67
68	350.753 376	3886.148 623	.000 257	.002 851	11.079 433	.090 257	68
69	382.321 179	4236.901 999	.000 236	.002 615	11.082 048	.090 236	69
70	416.730 086	4619.223 179	.000 216	.002 399	11.084 448	.090 216	70
71	454.235 793	5035.953 265	.000 198	.002 201	11.086 650	.090 198	71
72	495.117 015	5490.189 059	.000 182	.002 019	11.088 669	.090 182	72
73	539.677 546	5985.306 075	.000 167	.001 852	11.090 522	.090 167	73
74	588.248 525	6524.983 622	.000 153	.001 699	11.092 222	.090 153	74
75	641.190 893	7113.232 148	.000 140	.001 559	11.093 782	.090 140	75
76	698.898 073	7754.423 041	.000 128	.001 430	11.095 213	.090 128	76
77	761.798 900	8453.321 115	.000 118	.001 312	11.096 525	.090 118	77
78	830.360 801	9215.120 015	.000 108	.001 204	11.097 730	.090 108	78
79	905.093 273	10045.480 816	.000 099	.001 104	11.098 834	.090 099	79
80	986.551 668	10950.574 090	.000 091	.001 013	11.099 848	.090 091	80
81	1075.341 318	11937.125 758	.000 083	.000 929	11.100 778	.090 083	81
82	1172.122 036	13012.467 076	.000 076	.000 853	11.101 631	.090 076	82
83	1277.613 020	14184.589 113	.000 070	.000 782	11.102 414	.090 070	83
84	1392.598 192	15462.202 133	.000 064	.000 718	11.103 132	.090 064	84
85	1517.932 029	16854.800 325	.000 059	.000 658	11.103 791	.090 059	85
86	1654.545 911	18372.732 355	.000 054	.000 604	11.104 395	.090 054	86
87	1803.455 044	20027.278 267	.000 049	.000 554	11.104 950	.090 049	87
88	1965.765 998	21830.733 311	.000 045	.000 508	11.105 458	.090 045	88
89	2142.684 937	23796.499 309	.000 042	.000 466	11.105 925	.090 042	89
90	2335.526 582	25939.184 247	.000 038	.000 428	11.106 353	.090 038	90

N	$(1+i)^N$	$\dfrac{(1+i)^N-1}{i}$	$\dfrac{i}{(1+i)^N-1}$	$(1+i)^{-N}$	$\dfrac{1-(1+i)^{-N}}{i}$	$\dfrac{i}{1-(1+i)^{-N}}$
91	2545.723 974	28274.710 829	.000 035	.000 392	11.106 746	.090 035
92	2774.839 132	30820.434 803	.000 032	.000 360	11.107 106	.090 032
93	3024.574 654	33595.273 936	.000 029	.000 330	11.107 437	.090 029
94	3296.786 373	36619.848 590	.000 027	.000 303	11.107 740	.090 027
95	3593.497 146	39916.634 963	.000 025	.000 278	11.108 019	.090 025
96	3916.911 889	43510.132 110	.000 022	.000 255	11.108 274	.090 022
97	4269.433 960	47427.044 000	.000 021	.000 234	11.108 508	.090 021
98	4653.683 016	51696.477 960	.000 019	.000 214	11.108 723	.090 019
99	5072.514 487	56350.160 976	.000 017	.000 197	11.108 920	.090 017
100	5529.040 791	61422.675 464	.000 016	.000 181	11.109 101	.090 016
101	6026.654 463	66951.716 256	.000 014	.000 166	11.109 267	.090 014
102	6569.053 364	72978.370 719	.000 013	.000 152	11.109 419	.090 013
103	7160.268 167	79547.424 084	.000 012	.000 139	11.109 559	.090 012
104	7804.692 302	86707.692 252	.000 011	.000 128	11.109 687	.090 011
105	8507.114 609	94512.384 554	.000 010	.000 117	11.109 805	.090 010
106	9272.754 924	103019.499 164	.000 009	.000 108	11.109 912	.090 009
107	10107.302 868	112292.254 089	.000 008	.000 098	11.110 011	.090 008
108	11016.960 126	122399.556 957	.000 008	.000 090	11.110 102	.090 008
109	12008.486 537	133416.517 083	.000 007	.000 083	11.110 185	.090 007
110	13089.250 325	145425.003 621	.000 006	.000 076	11.110 262	.090 006
111	14267.282 855	158514.253 947	.000 006	.000 070	11.110 332	.090 006
112	15551.338 312	172781.536 802	.000 005	.000 064	11.110 396	.090 005
113	16950.958 760	188332.875 114	.000 005	.000 058	11.110 455	.090 005
114	18476.545 048	205283.833 874	.000 004	.000 054	11.110 509	.090 004
115	20139.434 103	223760.378 923	.000 004	.000 049	11.110 559	.090 004
116	21951.983 172	243899.813 026	.000 004	.000 045	11.110 604	.090 004
117	23927.661 657	265851.796 199	.000 003	.000 041	11.110 646	.090 003
118	26081.151 207	289779.457 857	.000 003	.000 038	11.110 685	.090 003
119	28428.454 815	315860.609 064	.000 003	.000 035	11.110 720	.090 003
120	30987.015 749	344289.063 879	.000 002	.000 032	11.110 752	.090 002

Source: *Financial Compound Interest and Annuity Tables*, 5th ed. (Boston: Financial Publishing Co., 1970).

TABLE 12

Rate of 10%

PERIODS	AMOUNT OF 1 How $1 left at compound interest will grow.	AMOUNT OF 1 PER PERIOD How $1 deposited periodically will grow.	SINKING FUND Periodic deposit that will grow to $1 at future date.	PRESENT WORTH OF 1 What $1 due in the future is worth today.	PRESENT WORTH OF 1 PER PERIOD What $1 payable periodically is worth today.	PARTIAL PAYMENT Annuity worth $1 today. Periodic payment necessary to pay off a loan of $1.	PERIODS
1	1.100 000	1.000 000	1.000 000	.909 090	.909 090	1.100 000	1
2	1.210 000	2.100 000	.476 190	.826 446	1.735 537	.576 190	2
3	1.331 000	3.310 000	.302 114	.751 314	2.486 851	.402 114	3
4	1.464 100	4.641 000	.215 470	.683 013	3.169 865	.315 470	4
5	1.610 510	6.105 100	.163 797	.620 921	3.790 786	.263 797	5
6	1.771 561	7.715 610	.129 607	.564 473	4.355 260	.229 607	6
7	1.948 717	9.487 171	.105 405	.513 158	4.868 418	.205 405	7
8	2.143 588	11.435 888	.087 444	.466 507	5.334 926	.187 444	8
9	2.357 947	13.579 476	.073 640	.424 097	5.759 023	.173 640	9
10	2.593 742	15.937 424	.062 745	.385 543	6.144 567	.162 745	10
11	2.853 116	18.531 167	.053 963	.350 493	6.495 061	.153 963	11
12	3.138 428	21.384 283	.046 763	.318 630	6.813 691	.146 763	12
13	3.452 271	24.522 712	.040 778	.289 664	7.103 356	.140 778	13
14	3.797 498	27.974 983	.035 746	.263 331	7.366 687	.135 746	14
15	4.177 248	31.772 481	.031 473	.239 392	7.606 079	.131 473	15
16	4.594 972	35.949 729	.027 816	.217 629	7.823 708	.127 816	16
17	5.054 470	40.544 702	.024 664	.197 844	8.021 553	.124 664	17
18	5.559 917	45.599 173	.021 930	.179 858	8.201 412	.121 930	18
19	6.115 909	51.159 090	.019 546	.163 507	8.364 920	.119 546	19
20	6.727 499	57.274 999	.017 459	.148 643	8.513 563	.117 459	20
21	7.400 249	64.002 499	.015 624	.135 130	8.648 694	.115 624	21
22	8.140 274	71.402 749	.014 005	.122 845	8.771 540	.114 005	22
23	8.954 302	79.543 024	.012 571	.111 678	8.883 218	.112 571	23
24	9.849 732	88.497 326	.011 299	.101 525	8.984 744	.111 299	24
25	10.834 705	98.347 059	.010 168	.092 295	9.077 040	.110 168	25
26	11.918 176	109.181 765	.009 159	.083 905	9.160 945	.109 159	26
27	13.109 994	121.099 941	.008 257	.076 277	9.237 223	.108 257	27
28	14.420 993	134.209 936	.007 451	.069 343	9.306 566	.107 451	28
29	15.863 092	148.630 929	.006 728	.063 039	9.369 605	.106 728	29
30	17.449 402	164.494 022	.006 079	.057 308	9.426 914	.106 079	30

N	$(1+i)^N$	$\dfrac{(1+i)^N-1}{i}$	$\dfrac{i}{(1+i)^N-1}$	$(1+i)^{-N}$	$\dfrac{1-(1+i)^{-N}}{i}$	$\dfrac{i}{1-(1+i)^{-N}}$	N
31	19.194 342	181.943 424	.005 496	.052 098	9.479 013	.105 496	31
32	21.113 776	201.137 767	.004 971	.047 362	9.526 375	.104 971	32
33	23.225 154	222.251 544	.004 499	.043 056	9.569 432	.104 499	33
34	25.547 669	245.476 698	.004 073	.039 142	9.608 574	.104 073	34
35	28.102 436	271.024 368	.003 689	.035 884	9.644 158	.103 689	35
36	30.912 680	299.126 805	.003 343	.032 349	9.676 508	.103 343	36
37	34.003 948	330.039 485	.003 029	.029 408	9.705 916	.103 029	37
38	37.404 343	364.043 434	.002 746	.026 734	9.732 651	.102 746	38
39	41.144 777	401.447 777	.002 490	.024 304	9.756 955	.102 490	39
40	45.259 255	442.592 555	.002 259	.022 094	9.779 050	.102 259	40
41	49.785 181	487.851 811	.002 049	.020 086	9.799 137	.102 049	41
42	54.763 699	537.636 992	.001 859	.018 260	9.817 397	.101 859	42
43	60.240 069	592.400 691	.001 688	.016 600	9.833 997	.101 688	43
44	66.264 076	652.640 760	.001 532	.015 091	9.849 088	.101 532	44
45	72.890 483	718.904 836	.001 391	.013 719	9.862 807	.101 391	45
46	80.179 532	791.795 320	.001 262	.012 472	9.875 279	.101 262	46
47	88.197 485	871.974 852	.001 146	.011 338	9.886 618	.101 146	47
48	97.017 233	960.172 337	.001 041	.010 307	9.896 925	.101 041	48
49	106.718 957	1057.189 571	.000 945	.009 370	9.906 295	.100 945	49
50	117.390 852	1163.908 528	.000 859	.008 518	9.914 814	.100 859	50
51	129.129 938	1281.299 381	.000 780	.007 744	9.922 558	.100 780	51
52	142.042 931	1410.429 319	.000 709	.007 040	9.929 598	.100 709	52
53	156.247 225	1552.472 251	.000 644	.006 400	9.935 998	.100 644	53
54	171.871 947	1708.719 477	.000 585	.005 818	9.941 817	.100 585	54
55	189.059 142	1880.591 424	.000 531	.005 289	9.947 106	.100 531	55
56	207.965 056	2069.650 567	.000 483	.004 808	9.951 914	.100 483	56
57	228.761 562	2277.615 623	.000 439	.004 371	9.956 286	.100 439	57
58	251.637 718	2506.377 186	.000 398	.003 974	9.960 260	.100 398	58
59	276.801 490	2758.014 904	.000 362	.003 613	9.963 873	.100 362	59
60	304.481 639	3034.816 395	.000 329	.003 284	9.967 157	.100 329	60

Source: *Financial Compound Interest and Annuity Tables*, 5th ed. (Boston: Financial Publishing Co., 1970).

TABLE 12 (continued)

Rate of 10%

PERIODS	AMOUNT OF 1 How $1 left at compound interest will grow.	AMOUNT OF 1 PER PERIOD How $1 deposited periodically will grow.	SINKING FUND Periodic deposit that will grow to $1 at future date.	PRESENT WORTH OF 1 What $1 due in the future is worth today.	PRESENT WORTH OF 1 PER PERIOD What $1 payable periodically is worth today.	PARTIAL PAYMENT Annuity worth $1 today. Periodic payment necessary to pay off a loan of $1.
61	334.929 803	3339.298 034	.000 299	.002 985	9.970 142	.100 299
62	368.422 783	3674.227 838	.000 272	.002 714	9.972 857	.100 272
63	405.265 062	4042.650 622	.000 247	.002 467	9.975 324	.100 247
64	445.791 568	4447.915 684	.000 224	.002 243	9.977 567	.100 224
65	490.370 725	4893.707 252	.000 204	.002 039	9.979 607	.100 204
66	539.407 797	5384.077 978	.000 185	.001 853	9.981 461	.100 185
67	593.348 577	5923.485 776	.000 168	.001 685	9.983 146	.100 168
68	652.683 435	6516.834 353	.000 153	.001 532	9.984 678	.100 153
69	717.951 778	7169.517 789	.000 139	.001 392	9.986 071	.100 139
70	789.746 956	7887.469 567	.000 126	.001 266	9.987 337	.100 126
71	868.721 652	8677.216 524	.000 115	.001 151	9.988 488	.100 115
72	955.593 817	9545.938 177	.000 104	.001 046	9.989 535	.100 104
73	1051.153 199	10501.531 995	.000 095	.000 951	9.990 486	.100 095
74	1156.268 519	11552.685 194	.000 086	.000 864	9.991 351	.100 086
75	1271.895 371	12708.953 713	.000 078	.000 786	9.992 137	.100 078
76	1399.084 908	13980.849 085	.000 071	.000 714	9.992 852	.100 071
77	1538.993 399	15379.933 993	.000 065	.000 649	9.993 502	.100 065
78	1692.892 739	16918.927 393	.000 059	.000 590	9.994 092	.100 059
79	1862.182 013	18611.820 132	.000 053	.000 537	9.994 629	.100 053
80	2048.400 214	20474.002 145	.000 048	.000 488	9.995 118	.100 048
81	2253.240 236	22522.402 360	.000 044	.000 443	9.995 561	.100 044
82	2478.564 259	24775.642 596	.000 040	.000 403	9.995 965	.100 040
83	2726.420 685	27254.206 856	.000 036	.000 366	9.996 332	.100 036
84	2999.062 754	29980.627 541	.000 033	.000 333	9.996 665	.100 033
85	3298.969 029	32979.690 295	.000 030	.000 303	9.996 968	.100 030
86	3628.865 932	36278.659 325	.000 027	.000 275	9.997 244	.100 027
87	3991.752 525	39907.525 258	.000 025	.000 250	9.997 494	.100 025
88	4390.927 778	43899.277 783	.000 022	.000 227	9.997 722	.100 022
89	4830.020 556	48290.205 562	.000 020	.000 207	9.997 929	.100 020
90	5313.022 611	53120.226 118	.000 018	.000 188	9.998 117	.100 018

N	$(1+i)^N$	$\dfrac{(1+i)^N-1}{i}$	$\dfrac{i}{(1+i)^N-1}$	$(1+i)^{-N}$	$\dfrac{1-(1+i)^{-N}}{i}$	$\dfrac{i}{1-(1+i)^{-N}}$
91	5844.524 873	58433.248 730	.000 017	.000 171	9.998 288	.100 017
92	6428.757 360	64277.573 603	.000 015	.000 155	9.998 444	.100 015
93	7071.633 096	70706.330 963	.000 014	.000 141	9.998 585	.100 014
94	7778.796 406	77777.964 060	.000 012	.000 128	9.998 714	.100 012
95	8556.676 046	85556.760 466	.000 011	.000 116	9.998 831	.100 011
96	9412.343 651	94113.436 512	.000 010	.000 106	9.998 937	.100 010
97	10353.578 016	103525.780 163	.000 009	.000 096	9.999 034	.100 009
98	11388.935 818	113879.358 180	.000 008	.000 087	9.999 121	.100 008
99	12527.829 399	125268.293 998	.000 007	.000 079	9.999 201	.100 007
100	13780.612 339	137796.123 398	.000 007	.000 072	9.999 274	.100 007
101	15158.673 573	151576.735 738	.000 006	.000 065	9.999 340	.100 006
102	16674.540 931	166735.409 311	.000 005	.000 059	9.999 400	.100 005
103	18341.995 024	183409.950 243	.000 005	.000 054	9.999 454	.100 005
104	20176.194 526	201751.945 267	.000 004	.000 049	9.999 504	.100 004
105	22193.813 979	221928.139 794	.000 004	.000 045	9.999 549	.100 004
106	24413.195 377	244121.953 773	.000 004	.000 040	9.999 590	.100 004
107	26854.514 915	268535.149 150	.000 003	.000 037	9.999 627	.100 003
108	29539.966 406	295389.664 065	.000 003	.000 033	9.999 661	.100 003
109	32493.963 047	324929.630 472	.000 003	.000 030	9.999 692	.100 003
110	35743.359 351	357423.593 519	.000 002	.000 027	9.999 720	.100 002
111	39317.695 287	393166.952 871	.000 002	.000 025	9.999 745	.100 002
112	43249.464 815	432484.648 158	.000 002	.000 023	9.999 768	.100 002
113	47574.411 297	475734.112 974	.000 002	.000 021	9.999 789	.100 002
114	52331.852 427	523308.524 272	.000 001	.000 019	9.999 808	.100 001
115	57565.037 669	575640.376 699	.000 001	.000 017	9.999 826	.100 001
116	63321.541 436	633205.414 369	.000 001	.000 015	9.999 842	.100 001
117	69653.695 580	696526.955 806	.000 001	.000 014	9.999 856	.100 001
118	76619.065 138	766180.651 387	.000 001	.000 013	9.999 869	.100 001
119	84280.971 652	842799.716 525	.000 001	.000 011	9.999 881	.100 001
120	92709.068 817	927080.688 178	.000 001	.000 010	9.999 892	.100 001

Source: *Financial Compound Interest and Annuity Tables*, 5th ed.
(Boston: Financial Publishing Co, 1970).

TABLE 13

Rate of 11%

PERIODS	AMOUNT OF 1 — How $1 left at compound interest will grow.	AMOUNT OF 1 PER PERIOD — How $1 deposited periodically will grow.	SINKING FUND — Periodic deposit that will grow to $1 at future date.	PRESENT WORTH OF 1 — What $1 due in the future is worth today.	PRESENT WORTH OF 1 PER PERIOD — What $1 payable periodically is worth today.	PARTIAL PAYMENT — Annuity worth $1 today. Periodic payment necessary to pay off a loan of $1.	PERIODS
1	1.110 000	1.000 000	1.000 000	.900 900	.900 900	1.110 000	1
2	1.232 100	2.110 000	.473 933	.811 622	1.712 523	.583 933	2
3	1.367 631	3.342 100	.299 213	.731 191	2.443 714	.409 213	3
4	1.518 070	4.709 731	.212 326	.658 730	3.102 445	.322 326	4
5	1.685 058	6.227 801	.160 570	.593 451	3.695 897	.270 570	5
6	1.870 414	7.912 859	.126 376	.534 640	4.230 537	.236 376	6
7	2.076 160	9.783 160	.102 215	.481 658	4.712 196	.212 215	7
8	2.304 537	11.859 434	.084 321	.433 926	5.146 122	.194 321	8
9	2.558 036	14.163 972	.070 601	.390 924	5.537 047	.180 601	9
10	2.839 420	16.722 008	.059 801	.352 184	5.889 232	.169 801	10
11	3.151 757	19.561 429	.051 121	.317 283	6.206 515	.161 121	11
12	3.498 450	22.713 187	.044 027	.285 840	6.492 356	.154 027	12
13	3.883 280	26.211 637	.038 150	.257 514	6.749 870	.148 150	13
14	4.310 440	30.094 918	.033 228	.231 994	6.981 865	.143 228	14
15	4.784 589	34.405 358	.029 065	.209 004	7.190 869	.139 065	15
16	5.310 894	39.189 948	.025 516	.188 292	7.379 161	.135 516	16
17	5.895 092	44.500 842	.022 471	.169 632	7.548 794	.132 471	17
18	6.543 552	50.395 935	.019 842	.152 822	7.701 616	.129 842	18
19	7.263 343	56.939 488	.017 562	.137 677	7.839 294	.127 562	19
20	8.062 311	64.202 832	.015 575	.124 033	7.963 328	.125 575	20
21	8.949 165	72.265 143	.013 837	.111 742	8.075 070	.123 837	21
22	9.933 574	81.214 309	.012 313	.100 668	8.175 739	.122 313	22
23	11.026 267	91.147 883	.010 971	.090 692	8.266 431	.120 971	23
24	12.239 156	102.174 150	.009 787	.081 704	8.348 136	.119 787	24
25	13.585 463	114.413 307	.008 740	.073 608	8.421 744	.118 740	25
26	15.079 864	127.998 771	.007 812	.066 313	8.488 058	.117 812	26
27	16.738 649	143.078 635	.006 989	.059 741	8.547 800	.116 989	27
28	18.579 901	159.817 285	.006 257	.053 821	8.601 621	.116 257	28
29	20.623 690	178.397 187	.005 605	.048 487	8.650 109	.115 605	29
30	22.892 296	199.020 877	.005 024	.043 682	8.693 792	.115 024	30

N	$(1+i)^N$	$\dfrac{(1+i)^N-1}{i}$	$\dfrac{i}{(1+i)^N-1}$	$(1+i)^{-N}$	$\dfrac{1-(1+i)^{-N}}{i}$	$\dfrac{i}{1-(1+i)^{-N}}$
31	25.410 449	221.913 174	.004 506	.039 353	8.733 146	.114 506
32	28.205 598	247.323 623	.004 043	.035 453	8.768 600	.114 043
33	31.308 214	275.529 222	.003 629	.031 940	8.800 540	.113 629
34	34.752 118	306.837 436	.003 259	.028 775	8.829 316	.113 259
35	38.574 851	341.589 554	.002 927	.025 923	8.855 239	.112 927
36	42.818 084	380.164 405	.002 630	.023 354	8.878 594	.112 630
37	47.528 073	422.982 490	.002 364	.021 040	8.899 634	.112 364
38	52.756 162	470.510 564	.002 125	.018 955	8.918 589	.112 125
39	58.559 339	523.266 726	.001 911	.017 076	8.935 666	.111 911
40	65.000 867	581.826 066	.001 718	.015 384	8.951 050	.111 718
41	72.150 962	646.826 933	.001 546	.013 859	8.964 910	.111 546
42	80.087 568	718.977 896	.001 390	.012 486	8.977 396	.111 390
43	88.897 201	799.065 465	.001 251	.011 248	8.988 645	.111 251
44	98.675 893	887.962 666	.001 126	.010 134	8.998 780	.111 126
45	109.530 241	986.638 559	.001 013	.009 129	9.007 910	.111 013
46	121.578 568	1096.168 801	.000 912	.008 225	9.016 135	.110 912
47	134.952 210	1217.747 369	.000 821	.007 410	9.023 545	.110 821
48	149.796 953	1352.699 579	.000 739	.006 675	9.030 220	.110 739
49	166.274 618	1502.496 533	.000 665	.006 014	9.036 235	.110 665
50	184.564 826	1668.771 152	.000 599	.005 418	9.041 653	.110 599
51	204.866 957	1853.335 978	.000 539	.004 881	9.046 534	.110 539
52	227.402 323	2058.202 936	.000 485	.004 397	9.050 931	.110 485
53	252.416 578	2285.605 259	.000 437	.003 961	9.054 893	.110 437
54	280.182 402	2538.021 838	.000 394	.003 569	9.058 462	.110 394
55	311.002 466	2818.204 240	.000 354	.003 215	9.061 678	.110 354
56	345.212 737	3129.206 706	.000 319	.002 896	9.064 574	.110 319
57	383.186 138	3474.419 444	.000 287	.002 609	9.067 184	.110 287
58	425.336 614	3857.605 583	.000 259	.002 351	9.069 535	.110 259
59	472.123 641	4282.942 197	.000 233	.002 118	9.071 653	.110 233
60	524.057 242	4755.065 839	.000 210	.001 908	9.073 561	.110 210

Source: *Financial Compound Interest and Annuity Tables*, 5th ed. (Boston: Financial Publishing Co., 1970).

TABLE 14

Rate of 12%

PERIODS	AMOUNT OF 1 How $1 left at compound interest will grow.	AMOUNT OF 1 PER PERIOD How $1 deposited periodically will grow.	SINKING FUND Periodic deposit that will grow to $1 at future date.	PRESENT WORTH OF 1 What $1 due in the future is worth today.	PRESENT WORTH OF 1 PER PERIOD What $1 payable periodically is worth today.	PARTIAL PAYMENT Annuity worth $1 today. Periodic payment necessary to pay off a loan of $1.	PERIODS
1	1.120 000	1.000 000	1.000 000	.892 857	.892 857	1.120 000	1
2	1.254 400	2.120 000	.471 698	.797 193	1.690 051	.591 698	2
3	1.404 928	3.374 400	.296 348	.711 780	2.401 831	.416 348	3
4	1.573 519	4.779 328	.209 234	.635 518	3.037 349	.329 349	4
5	1.762 341	6.352 847	.157 409	.567 426	3.604 776	.277 409	5
6	1.973 822	8.115 189	.123 225	.506 631	4.111 407	.243 225	6
7	2.210 681	10.089 011	.099 117	.452 349	4.563 756	.219 117	7
8	2.475 963	12.299 693	.081 302	.403 883	4.967 639	.201 302	8
9	2.773 078	14.775 656	.067 678	.360 610	5.328 249	.187 678	9
10	3.105 848	17.548 735	.056 984	.321 973	5.650 223	.176 984	10
11	3.478 549	20.654 583	.048 415	.287 476	5.937 699	.168 415	11
12	3.895 975	24.133 133	.041 436	.256 675	6.194 374	.161 436	12
13	4.363 493	28.029 109	.035 677	.229 174	6.423 548	.155 677	13
14	4.887 112	32.392 602	.030 871	.204 619	6.628 168	.150 871	14
15	5.473 565	37.279 714	.026 824	.182 696	6.810 864	.146 824	15
16	6.130 393	42.753 280	.023 390	.163 121	6.973 986	.143 390	16
17	6.866 040	48.883 674	.020 456	.145 644	7.119 630	.140 456	17
18	7.689 965	55.749 714	.017 937	.130 039	7.249 670	.137 937	18
19	8.612 761	63.439 680	.015 763	.116 106	7.365 776	.135 763	19
20	9.646 293	72.052 442	.013 878	.103 666	7.469 443	.133 878	20
21	10.803 848	81.698 735	.012 240	.092 559	7.562 003	.132 240	21
22	12.100 310	92.502 583	.010 810	.082 642	7.644 645	.130 810	22
23	13.552 347	104.602 893	.009 559	.073 787	7.718 433	.129 559	23
24	15.178 628	118.155 241	.008 463	.065 882	7.784 315	.128 463	24
25	17.000 064	133.333 870	.007 499	.058 823	7.843 139	.127 499	25
26	19.040 072	150.333 934	.006 651	.052 520	7.895 659	.126 651	26
27	21.324 880	169.374 006	.005 904	.046 893	7.942 553	.125 904	27
28	23.883 866	190.698 887	.005 243	.041 869	7.984 422	.125 243	28
29	26.749 930	214.582 753	.004 660	.037 383	8.021 806	.124 660	29
30	29.959 922	241.332 684	.004 143	.033 377	8.055 183	.124 143	30

N	$(1+i)^N$	$\dfrac{(1+i)^N-1}{i}$	$\dfrac{i}{(1+i)^N-1}$	$(1+i)^{-N}$	$\dfrac{1-(1+i)^{-N}}{i}$	$\dfrac{i}{1-(1+i)^{-N}}$
31	33.555 112	271.292 506	.003 686	.029 801	8.084 985	.123 686
32	37.581 726	304.847 719	.003 280	.026 608	8.111 594	.123 280
33	42.091 533	342.429 445	.002 920	.023 757	8.135 352	.122 920
34	47.142 517	384.520 979	.002 600	.021 212	8.156 564	.122 600
35	52.799 619	431.663 496	.002 316	.018 939	8.175 503	.122 316
36	59.135 573	484.463 116	.002 064	.016 910	8.192 414	.122 064
37	66.231 842	543.598 690	.001 839	.015 098	8.207 512	.121 839
38	74.179 663	609.830 532	.001 639	.013 480	8.220 993	.121 639
39	83.081 223	684.010 196	.001 461	.012 036	8.233 029	.121 461
40	93.050 970	767.091 420	.001 303	.010 746	8.243 776	.121 303
41	104.217 086	860.142 390	.001 162	.009 595	8.253 372	.121 162
42	116.723 137	964.359 477	.001 036	.008 567	8.261 939	.121 036
43	130.729 913	1081.082 615	.000 924	.007 649	8.269 588	.120 924
44	146.417 503	1211.812 528	.000 825	.006 829	8.276 418	.120 825
45	163.987 603	1358.230 032	.000 736	.006 098	8.282 516	.120 736
46	183.066 116	1522.217 636	.000 656	.005 444	8.287 961	.120 656
47	205.706 050	1705.883 752	.000 586	.004 861	8.292 822	.120 586
48	230.390 776	1911.589 802	.000 523	.004 340	8.297 162	.120 523
49	258.037 669	2141.980 579	.000 466	.003 875	8.301 038	.120 466
50	289.002 189	2400.018 248	.000 416	.003 460	8.304 498	.120 416
51	323.682 452	2689.020 438	.000 371	.003 089	8.307 587	.120 371
52	362.524 346	3012.702 891	.000 331	.002 758	8.310 346	.120 331
53	406.027 268	3375.227 237	.000 296	.002 462	8.312 809	.120 296
54	454.750 540	3781.254 506	.000 264	.002 199	8.315 008	.120 264
55	509.320 605	4236.005 047	.000 236	.001 963	8.316 971	.120 236
56	570.439 078	4745.325 652	.000 210	.001 753	8.318 724	.120 210
57	638.891 767	5315.764 731	.000 188	.001 565	8.320 289	.120 188
58	715.558 779	5954.656 499	.000 167	.001 397	8.321 687	.120 167
59	801.425 833	6670.215 278	.000 149	.001 247	8.322 935	.120 149
60	897.596 933	7471.641 112	.000 133	.001 114	8.324 049	.120 133

Source: *Financial Compound Interest and Annuity Tables*, 5th ed. (Boston: Financial Publishing Co., 1970).

TABLE 15
Rate of 13%

PERIODS	AMOUNT OF 1 — How $1 left at compound interest will grow.	AMOUNT OF 1 PER PERIOD — How $1 deposited periodically will grow.	SINKING FUND — Periodic deposit that will grow to $1 at future date.	PRESENT WORTH OF 1 — What $1 due in the future is worth today.	PRESENT WORTH OF 1 PER PERIOD — What $1 payable periodically is worth today.	PARTIAL PAYMENT — Annuity worth $1 today. Periodic payment necessary to pay off a loan of $1.	PERIODS
1	1.130 000	1.000 000	1.000 000	.884 955	.884 955	1.130 000	1
2	1.276 900	2.130 000	.469 483	.783 146	1.668 102	.599 483	2
3	1.442 897	3.406 900	.293 521	.693 050	2.361 152	.423 521	3
4	1.630 473	4.849 797	.206 194	.613 318	2.974 471	.336 194	4
5	1.842 435	6.480 270	.154 314	.542 759	3.517 231	.284 314	5
6	2.081 951	8.322 705	.120 153	.480 318	3.997 549	.250 153	6
7	2.352 605	10.404 657	.096 110	.425 060	4.422 610	.226 110	7
8	2.658 444	12.757 263	.078 386	.376 159	4.798 770	.208 386	8
9	3.004 041	15.415 707	.064 868	.332 884	5.131 655	.194 868	9
10	3.394 567	18.419 749	.054 289	.294 588	5.426 243	.184 289	10
11	3.835 861	21.814 316	.045 841	.260 697	5.686 941	.175 841	11
12	4.334 523	25.650 177	.038 986	.230 705	5.917 647	.168 986	12
13	4.898 011	29.984 700	.033 350	.204 164	6.121 811	.163 350	13
14	5.534 752	34.882 711	.028 667	.180 676	6.302 488	.158 667	14
15	6.254 270	40.417 464	.024 741	.159 890	6.462 378	.154 741	15
16	7.067 325	46.671 734	.021 426	.141 496	6.603 875	.151 426	16
17	7.986 077	53.739 060	.018 608	.125 217	6.729 092	.148 608	17
18	9.024 267	61.725 138	.016 200	.110 812	6.839 905	.146 200	18
19	10.197 422	70.749 406	.014 134	.098 063	6.937 969	.144 134	19
20	11.523 087	80.946 828	.012 353	.086 782	7.024 751	.142 353	20
21	13.021 089	92.469 916	.010 814	.076 798	7.101 550	.140 814	21
22	14.713 830	105.491 005	.009 479	.067 963	7.169 513	.139 479	22
23	16.626 628	120.204 836	.008 319	.060 144	7.229 657	.138 319	23
24	18.788 090	136.831 465	.007 308	.053 225	7.282 883	.137 308	24
25	21.230 542	155.619 555	.006 425	.047 101	7.329 984	.136 425	25
26	23.990 512	176.850 098	.005 654	.041 683	7.371 668	.135 654	26
27	27.109 279	200.840 610	.004 979	.036 887	7.408 555	.134 979	27
28	30.633 485	227.949 890	.004 386	.032 644	7.441 199	.134 386	28
29	34.615 838	258.583 376	.003 867	.028 888	7.470 088	.133 867	29
30	39.115 897	293.199 215	.003 410	.025 565	7.495 653	.133 410	30

N	$(1+i)^N$	$\dfrac{(1+i)^N-1}{i}$	$\dfrac{i}{(1+i)^N-1}$	$(1+i)^{-N}$	$\dfrac{1-(1+i)^{-N}}{i}$	$\dfrac{i}{1-(1+i)^{-N}}$
31	44.200 964	332.315 113	.003 009	.022 623	7.518 277	.133 009
32	49.947 090	376.516 077	.002 655	.020 021	7.538 298	.132 655
33	56.440 211	426.463 167	.002 344	.017 717	7.556 016	.132 344
34	63.777 439	482.903 379	.002 070	.015 679	7.571 695	.132 070
35	72.068 506	546.680 818	.001 829	.013 875	7.585 571	.131 829
36	81.437 412	618.749 325	.001 616	.012 279	7.597 851	.131 616
37	92.024 275	700.186 737	.001 428	.010 866	7.608 717	.131 428
38	103.987 431	792.211 013	.001 262	.009 616	7.618 334	.131 262
39	117.505 797	896.198 445	.001 115	.008 510	7.626 844	.131 115
40	132.781 551	1013.704 243	.000 986	.007 531	7.634 375	.130 986
41	150.043 153	1146.485 794	.000 872	.006 664	7.641 040	.130 872
42	169.548 763	1296.528 948	.000 771	.005 898	7.646 938	.130 771
43	191.590 102	1466.077 711	.000 682	.005 219	7.652 157	.130 682
44	216.496 815	1657.667 814	.000 603	.004 619	7.656 776	.130 603
45	244.641 401	1874.164 629	.000 533	.004 087	7.660 864	.130 533
46	276.444 784	2118.806 031	.000 471	.003 617	7.664 481	.130 471
47	312.382 606	2395.250 815	.000 417	.003 201	7.667 683	.130 417
48	352.992 344	2707.633 422	.000 369	.002 832	7.670 515	.130 369
49	398.881 349	3060.625 766	.000 326	.002 507	7.673 022	.130 326
50	450.735 925	3459.507 116	.000 289	.002 218	7.675 241	.130 289
51	509.331 595	3910.243 041	.000 255	.001 963	7.677 204	.130 255
52	575.544 702	4419.574 637	.000 226	.001 737	7.678 942	.130 226
53	650.365 514	4995.119 340	.000 200	.001 537	7.680 480	.130 200
54	734.913 031	5645.484 854	.000 177	.001 360	7.681 840	.130 177
55	830.451 725	6380.397 885	.000 156	.001 204	7.683 044	.130 156
56	938.410 449	7210.849 610	.000 138	.001 065	7.684 110	.130 138
57	1060.403 807	8149.260 059	.000 122	.000 943	7.685 053	.130 122
58	1198.256 302	9209.663 867	.000 108	.000 834	7.685 888	.130 108
59	1354.029 622	10407.920 170	.000 096	.000 738	7.686 626	.130 096
60	1530.053 473	11761.949 792	.000 085	.000 653	7.687 280	.130 085

Source: *Financial Compound Interest and Annuity Tables*, 5th ed. (Boston: Financial Publishing Co., 1970).

TABLE 16
Rate of 14%

PERIODS	PARTIAL PAYMENT Annuity worth $1 today. Periodic payment necessary to pay off a loan of $1.	PRESENT WORTH OF 1 PER PERIOD What $1 payable periodically is worth today.	PRESENT WORTH OF 1 What $1 due in the future is worth today.	SINKING FUND Periodic deposit that will grow to $1 at future date.	AMOUNT OF 1 PER PERIOD How $1 deposited periodically will grow.	AMOUNT OF 1 How $1 left at compound interest will grow.	PERIODS
1	1.140 000	.877 192	.877 192	1.000 000	1.000 000	1.140 000	1
2	.607 289	1.646 660	.769 467	.467 289	2.140 000	1.299 600	2
3	.430 731	2.321 632	.674 971	.290 731	3.439 600	1.481 544	3
4	.343 204	2.913 712	.592 080	.203 204	4.921 144	1.688 960	4
5	.291 283	3.433 080	.519 368	.151 283	6.610 104	1.925 414	5
6	.257 157	3.888 667	.455 586	.117 157	8.535 518	2.194 972	6
7	.233 192	4.288 304	.399 637	.093 192	10.730 491	2.502 268	7
8	.215 570	4.638 863	.350 559	.075 570	13.232 760	2.852 586	8
9	.202 168	4.946 371	.307 507	.062 168	16.085 346	3.251 948	9
10	.191 713	5.216 115	.269 743	.051 713	19.337 295	3.707 221	10
11	.183 394	5.452 733	.236 617	.043 394	23.044 516	4.226 232	11
12	.176 669	5.660 292	.207 559	.036 669	27.270 748	4.817 904	12
13	.171 163	5.842 361	.182 069	.031 163	32.088 653	5.492 411	13
14	.166 609	6.002 071	.159 709	.026 609	37.581 065	6.261 349	14
15	.162 808	6.142 167	.140 096	.022 808	43.842 414	7.137 937	15
16	.159 615	6.265 059	.122 891	.019 615	50.980 352	8.137 249	16
17	.156 915	6.372 859	.107 799	.016 915	59.117 601	9.276 464	17
18	.154 621	6.467 420	.094 561	.014 621	68.394 065	10.575 169	18
19	.152 663	6.550 368	.082 948	.012 663	78.969 234	12.055 692	19
20	.150 986	6.623 130	.072 761	.010 986	91.024 927	13.743 489	20
21	.149 544	6.686 956	.063 826	.009 544	104.768 417	15.667 578	21
22	.148 303	6.742 944	.055 987	.008 303	120.435 995	17.861 039	22
23	.147 230	6.792 056	.049 112	.007 230	138.297 035	20.361 584	23
24	.146 302	6.835 137	.043 080	.006 302	158.658 620	23.212 206	24
25	.145 498	6.872 927	.037 790	.005 498	181.870 827	26.461 915	25
26	.144 800	6.906 076	.033 149	.004 800	208.332 743	30.166 584	26
27	.144 192	6.935 154	.029 078	.004 192	238.499 327	34.389 905	27
28	.143 664	6.960 662	.025 507	.003 664	272.889 232	39.204 492	28
29	.143 204	6.983 037	.022 374	.003 204	312.093 725	44.693 121	29
30	.142 802	7.002 664	.019 627	.002 802	356.786 847	50.950 158	30

N	$(1+i)^N$	$\dfrac{(1+i)^N-1}{i}$	$\dfrac{i}{(1+i)^N-1}$	$(1+i)^{-N}$	$\dfrac{1-(1+i)^{-N}}{i}$	$\dfrac{i}{1-(1+i)^{-N}}$
31	58.083 180	407.737 005	.002 452	.017 216	7.019 880	.142 452
32	66.214 826	465.820 186	.002 146	.015 102	7.034 983	.142 146
33	75.484 901	532.035 012	.001 879	.013 247	7.048 230	.141 879
34	86.052 787	607.519 914	.001 646	.011 620	7.059 851	.141 646
35	98.100 178	693.572 702	.001 441	.010 193	7.070 045	.141 441
36	111.834 203	791.672 880	.001 263	.008 941	7.078 987	.141 263
37	127.490 991	903.507 083	.001 106	.007 843	7.086 830	.141 106
38	145.339 730	1030.998 075	.000 969	.006 880	7.093 711	.140 969
39	165.687 292	1176.337 806	.000 850	.006 035	7.099 746	.140 850
40	188.883 513	1342.025 098	.000 745	.005 294	7.105 040	.140 745
41	215.327 205	1530.908 612	.000 653	.004 644	7.109 685	.140 653
42	245.473 014	1746.235 818	.000 572	.004 073	7.113 758	.140 572
43	279.839 236	1991.708 833	.000 502	.003 573	7.117 332	.140 502
44	319.016 729	2271.548 069	.000 440	.003 134	7.120 466	.140 440
45	363.679 071	2590.564 799	.000 386	.002 749	7.123 216	.140 386
46	414.594 142	2954.243 871	.000 338	.002 411	7.125 628	.140 338
47	472.637 321	3368.838 013	.000 296	.002 115	7.127 744	.140 296
48	538.806 546	3841.475 335	.000 260	.001 855	7.129 600	.140 260
49	614.239 463	4380.281 882	.000 228	.001 628	7.131 228	.140 228
50	700.232 988	4994.521 346	.000 200	.001 428	7.132 656	.140 200
51	798.265 606	5694.754 334	.000 175	.001 252	7.133 909	.140 175
52	910.022 791	6493.019 941	.000 154	.001 098	7.135 008	.140 154
53	1037.425 982	7403.042 733	.000 135	.000 963	7.135 971	.140 135
54	1182.665 620	8440.468 715	.000 118	.000 845	7.136 817	.140 118
55	1348.238 807	9623.134 336	.000 103	.000 741	7.137 559	.140 103
56	1536.992 240	10971.373 143	.000 091	.000 650	7.138 209	.140 091
57	1752.171 153	12508.365 383	.000 079	.000 570	7.138 780	.140 079
58	1997.475 115	14260.536 536	.000 070	.000 500	7.139 281	.140 070
59	2277.121 631	16258.011 652	.000 061	.000 439	7.139 720	.140 061
60	2595.918 659	18535.133 283	.000 053	.000 385	7.140 105	.140 053

Source: *Financial Compound Interest and Annuity Tables*, 5th ed. (Boston: Financial Publishing Co., 1970).

TABLE 17
Rate of 15%

PERIODS	AMOUNT OF 1 — How $1 left at compound interest will grow.	AMOUNT OF 1 PER PERIOD — How $1 deposited periodically will grow.	SINKING FUND — Periodic deposit that will grow to $1 at future date.	PRESENT WORTH OF 1 — What $1 due in the future is worth today.	PRESENT WORTH OF 1 PER PERIOD — What $1 payable periodically is worth today.	PARTIAL PAYMENT — Annuity worth $1 today. Periodic payment necessary to pay off a loan of $1.
1	1.150 000	1.000 000	1.000 000	.869 565	.869 565	1.150 000
2	1.322 500	2.150 000	.465 116	.756 143	1.625 708	.615 116
3	1.520 875	3.472 500	.287 976	.657 516	2.283 225	.437 976
4	1.749 006	4.993 375	.200 265	.571 753	2.854 978	.350 265
5	2.011 357	6.742 381	.148 315	.497 176	3.352 155	.298 315
6	2.313 060	8.753 738	.114 236	.432 327	3.784 482	.264 236
7	2.660 019	11.066 799	.090 360	.375 937	4.160 419	.240 360
8	3.059 022	13.726 819	.072 850	.326 901	4.487 321	.222 850
9	3.517 876	16.785 841	.059 574	.284 262	4.771 583	.209 574
10	4.045 557	20.303 718	.049 252	.247 184	5.018 768	.199 252
11	4.652 391	24.349 275	.041 068	.214 943	5.233 711	.191 068
12	5.350 250	29.001 667	.034 480	.186 907	5.420 618	.184 480
13	6.152 787	34.351 917	.029 110	.162 527	5.583 146	.179 110
14	7.075 705	40.504 705	.024 688	.141 328	5.724 475	.174 688
15	8.137 061	47.580 410	.021 017	.122 894	5.847 370	.171 017
16	9.357 620	55.717 472	.017 947	.106 864	5.954 234	.167 947
17	10.761 264	65.075 093	.015 366	.092 925	6.047 160	.165 366
18	12.375 453	75.836 357	.013 186	.080 805	6.127 965	.163 186
19	14.231 771	88.211 810	.011 336	.070 265	6.198 231	.161 336
20	16.366 537	102.443 582	.009 761	.061 100	6.259 331	.159 761
21	18.821 518	118.810 120	.008 416	.053 130	6.312 462	.158 416
22	21.644 745	137.631 638	.007 265	.046 200	6.358 662	.157 265
23	24.891 457	159.276 383	.006 278	.040 174	6.398 837	.156 278
24	28.625 176	184.167 841	.005 429	.034 934	6.433 771	.155 429
25	32.918 952	212.793 017	.004 699	.030 377	6.464 149	.154 699
26	37.856 795	245.711 970	.004 069	.026 415	6.490 564	.154 069
27	43.535 314	283.568 765	.003 526	.022 969	6.513 534	.153 526
28	50.065 612	327.104 080	.003 057	.019 973	6.533 508	.153 057
29	57.575 453	377.169 692	.002 651	.017 368	6.550 876	.152 651
30	66.211 771	434.745 146	.002 300	.015 103	6.565 979	.152 300

N	$(1+i)^N$	$\dfrac{(1+i)^N-1}{i}$	$\dfrac{i}{(1+i)^N-1}$	$(1+i)^{-N}$	$\dfrac{1-(1+i)^{-N}}{i}$	$\dfrac{i}{1-(1+i)^{-N}}$
31	76.143 537	500.956 918	.001 996	.013 133	6.579 112	.151 996
32	87.565 068	577.100 456	.001 732	.011 420	6.590 532	.151 732
33	100.699 828	664.665 524	.001 504	.009 930	6.600 463	.151 504
34	115.804 802	765.365 353	.001 306	.008 635	6.609 098	.151 306
35	133.175 523	881.170 156	.001 134	.007 508	6.616 607	.151 134
36	153.151 851	1014.345 679	.000 985	.006 529	6.623 136	.150 985
37	176.124 629	1167.497 531	.000 856	.005 677	6.628 814	.150 856
38	202.543 324	1343.622 161	.000 744	.004 937	6.633 751	.150 744
39	232.924 822	1546.165 485	.000 646	.004 293	6.638 045	.150 646
40	267.863 546	1779.090 308	.000 562	.003 733	6.641 778	.150 562
41	308.043 078	2046.953 854	.000 488	.003 246	6.645 024	.150 488
42	354.249 539	2354.996 932	.000 424	.002 822	6.647 847	.150 424
43	407.386 970	2709.246 472	.000 369	.002 454	6.650 302	.150 369
44	468.495 016	3116.633 443	.000 320	.002 134	6.652 436	.150 320
45	538.769 268	3585.128 459	.000 278	.001 856	6.654 292	.150 278
46	619.584 659	4123.897 728	.000 242	.001 613	6.655 906	.150 242
47	712.522 358	4743.482 388	.000 210	.001 403	6.657 310	.150 210
48	819.400 711	5456.004 746	.000 183	.001 220	6.658 530	.150 183
49	942.310 818	6275.405 458	.000 159	.001 061	6.659 591	.150 159
50	1083.657 441	7217.716 277	.000 138	.000 922	6.660 514	.150 138
51	1246.206 057	8301.373 718	.000 120	.000 802	6.661 317	.150 120
52	1433.136 966	9547.579 776	.000 104	.000 697	6.662 014	.150 104
53	1648.107 511	10980.716 743	.000 091	.000 606	6.662 621	.150 091
54	1895.323 638	12628.824 254	.000 079	.000 527	6.663 149	.150 079
55	2179.622 183	14524.147 892	.000 068	.000 458	6.663 608	.150 068
56	2506.565 511	16703.770 076	.000 059	.000 398	6.664 006	.150 059
57	2882.550 338	19210.335 588	.000 052	.000 346	6.664 353	.150 052
58	3314.932 888	22092.885 926	.000 045	.000 301	6.664 655	.150 045
59	3812.172 822	25407.818 815	.000 039	.000 262	6.664 917	.150 039
60	4383.998 745	29219.991 637	.000 034	.000 228	6.665 145	.150 034

Source: *Financial Compound Interest and Annuity Tables*, 5th ed. (Boston: Financial Publishing Co., 1970).

TABLE 18
Rate of 16%

PERIODS	AMOUNT OF 1 How $1 left at compound interest will grow.	AMOUNT OF 1 PER PERIOD How $1 deposited periodically will grow.	SINKING FUND Periodic deposit that will grow to $1 at future date.	PRESENT WORTH OF 1 What $1 due in the future is worth today.	PRESENT WORTH OF 1 PER PERIOD What $1 payable periodically is worth today.	PARTIAL PAYMENT Annuity worth $1 today. Periodic payment necessary to pay off a loan of $1.	PERIODS
1	1.160 000	1.000 000	1.000 000	.862 068	.862 068	1.160 000	1
2	1.345 600	2.160 000	.462 962	.743 162	1.605 231	.622 962	2
3	1.560 896	3.505 660	.285 257	.640 657	2.245 889	.445 257	3
4	1.810 639	5.066 496	.197 375	.552 291	2.798 180	.357 375	4
5	2.100 341	6.877 135	.145 409	.476 113	3.274 293	.305 409	5
6	2.436 396	8.977 477	.111 389	.410 442	3.684 735	.271 389	6
7	2.826 219	11.413 873	.087 612	.353 829	4.038 565	.247 612	7
8	3.278 414	14.240 093	.070 224	.305 025	4.343 590	.230 224	8
9	3.802 961	17.518 507	.057 082	.262 952	4.606 543	.217 082	9
10	4.411 435	21.321 469	.046 901	.226 683	4.833 227	.206 901	10
11	5.117 264	25.732 904	.038 860	.195 416	5.028 644	.198 860	11
12	5.936 027	30.850 169	.032 414	.168 462	5.197 107	.192 414	12
13	6.885 791	36.786 196	.027 184	.145 226	5.342 333	.187 184	13
14	7.987 517	43.671 987	.022 897	.125 195	5.467 529	.182 897	14
15	9.265 520	51.659 505	.019 357	.107 927	5.575 456	.179 357	15
16	10.748 004	60.925 026	.016 413	.093 040	5.668 496	.176 413	16
17	12.467 684	71.673 030	.013 952	.080 207	5.748 704	.173 952	17
18	14.462 514	84.140 715	.011 884	.069 144	5.817 848	.171 884	18
19	16.776 516	98.603 229	.010 141	.059 607	5.877 455	.170 141	19
20	19.460 759	115.379 746	.008 667	.051 385	5.928 840	.168 667	20
21	22.574 480	134.840 506	.007 416	.044 297	5.973 138	.167 416	21
22	26.186 397	157.414 987	.006 352	.038 187	6.011 326	.166 352	22
23	30.376 221	183.601 384	.005 446	.032 920	6.044 246	.165 446	23
24	35.236 417	213.977 606	.004 673	.028 379	6.072 626	.164 673	24
25	40.874 243	249.214 023	.004 012	.024 465	6.097 091	.164 012	25
26	47.414 122	290.088 267	.003 447	.021 090	6.118 182	.163 447	26
27	55.000 382	337.502 390	.002 962	.018 181	6.136 364	.162 962	27
28	63.800 443	392.502 772	.002 547	.015 673	6.152 038	.162 547	28
29	74.008 514	456.303 216	.002 191	.013 511	6.165 550	.162 191	29
30	85.849 876	530.311 730	.001 885	.011 648	6.177 198	.161 885	30

N	$(1+i)^N$	$\dfrac{(1+i)^N-1}{i}$	$\dfrac{i}{(1+i)^N-1}$	$(1+i)^{-N}$	$\dfrac{1-(1+i)^{-N}}{i}$	$\dfrac{i}{1-(1+i)^{-N}}$
31	99.585 857	616.161 507	.001 622	.010 041	6.187 240	.161 622
32	115.519 594	715.747 464	.001 397	.008 656	6.195 896	.161 397
33	134.002 729	831.267 059	.001 202	.007 462	6.203 359	.161 202
34	155.443 166	965.269 788	.001 035	.006 433	6.209 792	.161 035
35	180.314 072	1120.712 954	.000 892	.005 545	6.215 338	.160 892
36	209.164 324	1301.027 027	.000 768	.004 780	6.220 119	.160 768
37	242.630 616	1510.191 352	.000 662	.004 121	6.224 240	.160 662
38	281.451 514	1752.821 968	.000 570	.003 553	6.227 793	.160 570
39	326.483 757	2034.273 483	.000 491	.003 062	6.230 856	.160 491
40	378.721 158	2360.757 240	.000 423	.002 640	6.233 497	.160 423
41	439.316 543	2739.478 399	.000 365	.002 276	6.235 773	.160 365
42	509.607 190	3178.794 942	.000 314	.001 962	6.237 735	.160 314
43	591.144 341	3688.402 133	.000 271	.001 691	6.239 427	.160 271
44	685.727 436	4279.546 475	.000 233	.001 458	6.240 885	.160 233
45	795.443 825	4965.273 911	.000 201	.001 257	6.242 142	.160 201
46	922.714 837	5760.717 737	.000 173	.001 083	6.243 226	.160 173
47	1070.349 211	6683.432 574	.000 149	.000 934	6.244 160	.160 149
48	1241.605 085	7753.781 786	.000 128	.000 805	6.244 966	.160 128
49	1440.261 899	8995.386 872	.000 111	.000 694	6.245 660	.160 111
50	1670.703 803	10435.648 772	.000 095	.000 598	6.246 259	.160 095
51	1938.016 412	12106.352 576	.000 082	.000 515	6.246 775	.160 082
52	2248.099 038	14044.368 988	.000 071	.000 444	6.247 219	.160 071
53	2607.794 884	16292.468 026	.000 061	.000 383	6.247 603	.160 061
54	3025.042 065	18900.262 910	.000 052	.000 330	6.247 933	.160 052
55	3509.048 796	21925.304 976	.000 045	.000 284	6.248 218	.160 045
56	4070.496 603	25434.353 772	.000 039	.000 245	6.248 464	.160 039
57	4721.776 060	29504.850 376	.000 033	.000 211	6.248 676	.160 033
58	5477.260 029	34226.626 436	.000 029	.000 182	6.248 858	.160 029
59	6353.621 866	39703.886 666	.000 025	.000 157	6.249 016	.160 025
60	7370.201 365	46057.503 532	.000 021	.000 135	6.249 151	.160 021

Source: *Financial Compound Interest and Annuity Tables*, 5th ed. (Boston: Financial Publishing Co., 1970).

TABLE 19
Rate of 17%

PERIODS	AMOUNT OF 1 How $1 left at compound interest will grow.	AMOUNT OF 1 PER PERIOD How $1 deposited periodically will grow.	SINKING FUND Periodic deposit that will grow to $1 at future date.	PRESENT WORTH OF 1 What $1 due in the future is worth today.	PRESENT WORTH OF 1 PER PERIOD What $1 payable periodically is worth today.	PARTIAL PAYMENT Annuity worth $1 today. Periodic payment necessary to pay off a loan of $1.	PERIODS
1	1.170 000	1.000 000	1.000 000	.854 700	.854 700	1.170 000	1
2	1.368 900	2.170 000	.460 829	.730 513	1.585 214	.630 829	2
3	1.601 613	3.538 900	.282 573	.624 370	2.209 584	.452 573	3
4	1.873 887	5.140 513	.194 533	.533 650	2.743 235	.364 533	4
5	2.192 448	7.014 400	.142 563	.456 111	3.199 346	.312 563	5
6	2.565 164	9.206 848	.108 614	.389 838	3.589 184	.278 614	6
7	3.001 242	11.772 012	.084 947	.333 195	3.922 380	.254 947	7
8	3.511 453	14.773 254	.067 689	.284 782	4.207 162	.237 689	8
9	4.108 400	18.284 707	.054 690	.243 403	4.450 566	.224 690	9
10	4.806 828	22.393 108	.044 656	.208 037	4.658 603	.214 656	10
11	5.623 989	27.199 936	.036 764	.177 809	4.836 413	.206 764	11
12	6.580 067	32.823 925	.030 465	.151 974	4.988 387	.200 465	12
13	7.698 678	39.403 993	.025 378	.129 892	5.118 279	.195 378	13
14	9.007 454	47.102 671	.021 230	.111 019	5.229 299	.191 230	14
15	10.538 721	56.110 126	.017 822	.094 888	5.324 187	.187 822	15
16	12.330 304	66.648 847	.015 004	.081 101	5.405 288	.185 004	16
17	14.426 455	78.979 151	.012 661	.069 317	5.474 605	.182 661	17
18	16.878 953	93.405 607	.010 705	.059 245	5.533 850	.180 705	18
19	19.748 375	110.284 560	.009 067	.050 637	5.584 487	.179 067	19
20	23.105 599	130.032 936	.007 690	.043 279	5.627 767	.177 690	20
21	27.033 551	153.138 535	.006 530	.036 991	5.664 758	.176 530	21
22	31.629 254	180.172 086	.005 550	.031 616	5.696 374	.175 550	22
23	37.006 227	211.801 341	.004 721	.027 022	5.723 397	.174 721	23
24	43.297 286	248.807 569	.004 019	.023 096	5.746 493	.174 019	24
25	50.657 825	292.104 855	.003 423	.019 740	5.766 233	.173 423	25
26	59.269 655	342.762 681	.002 917	.016 872	5.783 105	.172 917	26
27	69.345 497	402.032 337	.002 487	.014 420	5.797 526	.172 487	27
28	81.134 231	471.377 834	.002 121	.012 325	5.809 851	.172 121	28
29	94.927 051	552.512 066	.001 809	.010 534	5.820 385	.171 809	29
30	111.064 650	647.439 117	.001 544	.009 003	5.829 389	.171 544	30

N	$(1+i)^N$	$\dfrac{(1+i)^N-1}{i}$	$\dfrac{i}{(1+i)^N-1}$	$(1+i)^{-N}$	$\dfrac{1-(1+i)^{-N}}{i}$	$\dfrac{i}{1-(1+i)^{-N}}$
31	129.945 640	758.503 767	.001 318	.007 695	5.837 085	.171 318
32	152.036 399	888.449 408	.001 125	.006 577	5.843 662	.171 125
33	177.882 587	1040.485 807	.000 961	.005 621	5.849 284	.170 961
34	208.122 627	1218.368 394	.000 820	.004 804	5.854 089	.170 820
35	243.503 473	1426.491 022	.000 701	.004 106	5.858 195	.170 701
36	284.899 064	1669.994 495	.000 598	.003 510	5.861 705	.170 598
37	333.331 905	1954.893 560	.000 511	.003 000	5.864 705	.170 511
38	389.998 329	2288.225 465	.000 437	.002 564	5.867 269	.170 437
39	456.298 045	2678.223 794	.000 373	.002 191	5.869 461	.170 373
40	533.868 712	3134.521 839	.000 319	.001 873	5.871 334	.170 319
41	624.626 393	3668.390 552	.000 272	.001 600	5.872 935	.170 272
42	730.812 880	4293.016 946	.000 232	.001 368	5.874 303	.170 232
43	855.051 070	5023.829 826	.000 199	.001 169	5.875 473	.170 199
44	1000.409 752	5878.880 897	.000 170	.000 999	5.876 472	.170 170
45	1170.479 410	6879.290 650	.000 145	.000 854	5.877 327	.170 145
46	1369.460 910	8049.770 060	.000 124	.000 730	5.878 057	.170 124
47	1602.269 265	9419.230 970	.000 106	.000 624	5.878 681	.170 106
48	1874.655 040	11021.500 235	.000 090	.000 533	5.879 215	.170 090
49	2193.346 396	12896.155 275	.000 077	.000 455	5.879 671	.170 077
50	2566.215 284	15089.501 672	.000 066	.000 389	5.880 060	.170 066
51	3002.471 882	17655.716 957	.000 056	.000 333	5.880 393	.170 056
52	3512.892 102	20658.188 840	.000 048	.000 284	5.880 678	.170 048
53	4110.083 760	24171.080 942	.000 041	.000 243	5.880 921	.170 041
54	4808.797 999	28281.164 703	.000 035	.000 207	5.881 129	.170 035
55	5626.293 659	33089.962 702	.000 030	.000 177	5.881 307	.170 030
56	6582.763 581	38716.256 362	.000 025	.000 151	5.881 459	.170 025
57	7701.833 390	45299.019 943	.000 022	.000 129	5.881 589	.170 022
58	9011.145 066	53000.853 334	.000 018	.000 110	5.881 700	.170 018
59	10543.039 728	62011.998 400	.000 016	.000 094	5.881 795	.170 016
60	12335.356 481	72555.038 128	.000 013	.000 061	5.881 876	.170 013

Source: *Financial Compound Interest and Annuity Tables*, 5th ed.
(Boston: Financial Publishing Co., 1970).

TABLE 20
Rate of 18%

PERIODS	AMOUNT OF 1 — How $1 left at compound interest will grow.	AMOUNT OF 1 PER PERIOD — How $1 deposited periodically will grow.	SINKING FUND — Periodic deposit that will grow to $1 at future date.	PRESENT WORTH OF 1 — What $1 due in the future is worth today.	PRESENT WORTH OF 1 PER PERIOD — What $1 payable periodically is worth today.	PARTIAL PAYMENT — Annuity worth $1 today. Periodic payment necessary to pay off a loan of $1.	PERIODS
1	1.180 000	1.000 000	1.000 000	.847 457	.847 457	1.180 000	1
2	1.392 400	2.180 000	.458 715	.718 184	1.565 642	.638 715	2
3	1.643 032	3.572 400	.279 923	.608 630	2.174 272	.459 923	3
4	1.938 777	5.215 432	.191 738	.515 788	2.690 061	.371 738	4
5	2.287 757	7.154 209	.139 777	.437 109	3.127 171	.319 777	5
6	2.699 554	9.441 967	.105 910	.370 431	3.497 602	.285 910	6
7	3.185 473	12.141 521	.082 361	.313 925	3.811 527	.262 361	7
8	3.758 859	15.326 995	.065 244	.266 038	4.077 565	.245 244	8
9	4.435 453	19.085 854	.052 394	.225 456	4.303 021	.232 394	9
10	5.233 835	23.521 308	.042 514	.191 064	4.494 086	.222 514	10
11	6.175 925	28.755 144	.034 776	.161 919	4.656 005	.214 776	11
12	7.287 592	34.931 070	.028 627	.137 219	4.793 224	.208 627	12
13	8.599 359	42.218 662	.023 686	.116 287	4.909 512	.203 686	13
14	10.147 243	50.818 022	.019 678	.098 548	5.008 061	.199 678	14
15	11.973 747	60.965 266	.016 402	.083 516	5.091 577	.196 402	15
16	14.129 022	72.939 013	.013 710	.070 776	5.162 353	.193 710	16
17	16.672 246	87.068 036	.011 485	.059 979	5.222 333	.191 485	17
18	19.673 250	103.740 282	.009 639	.050 830	5.273 164	.189 639	18
19	23.214 436	123.413 533	.008 102	.043 076	5.316 240	.188 102	19
20	27.393 034	146.627 970	.006 819	.036 505	5.352 746	.186 819	20
21	32.323 780	174.021 004	.005 746	.030 936	5.383 683	.185 746	21
22	38.142 061	206.344 785	.004 846	.026 217	5.409 901	.184 846	22
23	45.007 632	244.486 846	.004 090	.022 218	5.432 119	.184 090	23
24	53.109 006	289.494 479	.003 454	.018 829	5.450 948	.183 454	24
25	62.668 627	342.603 485	.002 918	.015 956	5.466 905	.182 918	25
26	73.948 980	405.272 112	.002 467	.013 522	5.480 428	.182 467	26
27	87.259 796	479.221 093	.002 086	.011 460	5.491 888	.182 086	27
28	102.966 560	566.480 890	.001 765	.009 711	5.501 600	.181 765	28
29	121.500 541	669.447 450	.001 493	.008 230	5.509 831	.181 493	29
30	143.370 638	790.947 991	.001 264	.006 974	5.516 805	.181 264	30

N	$(1+i)^N$	$\frac{(1+i)^N-1}{i}$	$\frac{i}{(1+i)^N-1}$	$(1+i)^{-N}$	$\frac{1-(1+i)^{-N}}{i}$	$\frac{i}{1-(1+i)^{-N}}$	N
31	169.177 353	934.318 629	.001 070	.005 910	5.522 716	.181 070	31
32	199.629 276	1103.495 983	.000 906	.005 009	5.527 726	.180 906	32
33	235.562 546	1303.125 260	.000 767	.004 245	5.531 971	.180 767	33
34	277.963 805	1538.687 806	.000 649	.003 597	5.535 568	.180 649	34
35	327.997 290	1816.651 612	.000 550	.003 048	5.538 617	.180 550	35
36	387.036 802	2144.648 902	.000 466	.002 583	5.541 201	.180 466	36
37	456.703 426	2531.685 704	.000 394	.002 189	5.543 391	.180 394	37
38	538.910 043	2988.389 131	.000 334	.001 855	5.545 246	.180 334	38
39	635.913 851	3527.299 175	.000 283	.001 572	5.546 819	.180 283	39
40	750.378 344	4163.213 026	.000 240	.001 332	5.548 151	.180 240	40
41	885.446 446	4913.591 371	.000 203	.001 129	5.549 281	.180 203	41
42	1044.826 807	5799.037 818	.000 172	.000 957	5.550 238	.180 172	42
43	1232.895 632	6843.864 625	.000 146	.000 811	5.551 049	.180 146	43
44	1454.816 846	8076.760 258	.000 123	.000 687	5.551 736	.180 123	44
45	1716.683 878	9531.577 105	.000 104	.000 582	5.552 319	.180 104	45
46	2025.686 977	11248.260 983	.000 086	.000 493	5.552 813	.180 088	46
47	2390.310 632	13273.947 961	.000 075	.000 418	5.553 231	.180 075	47
48	2820.566 546	15664.258 594	.000 063	.000 354	5.553 585	.180 063	48
49	3328.268 525	18484.825 141	.000 054	.000 300	5.553 886	.180 054	49
50	3927.356 859	21813.093 666	.000 045	.000 254	5.554 140	.180 045	50
51	4634.281 094	25740.450 526	.000 038	.000 215	5.554 356	.180 038	51
52	5468.451 691	30374.731 621	.000 032	.000 182	5.554 539	.180 032	52
53	6452.772 996	35843.183 312	.000 027	.000 154	5.554 694	.180 027	53
54	7614.272 135	42295.956 309	.000 023	.000 131	5.554 825	.180 023	54
55	8984.841 120	49910.228 444	.000 020	.000 111	5.554 937	.180 020	55
56	10602.112 521	58895.069 565	.000 016	.000 094	5.555 031	.180 016	56
57	12510.492 775	69497.182 086	.000 014	.000 079	5.555 111	.180 014	57
58	14762.381 475	82007.674 862	.000 012	.000 067	5.555 179	.180 012	58
59	17419.610 140	96770.056 337	.000 010	.000 057	5.555 236	.180 010	59
60	20555.139 966	114189.666 478	.000 008	.000 048	5.555 285	.180 008	60

Source: *Financial Compound Interest and Annuity Tables*, 5th ed. (Boston: Financial Publishing Co., 1970).

Appendix 2

Logarithms

The use of logarithms (logs) provides a mathematical short cut for multiplying, dividing, taking square roots, and finding powers of numbers. Most log tables are to the base 10, which means that the log of a number is as follows:

$$10^y = x$$
where x is the number
and y is its log.

For example:

$10^0 = 1$, and the log of 1 is zero; $10^1 = 10$ and the log of 10 is 1; $10^2 = 100$ and the log of 100 is 2.0; $10^3 = 1,000$ and the log of 1,000 is 3; $10^4 = 10,000$ and the log of 10,000 is 4; $10^{-1} = 0.1$ and the log of 0.1 is $0.0000 - 1$; $10^{-2} = 0.01$ and the log of 0.01 is $0.0000 - 2$ (often expressed as $8.0000 - 10$).

Every log consists of two parts: the characteristic and the mantissa. As we saw above, the log of 1,000 is 3.0000. The part of the log to the left of the decimal is the characteristic and the part after the decimal is the mantissa. Log tables provide the *mantissas* only of the

161

logarithms of numbers. The person doing the calculation must provide the characteristic. However, it is simple to determine the characteristic. The following chart shows, for various numbers, the log characteristic:

Number	Log characteristic
100,000.0026....................	5
20,000.0035....................	4
6,000.8718....................	3
200.6556....................	2
17.0124....................	1
8.3112....................	0
0.8372....................	−1 or 9. xxxx − 10
0.0654....................	−2 or 8. xxxx − 10.

The rule for determining the characteristic follows:

Put a slash mark after the first significant figure of the number whose characteristic is desired. The first significant figure is the first whole number greater than zero.

EXAMPLES:

Number	Characteristic
1/234.007................	3
1/063.005................	3
7/23.001................	2
8/2.056................	1
9/.711................	0
0.8/37................	(−1) 9. xxxx − 10
0.05/6................	(−2) 8. xxxx − 10
0.007/................	(−3) 7. xxxx − 10

The number of digits to the left of the actual decimal and before the slash mark is the plus or positive characteristic. If the slash mark is to the right of the actual decimal, then the characteristic is negative, but is still the number of digits between the decimal and the slash mark.

The following tables contain the logs of numbers between 1.000 to 9.999. These numbers are shown under the column headed "N." The decimal after the 1 and the 9, and so on, is omitted.

Since the mantissa portion of the log is the same for the number 8 as it is for 80 or 800 or 0.8, it should be noted, the tables are used to determine the log of any number. Only the characteristic (which is zero for all the numbers in the table) and the decimal after the characteristic (which is not shown to save space) need to be added.

EXAMPLE:

Use the first page of the tables to determine the log of the following numbers:

Number	--------- *Log* ---------	
	Characteristic	*Mantissa*
105.000...............	2.	02119
103.000...............	2.	01284
10.300...............	1.	01284
0.102...............	9.	00860 −10

Note that the mantissas, to save space, omit the first two figures except that the first two figures are shown on the first available line under the column headed "0" after a change in those first two digits has occurred. Horizontal underlinings in the tables separate logs beginning with 1 pair of digits from those beginning with another pair.

The rules for finding powers, multiplying, dividing, and other operations are as follows:

Powers:

The log of 2^{10} is 10 times log 2.0.

Division:

The log of (70 divided by 10) is log 70 minus log 10.

Multiplication:

The log of (7 times 100) is log 7 plus log 100.

Roots:

The log of the 5th root of 32 ($\sqrt[5]{32}$) is log 32 divided by 5.

EXAMPLE:

Find 2^{10} with logs.

$$\text{Log } 2^{10} = 10 \ (\log \ 2.0) \quad \text{(the log of 2.0 is}$$
$$0.30103)$$
$$= 10 \ (0.30103)$$
$$= 3.0103$$

To find the actual number (x) whose log is 3.0103 ($x = 10^{3.01030}$),

1. Note that for the number (x) we wish to find, its log has a characteristic of 3 and a mantissa of .01030. Since the characteristic is plus 3, the number x must have 4 digits to the left of its decimal, that is the form is: xxxx.xx.

2. The digits of the number N are determined by finding the number N in the tables whose mantissa is .01030. Searching the tables, one finds that N is 1024.

3. Thus, the number is 1024, which is 2^{10}.

EXAMPLE:

Find 70 divided by 10 with logs.

(1) $\qquad \log \dfrac{70}{10} = \log 70$ minus $\log 10.$

$$\log 70 = 1.84510$$
$$\log 10 = 1.000000$$
$$\log 70 - \log 10 = \overline{0.84510}$$

(2) Find, in the tables, the number N whose mantissa is 84510. Since the characteristic is zero, the number is of the form x.xx.

(3) The number whose mantissa is 84510 is 7000. Hence, the number is 7.000.

EXAMPLE:

Find 7 times 100 with logs.

(1) $\log$ (7 x 100)　　$= \log 7$ plus $\log 100$
$\quad \log 7 \qquad\qquad\quad = 0.84510$
$\quad \log 100 \qquad\qquad = 2.000000$
$\quad \log 7 + \log 100 = \overline{2.84510}$

(2) Since the characteristic is 2, the number is of the form xxx.xx.

(3) Find in the tables the number N whose mantissa is 84510, which is 7000. Hence, the number is 700.00.

EXAMPLE:

Find $\sqrt[5]{32}.$

(1) $\log \sqrt[5]{32}\ = \log 32$ divided by 5
$\quad \log 32 \quad\ \ = 1.50515$
$\quad \log 32/5 = 0.30101.$

(2) Since the characteristic is 0, the number is of the form x.xx.

(3) Searching the tables, one finds that the number, N, whose mantissa is .30101 is 2000. Hence, the number must be 2.00.

EXAMPLE:

Find 62 x 41 by logs.

(1) log (62 x 41)   = log 62 plus log 41
     log 62   = 1.79239
     log 41   = 1.61278
     log 62 + log 41 = 3.40517

(2) Since the characteristic is 3, the number must be of the form xxxx.xx.

(3) Searching the tables, one finds that the number, N, whose mantissa is 405176 is 2542. Hence, the answer is 2542.

EXAMPLE:

Find, by logs, 1735 divided by 146.

(1) log (1735 divided
     by 146)   = log 1735 minus log 146

(2)   log 1735   = 3.23930
           log 146   = 2.16435
     log 1735 — log 146 = 1.07495

(3) Since the characteristic is 1, the number is of the form xx.xxx.

(4) Searching the tables for the number N, whose mantissa is 07495, one finds that there is no mantissa, 07495. There is, however:
     07482 for N = 1188, and
     07518 for N = 1189.

(5) The mantissa of our number (07495) is between 07482 and 07518, hence our number is between 1188 and 1189. The approximate number can be found by interpolation, which is finding the pro-rata distance of our number's mantissa and those of the two in the table.

$$
\left.\begin{array}{ll}
1189 & 07518 \\
\text{our number} & 07495 \\
1188 & 07482
\end{array}\;A\right]\quad B\Bigg]
$$

(6) The fifth digit of our number is the same distance between 11880 and 11890 as A (07495 minus 07482) divided by B (07518 minus 07482).

This is $\dfrac{13}{36}$ or .36, which rounds off to .4

(7) Hence, our number is 11.884.

(8) Rather than divide 13 by 36, one may use the proportional parts table. B above, the difference between the two mantissas, in the table is 36. Look in the proportional parts table, under the "diff" column, for 36. Then move horizontally on that line until the closest number to A above, the difference between the smaller mantissa and the mantissa of our number (13) is found. The closest number is 14.4, which is in the "4" column. Hence the proportion is .4 and the number, by this method, is 11.884.

TABLE 21

Five-place logarithms

N.	0	1	2	3	4	5	6	7	8	9
100	00 000	043	087	130	173	217	260	303	346	389
101	432	475	518	561	604	647	689	732	775	817
102	860	903	945	988	*030	*072	*115	*157	*199	*242
103	01 284	326	368	410	452	494	536	578	620	662
104	703	745	787	828	870	912	953	995	*036	*078
105	02 119	160	202	243	284	325	366	407	449	490
106	531	572	612	653	694	735	776	816	857	898
107	938	979	*019	*060	*100	*141	*181	*222	*262	*302
108	03 342	383	423	463	503	543	583	623	663	703
109	743	782	822	862	902	941	981	*021	*060	*100
110	04 139	179	218	258	297	336	376	415	454	493
111	532	571	610	650	689	727	766	805	844	883
112	922	961	999	*038	*077	*115	*154	*192	*231	*269
113	05 308	346	385	423	461	500	538	576	614	652
114	690	729	767	805	843	881	918	956	994	*032
115	06 070	108	145	183	221	258	296	333	371	408
116	446	483	521	558	595	633	670	707	744	781
117	819	856	893	930	967	*004	*041	*078	*115	*151
118	07 188	225	262	298	335	372	408	445	482	518
119	555	591	628	664	700	737	773	809	846	882
120	918	954	990	*027	*063	*099	*135	*171	*207	*243
121	08 279	314	350	386	422	458	493	529	565	600
122	636	672	707	743	778	814	849	884	920	955
123	991	*026	*061	*096	*132	*167	*202	*237	*272	*307
124	09 342	377	412	447	482	517	552	587	621	656
125	691	726	760	795	830	864	899	934	968	*003
126	10 037	072	106	140	175	209	243	278	312	346
127	380	415	449	483	517	551	585	619	653	687
128	721	755	789	823	857	890	924	958	992	*025
129	11 059	093	126	160	193	227	261	294	327	361
130	394	428	461	494	528	561	594	628	661	694
131	727	760	793	826	860	893	926	959	992	*024
132	12 057	090	123	156	189	222	254	287	320	352
133	385	418	450	483	516	548	581	613	646	678
134	710	743	775	808	840	872	905	937	969	*001
135	13 033	066	098	130	162	194	226	258	290	322
136	354	386	418	450	481	513	545	577	609	640
137	672	704	735	767	799	830	862	893	925	956
138	988	*019	*051	*082	*114	*145	*176	*208	*239	*270
139	14 301	333	364	395	426	457	489	520	551	582
140	613	644	675	706	737	768	799	829	860	891
141	922	953	983	*014	*045	*076	*106	*137	*168	*198
142	15 229	259	290	320	351	381	412	442	473	503
143	534	564	594	625	655	685	715	746	776	806
144	836	866	897	927	957	987	*017	*047	*077	*107
145	16 137	167	197	227	256	286	316	346	376	406
146	435	465	495	524	554	584	613	643	673	702
147	732	761	791	820	850	879	909	938	967	997
148	17 026	056	085	114	143	173	202	231	260	289
149	319	348	377	406	435	464	493	522	551	580
150	609	638	667	696	725	754	782	811	840	869

N.	0	1	2	3	4	5	6	7	8	9

Proportional Parts

	44	43	42
1	4.4	4.3	4.2
2	8.8	8.6	8.4
3	13.2	12.9	12.6
4	17.6	17.2	16.8
5	22.0	21.5	21.0
6	26.4	25.8	25.2
7	30.8	30.1	29.4
8	35.2	34.4	33.6
9	39.6	38.7	37.8

	41	40	39
1	4.1	4.0	3.9
2	8.2	8.0	7.8
3	12.3	12.0	11.7
4	16.4	16.0	15.6
5	20.5	20.0	19.5
6	24.6	24.0	23.4
7	28.7	28.0	27.3
8	32.8	32.0	31.2
9	36.9	36.0	35.1

	38	37	36
1	3.8	3.7	3.6
2	7.6	7.4	7.2
3	11.4	11.1	10.8
4	15.2	14.8	14.4
5	19.0	18.5	18.0
6	22.8	22.2	21.6
7	26.6	25.9	25.2
8	30.4	29.6	28.8
9	34.2	33.3	32.4

	35	34	33
1	3.5	3.4	3.3
2	7.0	6.8	6.6
3	10.5	10.2	9.9
4	14.0	13.6	13.2
5	17.5	17.0	16.5
6	21.0	20.4	19.8
7	24.5	23.8	23.1
8	28.0	27.2	26.4
9	31.5	30.6	29.7

	32	31	30
1	3.2	3.1	3.0
2	6.4	6.2	6.0
3	9.6	9.3	9.0
4	12.8	12.4	12.0
5	16.0	15.5	15.0
6	19.2	18.6	18.0
7	22.4	21.7	21.0
8	25.6	24.8	24.0
9	28.8	27.9	27.0

TABLE 21 (continued)

Five-place logarithms (continued)

N.	0	1	2	3	4	5	6	7	8	9
150	17 609	638	667	696	725	754	782	811	840	869
151	898	926	955	984	*013	*041	*070	*099	*127	*156
152	18 184	213	241	270	298	327	355	384	412	441
153	469	498	526	554	583	611	639	667	696	724
154	752	780	808	837	865	893	921	949	977	*005
155	19 033	061	089	117	145	173	201	229	257	285
156	312	340	368	396	424	451	479	507	535	562
157	590	618	645	673	700	728	756	783	811	838
158	866	893	921	948	976	*003	*030	*058	*085	*112
159	20 140	167	194	222	249	276	303	330	358	385
160	412	439	466	493	520	548	575	602	629	656
161	683	710	737	763	790	817	844	871	898	925
162	952	978	*005	*032	*059	*085	*112	*139	*165	*192
163	21 219	245	272	299	325	352	378	405	431	458
164	484	511	537	564	590	617	643	669	696	722
165	748	775	801	827	854	880	906	932	958	985
166	22 011	037	063	089	115	141	167	194	220	246
167	272	298	324	350	376	401	427	453	479	505
168	531	557	583	608	634	660	686	712	737	763
169	789	814	840	866	891	917	943	968	994	*019
170	23 045	070	096	121	147	172	198	223	249	274
171	300	325	350	376	401	426	452	477	502	528
172	553	578	603	629	654	679	704	729	754	779
173	805	830	855	880	905	930	955	980	*005	*030
174	24 055	080	105	130	155	180	204	229	254	279
175	304	329	353	378	403	428	452	477	502	527
176	551	576	601	625	650	674	699	724	748	773
177	797	822	846	871	895	920	944	969	993	*018
178	25 042	066	091	115	139	164	188	212	237	261
179	285	310	334	358	382	406	431	455	479	503
180	527	551	575	600	624	648	672	696	720	744
181	768	792	816	840	864	888	912	935	959	983
182	26 007	031	055	079	102	126	150	174	198	221
183	245	269	293	316	340	364	387	411	435	458
184	482	505	529	553	576	600	623	647	670	694
185	717	741	764	788	811	834	858	881	905	928
186	951	975	998	*021	*045	*068	*091	*114	*138	*161
187	27 184	207	231	254	277	300	323	346	370	393
188	416	439	462	485	508	531	554	577	600	623
189	646	669	692	715	738	761	784	807	830	852
190	875	898	921	944	967	989	*012	*035	*058	*081
191	28 103	126	149	171	194	217	240	262	285	307
192	330	353	375	398	421	443	466	488	511	533
193	556	578	601	623	646	668	691	713	735	758
194	780	803	825	847	870	892	914	937	959	981
195	29 003	026	048	070	092	115	137	159	181	203
196	226	248	270	292	314	336	358	380	403	425
197	447	469	491	513	535	557	579	601	623	645
198	667	688	710	732	754	776	798	820	842	863
199	885	907	929	951	973	994	*016	*038	*060	*081
200	30 103	125	146	168	190	211	233	255	276	298

N.	0	1	2	3	4	5	6	7	8	9

Proportional parts

	29	28		27	26		25		24	23		22	21
1	2.9	2.8	1	2.7	2.6	1	2.5	1	2.4	2.3	1	2.2	2.1
2	5.8	5.6	2	5.4	5.2	2	5.0	2	4.8	4.6	2	4.4	4.2
3	8.7	8.4	3	8.1	7.8	3	7.5	3	7.2	6.9	3	6.6	6.3
4	11.6	11.2	4	10.8	10.4	4	10.0	4	9.6	9.2	4	8.8	8.4
5	14.5	14.0	5	13.5	13.0	5	12.5	5	12.0	11.5	5	11.0	10.5
6	17.4	16.8	6	16.2	15.6	6	15.0	6	14.4	13.8	6	13.2	12.6
7	20.3	19.6	7	18.9	18.2	7	17.5	7	16.8	16.1	7	15.4	14.7
8	23.2	22.4	8	21.6	20.8	8	20.0	8	19.2	18.4	8	17.6	16.8
9	26.1	25.2	9	24.3	23.4	9	22.5	9	21.6	20.7	9	19.8	18.9

170

TABLE 21 (continued)

Five-place logarithms (continued)

N.	0	1	2	3	4	5	6	7	8	9
200	30 103	125	146	168	190	211	233	255	276	298
201	320	341	363	384	406	428	449	471	492	514
202	535	557	578	600	621	643	664	685	707	728
203	750	771	792	814	835	856	878	899	920	942
204	963	984	*006	*027	*048	*069	*091	*112	*133	*154
205	31 175	197	218	239	260	281	302	323	345	366
206	387	408	429	450	471	492	513	534	555	576
207	597	618	639	660	681	702	723	744	765	785
208	806	827	848	869	890	911	931	952	973	994
209	32 015	035	056	077	098	118	139	160	181	201
210	222	243	263	284	305	325	346	366	387	408
211	428	449	469	490	510	531	552	572	593	613
212	634	654	675	695	715	736	756	777	797	818
213	838	858	879	899	919	940	960	980	*001	*021
214	33 041	062	082	102	122	143	163	183	203	224
215	244	264	284	304	325	345	365	385	405	425
216	445	465	486	506	526	546	566	586	606	626
217	646	666	686	706	726	746	766	786	806	826
218	846	866	885	905	925	945	965	985	*005	*025
219	34 044	064	084	104	124	143	163	183	203	223
220	242	262	282	301	321	341	361	380	400	420
221	439	459	479	498	518	537	557	577	596	616
222	635	655	674	694	713	733	753	772	792	811
223	830	850	869	889	908	928	947	967	986	*005
224	35 025	044	064	083	102	122	141	160	180	199
225	218	238	257	276	295	315	334	353	372	392
226	411	430	449	468	488	507	526	545	564	583
227	603	622	641	660	679	698	717	736	755	774
228	793	813	832	851	870	889	908	927	946	965
229	984	*003	*021	*040	*059	*078	*097	*116	*135	*154
230	36 173	192	211	229	248	267	286	305	324	342
231	361	380	399	418	436	455	474	493	511	530
232	549	568	586	605	624	642	661	680	698	717
233	736	754	773	791	810	829	847	866	884	903
234	922	940	959	977	996	*014	*033	*051	*070	*088
235	37 107	125	144	162	181	199	218	236	254	273
236	291	310	328	346	365	383	401	420	438	457
237	475	493	511	530	548	566	585	603	621	639
238	658	676	694	712	731	749	767	785	803	822
239	840	858	876	894	912	931	949	967	985	*003
240	38 021	039	057	075	093	112	130	148	166	184
241	202	220	238	256	274	292	310	328	346	364
242	382	399	417	435	453	471	489	507	525	543
243	561	578	596	614	632	650	668	686	703	721
244	739	757	775	792	810	828	846	863	881	899
245	917	934	952	970	987	*005	*023	*041	*058	*076
246	39 094	111	129	146	164	182	199	217	235	252
247	270	287	305	322	340	358	375	393	410	428
248	445	463	480	498	515	533	550	568	585	602
249	620	637	655	672	690	707	724	742	759	777
250	794	811	829	846	863	881	898	915	933	950

Proportional parts

	22	21
1	2.2	2.1
2	4.4	4.2
3	6.6	6.3
4	8.8	8.4
5	11.0	10.5
6	13.2	12.6
7	15.4	14.7
8	17.6	16.8
9	19.8	18.9

	20
1	2.0
2	4.0
3	6.0
4	8.0
5	10.0
6	12.0
7	14.0
8	16.0
9	18.0

	19
1	1.9
2	3.8
3	5.7
4	7.6
5	9.5
6	11.4
7	13.3
8	15.2
9	17.1

	18
1	1.8
2	3.6
3	5.4
4	7.2
5	9.0
6	10.8
7	12.6
8	14.4
9	16.2

	17
1	1.7
2	3.4
3	5.1
4	6.8
5	8.5
6	10.2
7	11.9
8	13.6
9	15.3

N.	0	1	2	3	4	5	6	7	8	9	Proportional parts

TABLE 21 (continued)

Five-place logarithms (continued)

N.	0	1	2	3	4	5	6	7	8	9
250	39 794	811	829	846	863	881	898	915	933	950
251	967	985	*002	*019	*037	*054	*071	*088	*106	*123
252	40 140	157	175	192	209	226	243	261	278	295
253	312	329	346	364	381	398	415	432	449	466
254	483	500	518	535	552	569	586	603	620	637
255	654	671	688	705	722	739	756	773	790	807
256	824	841	858	875	892	909	926	943	960	976
257	993	*010	*027	*044	*061	*078	*095	*111	*128	*145
258	41 162	179	196	212	229	246	263	280	296	313
259	330	347	363	380	397	414	430	447	464	481
260	497	514	531	547	564	581	597	614	631	647
261	664	681	697	714	731	747	764	780	797	814
262	830	847	863	880	896	913	929	946	963	979
263	996	*012	*029	*045	*062	*078	*095	*111	*127	*144
264	42 160	177	193	210	226	243	259	275	292	308
265	325	341	357	374	390	406	423	439	455	472
266	488	504	521	537	553	570	586	602	619	635
267	651	667	684	700	716	732	749	765	781	797
268	813	830	846	862	878	894	911	927	943	959
269	975	991	*008	*024	*040	*056	*072	*088	*104	*120
270	43 136	152	169	185	201	217	233	249	265	281
271	297	313	329	345	361	377	393	409	425	441
272	457	473	489	505	521	537	553	569	584	600
273	616	632	648	664	680	696	712	727	743	759
274	775	791	807	823	838	854	870	886	902	917
275	933	949	965	981	996	*012	*028	*044	*059	*075
276	44 091	107	122	138	154	170	185	201	217	232
277	248	264	279	295	311	326	342	358	373	389
278	404	420	436	451	467	483	498	514	529	545
279	560	576	592	607	623	638	654	669	685	700
280	716	731	747	762	778	793	809	824	840	855
281	871	886	902	917	932	948	963	979	994	*010
282	45 025	040	056	071	086	102	117	130	148	163
283	179	194	209	225	240	255	271	286	301	317
284	332	347	362	378	393	408	423	439	454	469
285	484	500	515	530	545	561	576	591	606	621
286	637	652	667	682	697	712	728	743	758	773
287	788	803	818	834	849	864	879	894	909	924
288	939	954	969	984	*000	*015	*030	*045	*060	*075
289	46 090	105	120	135	150	165	180	195	210	225
290	240	255	270	285	300	315	330	345	359	374
291	389	404	419	434	449	464	479	494	509	523
292	538	553	568	583	598	613	627	642	657	672
293	687	702	716	731	746	761	776	790	805	820
294	835	850	864	879	894	909	923	938	953	967
295	982	997	*012	*026	*041	*056	*070	*085	*100	*114
296	47 129	144	159	173	188	202	217	232	246	261
297	276	290	305	319	334	349	363	378	392	407
298	422	436	451	465	480	494	509	524	538	553
299	567	582	596	611	625	640	654	669	683	698
300	712	727	741	756	770	784	799	813	828	842

| N. | 0 | 1 | 2 | 3 | 4 | 5 | 6 | 7 | 8 | 9 |

Proportional parts

18		17		16		15		14	
1	1.8	1	1.7	1	1.6	1	1.5	1	1.4
2	3.6	2	3.4	2	3.2	2	3.0	2	2.8
3	5.4	3	5.1	3	4.8	3	4.5	3	4.2
4	7.2	4	6.8	4	6.4	4	6.0	4	5.6
5	9.0	5	8.5	5	8.0	5	7.5	5	7.0
6	10.8	6	10.2	6	9.6	6	9.0	6	8.4
7	12.6	7	11.9	7	11.2	7	10.5	7	9.8
8	14.4	8	13.6	8	12.8	8	12.0	8	11.2
9	16.2	9	15.3	9	14.4	9	13.5	9	12.6

TABLE 21 (continued)

Five-place logarithms (continued)

N.	0	1	2	3	4	5	6	7	8	9
300	47 712	727	741	756	770	784	799	813	828	842
301	857	871	885	900	914	929	943	958	972	986
302	48 001	015	029	044	058	073	087	101	116	130
303	144	159	173	187	202	216	230	244	259	273
304	287	302	316	330	344	359	373	387	401	416
305	430	444	458	473	487	501	515	530	544	558
306	572	586	601	615	629	643	657	671	686	700
307	714	728	742	756	770	785	799	813	827	841
308	855	869	883	897	911	926	940	954	968	982
309	996	*010	*024	*038	*052	*066	*080	*094	*108	*122
310	49 136	150	164	178	192	206	220	234	248	262
311	276	290	304	318	332	346	360	374	388	402
312	415	429	443	457	471	485	499	513	527	541
313	554	568	582	596	610	624	638	651	665	679
314	693	707	721	734	748	762	776	790	803	817
315	831	845	859	872	886	900	914	927	941	955
316	969	982	996	*010	*024	*037	*051	*065	*079	*092
317	50 106	120	133	147	161	174	188	202	215	229
318	243	256	270	284	297	311	325	338	352	365
319	379	393	406	420	433	447	461	474	488	501
320	515	529	542	556	569	583	596	610	623	637
321	651	664	678	691	705	718	732	745	759	772
322	786	799	813	826	840	853	866	880	893	907
323	920	934	947	961	974	987	*001	*014	*028	*041
324	51 055	068	081	095	108	121	135	148	162	175
325	188	202	215	228	242	255	268	282	295	308
326	322	335	348	362	375	388	402	415	428	441
327	455	468	481	495	508	521	534	548	561	574
328	587	601	614	627	640	654	667	680	693	706
329	720	733	746	759	772	786	799	812	825	838
330	851	865	878	891	904	917	930	943	957	970
331	983	996	*009	*022	*035	*048	*061	*075	*088	*101
332	52 114	127	140	153	166	179	192	205	218	231
333	244	257	270	284	297	310	323	336	349	362
334	375	388	401	414	427	440	453	466	479	492
335	504	517	530	543	556	569	582	595	608	621
336	634	647	660	673	686	699	711	724	737	750
337	763	776	789	802	815	827	840	853	866	879
338	892	905	917	930	943	956	969	982	994	*007
339	53 020	033	046	058	071	084	097	110	122	135
340	148	161	173	186	199	212	224	237	250	263
341	275	288	301	314	326	339	352	364	377	390
342	403	415	428	441	453	466	479	491	504	517
343	529	542	555	567	580	593	605	618	631	643
344	656	668	681	694	706	719	732	744	757	769
345	782	794	807	820	832	845	857	870	882	895
346	908	920	933	945	958	970	983	995	*008	*020
347	54 033	045	058	070	083	095	108	120	133	145
348	158	170	183	195	208	220	233	245	258	270
349	283	295	307	320	332	345	357	370	382	394
350	407	419	432	444	456	469	481	494	506	518

| N. | 0 | 1 | 2 | 3 | 4 | 5 | 6 | 7 | 8 | 9 |

Proportional parts

	15		14		13		12
1	1.5	1	1.4	1	1.3	1	1.2
2	3.0	2	2.8	2	2.6	2	2.4
3	4.5	3	4.2	3	3.9	3	3.6
4	6.0	4	5.6	4	5.2	4	4.8
5	7.5	5	7.0	5	6.5	5	6.0
6	9.0	6	8.4	6	7.8	6	7.2
7	10.5	7	9.8	7	9.1	7	8.4
8	12.0	8	11.2	8	10.4	8	9.6
9	13.5	9	12.6	9	11.7	9	10.8

TABLE 21 (continued)

Five-place logarithms (continued)

N.	0	1	2	3	4	5	6	7	8	9
350	54 407	419	432	444	456	469	481	494	506	518
351	531	543	555	568	580	593	605	617	630	642
352	654	667	679	691	704	716	728	741	753	765
353	777	790	802	814	827	839	851	864	876	888
354	900	913	925	937	949	962	974	986	998	*011
355	55 023	035	047	060	072	084	096	108	121	133
356	145	157	169	182	194	206	218	230	242	255
357	267	279	291	303	315	328	340	352	364	376
358	388	400	413	425	437	449	461	473	485	497
359	509	522	534	546	558	570	582	594	606	618
360	630	642	654	666	678	691	703	715	727	739
361	751	763	775	787	799	811	823	835	847	859
362	871	883	895	907	919	931	943	955	967	979
363	991	*003	*015	*027	*038	*050	*062	*074	*086	*098
364	56 110	122	134	146	158	170	182	194	205	217
365	229	241	253	265	277	289	301	312	324	336
366	348	360	372	384	396	407	419	431	443	455
367	467	478	490	502	514	526	538	549	561	573
368	585	597	608	620	632	644	656	667	679	691
369	703	714	726	738	750	761	773	785	797	808
370	820	832	844	855	867	879	891	902	914	926
371	937	949	961	972	984	996	*008	*019	*031	*043
372	57 054	066	078	089	101	113	124	136	148	159
373	171	183	194	206	217	229	241	252	264	276
374	287	299	310	322	334	345	357	368	380	392
375	403	415	426	438	449	461	473	484	496	507
376	519	530	542	553	565	576	588	600	611	623
377	634	646	657	669	680	692	703	715	726	738
378	749	761	772	784	795	807	818	830	841	852
379	864	875	887	898	910	921	933	944	955	967
380	978	990	*001	*013	*024	*035	*047	*058	*070	*081
381	58 092	104	115	127	138	149	161	172	184	195
382	206	218	229	240	252	263	274	286	297	309
383	320	331	343	354	365	377	388	399	410	422
384	433	444	456	467	478	490	501	512	524	535
385	546	557	569	580	591	602	614	625	636	647
386	659	670	681	692	704	715	726	737	749	760
387	771	782	794	805	816	827	838	850	861	872
388	883	894	906	917	928	939	950	961	973	984
389	995	*006	*017	*028	*040	*051	*062	*073	*084	*095
390	59 106	118	129	140	151	162	173	184	195	207
391	218	229	240	251	262	273	284	295	306	318
392	329	340	351	362	373	384	395	406	417	428
393	439	450	461	472	483	494	506	517	528	539
394	550	561	572	583	594	605	616	627	638	649
395	660	671	682	693	704	715	726	737	748	759
396	770	780	791	802	813	824	835	846	857	868
397	879	890	901	912	923	934	945	956	966	977
398	988	999	*010	*021	*032	*043	*054	*065	*076	*086
399	60 097	108	119	130	141	152	163	173	184	195
400	206	217	228	239	249	260	271	282	293	304

N.	0	1	2	3	4	5	6	7	8	9

Proportional parts

	13		**12**		**11**		**10**
1	1.3		1.2		1.1		1.0
2	2.6		2.4		2.2		2.0
3	3.9		3.6		3.3		3.0
4	5.2		4.8		4.4		4.0
5	6.5		6.0		5.5		5.0
6	7.8		7.2		6.6		6.0
7	9.1		8.4		7.7		7.0
8	10.4		9.6		8.8		8.0
9	11.7		10.8		9.9		9.0

174

TABLE 21 (continued)

Five-place logarithms (continued)

N.	0	1	2	3	4	5	6	7	8	9	Proportional parts
400	60 206	217	228	239	249	260	271	282	293	304	
401	314	325	336	347	358	369	379	390	401	412	
402	423	433	444	455	466	477	487	498	509	520	
403	531	541	552	563	574	584	595	606	617	627	
404	638	649	660	670	681	692	703	713	724	735	
405	746	756	767	778	788	799	810	821	831	842	
406	853	863	874	885	895	906	917	927	938	949	
407	959	970	981	991	*002	*013	*023	*034	*045	*055	**11**
408	61 066	077	087	098	109	119	130	140	151	162	1 1.1
409	172	183	194	204	215	225	236	247	257	268	2 2.2
410	278	289	300	310	321	331	342	352	363	374	3 3.3 / 4 4.4
411	384	395	405	416	426	437	448	458	469	479	5 5.5
412	490	500	511	521	532	542	553	563	574	584	6 6.6
413	595	606	616	627	637	648	658	669	679	690	7 7.7
414	700	711	721	731	742	752	763	773	784	794	8 8.8 / 9 9.9
415	805	815	826	836	847	857	868	878	888	899	
416	909	920	930	941	951	962	972	982	993	*003	
417	62 014	024	034	045	055	066	076	086	097	107	
418	118	128	138	149	159	170	180	190	201	211	
419	221	232	242	252	263	273	284	294	304	315	
420	325	335	346	356	366	377	387	397	408	418	
421	428	439	449	459	469	480	490	500	511	521	**10**
422	531	542	552	562	572	583	593	603	613	624	1 1.0
423	634	644	655	665	675	685	696	706	716	726	2 2.0
424	737	747	757	767	778	788	798	808	818	829	3 3.0 / 4 4.0
425	839	849	859	870	880	890	900	910	921	931	5 5.0
426	941	951	961	972	982	992	*002	*012	*022	*033	6 6.0
427	63 043	053	063	073	083	094	104	114	124	134	7 7.0
428	144	155	165	175	185	195	205	215	225	236	8 8.0
429	246	256	266	276	286	296	306	317	327	337	9 9.0
430	347	357	367	377	387	397	407	417	428	438	
431	448	458	468	478	488	498	508	518	528	538	
432	548	558	568	579	589	599	609	619	629	639	
433	649	659	669	679	689	699	709	719	729	739	
434	749	759	769	779	789	799	809	819	829	839	
435	849	859	869	879	889	899	909	919	929	939	**9**
436	949	959	969	979	988	998	*008	*018	*028	*038	1 0.9
437	64 048	058	068	078	088	098	108	118	128	137	2 1.8
438	147	157	167	177	187	197	207	217	227	237	3 2.7
439	246	256	266	276	286	296	306	316	326	335	4 3.6 / 5 4.5
440	345	355	365	375	385	395	404	414	424	434	6 5.4
441	444	454	464	473	483	493	503	513	523	532	7 6.3
442	542	552	562	572	582	591	601	611	621	631	8 7.2
443	640	650	660	670	680	689	699	709	719	729	9 8.1
444	738	748	758	768	777	787	797	807	816	826	
445	836	846	856	865	875	885	895	904	914	924	
446	933	943	953	963	972	982	992	*002	*011	*021	
447	65 031	040	050	060	070	079	089	099	108	118	
448	128	137	147	157	167	176	186	196	205	215	
449	225	234	244	254	263	273	283	292	302	312	
450	321	331	341	350	360	369	379	389	398	408	

N.	0	1	2	3	4	5	6	7	8	9	Proportional parts

TABLE 21 (continued)

Five-place logarithms (continued)

N.	0	1	2	3	4	5	6	7	8	9
450	65 321	331	341	350	360	369	379	389	398	408
451	418	427	437	447	456	466	475	485	495	504
452	514	523	533	543	552	562	571	581	591	600
453	610	619	629	639	648	658	667	677	686	696
454	706	715	725	734	744	753	763	772	782	792
455	801	811	820	830	839	849	858	868	877	887
456	896	906	916	925	935	944	954	963	973	982
457	992	*001	*011	*020	*030	*039	*049	*058	*068	*077
458	66 087	096	106	115	124	134	143	153	162	172
459	181	191	200	210	219	229	238	247	257	266
460	276	285	295	304	314	323	332	342	351	361
461	370	380	389	398	408	417	427	436	445	455
462	464	474	483	492	502	511	521	530	539	549
463	558	567	577	586	596	605	614	624	633	642
464	652	661	671	680	689	699	708	717	727	736
465	745	755	764	773	783	792	801	811	820	829
466	839	848	857	867	876	885	894	904	913	922
467	932	941	950	960	969	978	987	997	*006	*015
468	67 025	034	043	052	062	071	080	089	099	108
469	117	127	136	145	154	164	173	182	191	201
470	210	219	228	237	247	256	265	274	284	293
471	302	311	321	330	339	348	357	367	376	385
472	394	403	413	422	431	440	449	459	468	477
473	486	495	504	514	523	532	541	550	560	569
474	578	587	596	605	614	624	633	642	651	660
475	669	679	688	697	706	715	724	733	742	752
476	761	770	779	788	797	806	815	825	834	843
477	852	861	870	879	888	897	906	916	925	934
478	943	952	961	970	979	988	997	*006	*015	*024
479	68 034	043	052	061	070	079	088	097	106	115
480	124	133	142	151	160	169	178	187	196	205
481	215	224	233	242	251	260	269	278	287	296
482	305	314	323	332	341	350	359	368	377	386
483	395	404	413	422	431	440	449	458	467	476
484	485	494	502	511	520	529	538	547	556	565
485	574	583	592	601	610	619	628	637	646	655
486	664	673	681	690	699	708	717	726	735	744
487	753	762	771	780	789	797	806	815	824	833
488	842	851	860	869	878	886	895	904	913	922
489	931	940	949	958	966	975	984	993	*002	*011
490	69 020	028	037	046	055	064	073	082	090	099
491	108	117	126	135	144	152	161	170	179	188
492	197	205	214	223	232	241	249	258	267	276
493	285	294	302	311	320	329	338	346	355	364
494	373	381	390	399	408	417	425	434	443	452
495	461	469	478	487	496	504	513	522	531	539
496	548	557	566	574	583	592	601	609	618	627
497	636	644	653	662	671	679	688	697	705	714
498	723	732	740	749	758	767	775	784	793	801
499	810	819	827	836	845	854	862	871	880	888
500	897	906	914	923	932	940	949	958	966	975
N.	0	1	2	3	4	5	6	7	8	9

Proportional parts

	10
1	1.0
2	2.0
3	3.0
4	4.0
5	5.0
6	6.0
7	7.0
8	8.0
9	9.0

	9
1	0.9
2	1.8
3	2.7
4	3.6
5	4.5
6	5.4
7	6.3
8	7.2
9	8.1

	8
1	0.8
2	1.6
3	2.4
4	3.2
5	4.0
6	4.8
7	5.6
8	6.4
9	7.2

TABLE 21 (continued)

Five-place logarithms (continued)

N.	0	1	2	3	4	5	6	7	8	9
500	69 897	906	914	923	932	940	949	958	966	975
501	984	992	*001	*010	*018	*027	*036	*044	*053	*062
502	70 070	079	088	096	105	114	122	131	140	148
503	157	165	174	183	191	200	209	217	226	234
504	243	252	260	269	278	286	295	303	312	321
505	329	338	346	355	364	372	381	389	398	406
506	415	424	432	441	449	458	467	475	484	492
507	501	509	518	526	535	544	552	561	569	578
508	586	595	603	612	621	629	638	646	655	663
509	672	680	689	697	706	714	723	731	740	749
510	757	766	774	783	791	800	808	817	825	834
511	842	851	859	868	876	885	893	902	910	919
512	927	935	944	952	961	969	978	986	995	*003
513	71 012	020	029	037	046	054	063	071	079	088
514	096	105	113	122	130	139	147	155	164	172
515	181	189	198	206	214	223	231	240	248	257
516	265	273	282	290	299	307	315	324	332	341
517	349	357	366	374	383	391	399	408	416	425
518	433	441	450	458	466	475	483	492	500	508
519	517	525	533	542	550	559	567	575	584	592
520	600	609	617	625	634	642	650	659	667	675
521	684	692	700	709	717	725	734	742	750	759
522	767	775	784	792	800	809	817	825	834	842
523	850	858	867	875	883	892	900	908	917	925
524	933	941	950	958	966	975	983	991	999	*008
525	72 016	024	032	041	049	057	066	074	082	090
526	099	107	115	123	132	140	148	156	165	173
527	181	189	198	206	214	222	230	239	247	255
528	263	272	280	288	296	304	313	321	329	337
529	346	354	362	370	378	387	395	403	411	419
530	428	436	444	452	460	469	477	485	493	501
531	509	518	526	534	542	550	558	567	575	583
532	591	599	607	616	624	632	640	648	656	665
533	673	681	689	697	705	713	722	730	738	746
534	754	762	770	779	787	795	803	811	819	827
535	835	843	852	860	868	876	884	892	900	908
536	916	925	933	941	949	957	965	973	981	989
537	997	*006	*014	*022	*030	*038	*046	*054	*062	*070
538	73 078	086	094	102	111	119	127	135	143	151
539	159	167	175	183	191	199	207	215	223	231
540	239	247	255	263	272	280	288	296	304	312
541	320	328	336	344	352	360	368	376	384	392
542	400	408	416	424	432	440	448	456	464	472
543	480	488	496	504	512	520	528	536	544	552
544	560	568	576	584	592	600	608	616	624	632
545	640	648	656	664	672	679	687	695	703	711
546	719	727	735	743	751	759	767	775	783	791
547	799	807	815	823	830	838	846	854	862	870
548	878	886	894	902	910	918	926	933	941	949
549	957	965	973	981	989	997	*005	*013	*020	*028
550	74 036	044	052	060	068	076	084	092	099	107

Proportional parts

	9
1	0.9
2	1.8
3	2.7
4	3.6
5	4.5
6	5.4
7	6.3
8	7.2
9	8.1

	8
1	0.8
2	1.6
3	2.4
4	3.2
5	4.0
6	4.8
7	5.6
8	6.4
9	7.2

	7
1	0.7
2	1.4
3	2.1
4	2.8
5	3.5
6	4.2
7	4.9
8	5.6
9	6.3

TABLE 21 (continued)

Five-place logarithms (continued)

N.	0	1	2	3	4	5	6	7	8	9
550	74 086	044	052	060	068	076	084	092	099	107
551	115	123	131	139	147	155	162	170	178	186
552	194	202	210	218	225	233	241	249	257	265
553	273	280	288	296	304	312	320	327	335	343
554	351	359	367	374	382	390	398	406	414	421
555	429	437	445	453	461	468	476	484	492	500
556	507	515	523	531	539	547	554	562	570	578
557	586	593	601	609	617	624	632	640	648	656
558	663	671	679	687	695	702	710	718	726	733
559	741	749	757	764	772	780	788	796	803	811
560	819	827	834	842	850	858	865	873	881	889
561	896	904	912	920	927	935	943	950	958	966
562	974	981	989	997	*005	*012	*020	*028	*035	*043
563	75 051	059	066	074	082	089	097	105	113	120
564	128	136	143	151	159	166	174	182	189	197
565	205	213	220	228	236	243	251	259	266	274
566	282	289	297	305	312	320	328	335	343	351
567	358	366	374	381	389	397	404	412	420	427
568	435	442	450	458	465	473	481	488	496	504
569	511	519	526	534	542	549	557	565	572	580
570	587	595	603	610	618	626	633	641	648	656
571	664	671	679	686	694	702	709	717	724	732
572	740	747	755	762	770	778	785	793	800	808
573	815	823	831	838	846	853	861	868	876	884
574	891	899	906	914	921	929	937	944	952	959
575	967	974	982	989	997	*005	*012	*020	*027	*035
576	76 042	050	057	065	072	080	087	095	103	110
577	118	125	133	140	148	155	163	170	178	185
578	193	200	208	215	223	230	238	245	253	260
579	268	275	283	290	298	305	313	320	328	335
580	343	350	358	365	373	380	388	395	403	410
581	418	425	433	440	448	455	462	470	477	485
582	492	500	507	515	522	530	537	545	552	559
583	567	574	582	589	597	604	612	619	626	634
584	641	649	656	664	671	678	686	693	701	708
585	716	723	730	738	745	753	760	768	775	782
586	790	797	805	812	819	827	834	842	849	856
587	864	871	879	886	893	901	908	916	923	930
588	938	945	953	960	967	975	982	989	997	*004
589	77 012	019	026	034	041	048	056	063	070	078
590	065	093	100	107	115	122	129	137	144	151
591	159	166	173	181	188	195	203	210	217	225
592	232	240	247	254	262	269	276	283	291	298
593	305	313	320	327	335	342	349	357	364	371
594	379	386	393	401	408	415	422	430	437	444
595	452	459	466	474	481	488	495	503	510	517
596	525	532	539	546	554	561	568	576	583	590
597	597	605	612	619	627	634	641	648	656	663
598	670	677	685	692	699	706	714	721	728	735
599	743	750	757	764	772	779	786	793	801	808
600	815	822	830	837	844	851	859	866	873	880
N	0	1	2	3	4	5	6	7	8	9

Proportional parts

	8
1	0.8
2	1.6
3	2.4
4	3.2
5	4.0
6	4.8
7	5.6
8	6.4
9	7.2

	7
1	0.7
2	1.4
3	2.1
4	2.8
5	3.5
6	4.2
7	4.9
8	5.6
9	6.3

TABLE 21 (continued)

Five-place logarithms (continued)

N.	0	1	2	3	4	5	6	7	8	9
600	77 815	822	830	837	844	851	859	866	873	880
601	887	895	902	909	916	924	931	938	945	952
602	960	967	974	981	988	996	*003	*010	*017	*025
603	78 032	039	046	053	061	068	075	082	089	097
604	104	111	118	125	132	140	147	154	161	168
605	176	183	190	197	204	211	219	226	233	240
606	247	254	262	269	276	283	290	297	305	312
607	319	326	333	340	347	355	362	369	376	383
608	390	398	405	412	419	426	433	440	447	455
609	462	469	476	483	490	497	504	512	519	526
610	533	540	547	554	561	569	576	583	590	597
611	604	611	618	625	633	640	647	654	661	668
612	675	682	689	696	704	711	718	725	732	739
613	746	753	760	767	774	781	789	796	803	810
614	817	824	831	838	845	852	859	866	873	880
615	888	895	902	909	916	923	930	937	944	951
616	958	965	972	979	986	993	*000	*007	*014	*021
617	79 029	036	043	050	057	064	071	078	085	092
618	099	106	113	120	127	134	141	148	155	162
619	169	176	183	190	197	204	211	218	225	232
620	239	246	253	260	267	274	281	288	295	302
621	309	316	323	330	337	344	351	358	365	372
622	379	386	393	400	407	414	421	428	435	442
623	449	456	463	470	477	484	491	498	505	511
624	518	525	532	539	546	553	560	567	574	581
625	588	595	602	609	616	623	630	637	644	650
626	657	664	671	678	685	692	699	706	713	720
627	727	734	741	748	754	761	768	775	782	789
628	796	803	810	817	824	831	837	844	851	858
629	865	872	879	886	893	900	906	913	920	927
630	934	941	948	955	962	969	975	982	989	996
631	80 003	010	017	024	030	037	044	051	058	065
632	072	079	085	092	099	106	113	120	127	134
633	140	147	154	161	168	175	182	188	195	202
634	209	216	223	229	236	243	250	257	264	271
635	277	284	291	298	305	312	318	325	332	339
636	346	353	359	366	373	380	387	393	400	407
637	414	421	428	434	441	448	455	462	468	475
638	482	489	496	502	509	516	523	530	536	543
639	550	557	564	570	577	584	591	598	604	611
640	618	625	632	638	645	652	659	665	672	679
641	686	693	699	706	713	720	726	733	740	747
642	754	760	767	774	781	787	794	801	808	814
643	821	828	835	841	848	855	862	868	875	882
644	889	895	902	909	916	922	929	936	943	949
645	956	963	969	976	983	990	996	*003	*010	*017
646	81 023	030	037	043	050	057	064	070	077	084
647	090	097	104	111	117	124	131	137	144	151
648	158	164	171	178	184	191	198	204	211	218
649	224	231	238	245	251	258	265	271	278	285
650	291	298	305	311	318	325	331	338	345	351

N.	0	1	2	3	4	5	6	7	8	9

Proportional parts

	8
1	0.8
2	1.6
3	2.4
4	3.2
5	4.0
6	4.8
7	5.6
8	6.4
9	7.2

	7
1	0.7
2	1.4
3	2.1
4	2.8
5	3.5
6	4.2
7	4.9
8	5.6
9	6.3

	6
1	0.6
2	1.2
3	1.8
4	2.4
5	3.0
6	3.6
7	4.2
8	4.8
9	5.4

TABLE 21 (continued)

Five-place logarithms (continued)

N.	0	1	2	3	4	5	6	7	8	9	Proportional parts
650	81 291	298	305	311	318	325	331	338	345	351	
651	358	365	371	378	385	391	398	405	411	418	
652	425	431	438	445	451	458	465	471	478	485	
653	491	498	505	511	518	525	531	538	544	551	
654	558	564	571	578	584	591	598	604	611	617	
655	624	631	637	644	651	657	664	671	677	684	
656	690	697	704	710	717	723	730	737	743	750	
657	757	763	770	776	783	790	796	803	809	816	
658	823	829	836	842	849	856	862	869	875	882	
659	889	895	902	908	915	921	928	935	941	948	
660	954	961	968	974	981	987	994	*000	*007	*014	**7**
661	82 020	027	033	040	046	053	060	066	073	079	1 0.7
662	086	092	099	105	112	119	125	132	138	145	2 1.4
663	151	158	164	171	178	184	191	197	204	210	3 2.1
664	217	223	230	236	243	249	256	263	269	276	4 2.8
											5 3.5
665	282	289	295	302	308	315	321	328	334	341	6 4.2
666	347	354	360	367	373	380	387	393	400	406	7 4.9
667	413	419	426	432	439	445	452	458	465	471	8 5.6
668	478	484	491	497	504	510	517	523	530	536	9 6.3
669	543	549	556	562	569	575	582	588	595	601	
670	607	614	620	627	633	640	646	653	659	666	
671	672	679	685	692	698	705	711	718	724	730	
672	737	743	750	756	763	769	776	782	789	795	
673	802	808	814	821	827	834	840	847	853	860	
674	866	872	879	885	892	898	905	911	918	924	
675	930	937	943	950	956	963	969	975	982	988	
676	995	*001	*008	*014	*020	*027	*033	*040	*046	*052	
677	83 059	065	072	078	085	091	097	104	110	117	
678	123	129	136	142	149	155	161	168	174	181	
679	187	193	200	206	213	219	225	232	238	245	
680	251	257	264	270	276	283	289	296	302	308	**6**
681	315	321	327	334	340	347	353	359	366	372	1 0.6
682	378	385	391	398	404	410	417	423	429	436	2 1.2
683	442	448	455	461	467	474	480	487	493	499	3 1.8
684	506	512	518	525	531	537	544	550	556	563	4 2.4
											5 3.0
685	569	575	582	588	594	601	607	613	620	626	6 3.6
686	632	639	645	651	658	664	670	677	683	689	7 4.2
687	696	702	708	715	721	727	734	740	746	753	8 4.8
688	759	765	771	778	784	790	797	803	809	816	9 5.4
689	822	828	835	841	847	853	860	866	872	879	
690	885	891	897	904	910	916	923	929	935	942	
691	948	954	960	967	973	979	985	992	998	*004	
692	84 011	017	023	029	036	042	048	055	061	067	
693	073	080	086	092	098	105	111	117	123	130	
694	136	142	148	155	161	167	173	180	186	192	
695	198	205	211	217	223	230	236	242	248	255	
696	261	267	273	280	286	292	298	305	311	317	
697	323	330	336	342	348	354	361	367	373	379	
698	386	392	398	404	410	417	423	429	435	442	
699	448	454	460	466	473	479	485	491	497	504	
700	510	516	522	528	535	541	547	553	559	566	

N.	0	1	2	3	4	5	6	7	8	9	Proportional parts

TABLE   21   (continued)

Five-place logarithms (continued)

N.	0	1	2	3	4	5	6	7	8	9	Proportional parts
700	84 510	516	522	528	535	541	547	553	559	566	
701	572	578	584	590	597	603	609	615	621	628	
702	634	640	646	652	658	665	671	677	683	689	
703	696	702	708	714	720	726	733	739	745	751	
704	757	763	770	776	782	788	794	800	807	813	
705	819	825	831	837	844	850	856	862	868	874	
706	880	887	893	899	905	911	917	924	930	936	
707	942	948	954	960	967	973	979	985	991	997	**7**
708	85 003	009	016	022	028	034	040	046	052	058	1 0.7
709	065	071	077	083	089	095	101	107	114	120	2 1.4
											3 2.1
710	126	132	138	144	150	156	163	169	175	181	4 2.8
711	187	193	199	205	211	217	224	230	236	242	5 3.5
712	248	254	260	266	272	278	285	291	297	303	6 4.2
713	309	315	321	327	333	339	345	352	358	364	7 4.9
714	370	376	382	388	394	400	406	412	418	425	8 5.6
											9 6.3
715	431	437	443	449	455	461	467	473	479	485	
716	491	497	503	509	516	522	528	534	540	546	
717	552	558	564	570	576	582	588	594	600	606	
718	612	618	625	631	637	643	649	655	661	667	
719	673	679	685	691	697	703	709	715	721	727	
720	733	739	745	751	757	763	769	775	781	788	
721	794	800	806	812	818	824	830	836	842	848	**6**
722	854	860	866	872	878	884	890	896	902	908	1 0.6
723	914	920	926	932	938	944	950	956	962	968	2 1.2
724	974	980	986	992	998	*004	*010	*016	*022	*028	3 1.8
											4 2.4
725	86 034	040	046	052	058	064	070	076	082	088	5 3.0
726	094	100	106	112	118	124	130	136	141	147	6 3.6
727	153	159	165	171	177	183	189	195	201	207	7 4.2
728	213	219	225	231	237	243	249	255	261	267	8 4.8
729	273	279	285	291	297	303	308	314	320	326	9 5.4
730	332	338	344	350	356	362	368	374	380	386	
731	392	398	404	410	415	421	427	433	439	445	
732	451	457	463	469	475	481	487	493	499	504	
733	510	516	522	528	534	540	546	552	558	564	
734	570	576	581	587	593	599	605	611	617	623	
735	629	635	641	646	652	658	664	670	676	682	**5**
736	688	694	700	705	711	717	723	729	735	741	1 0.5
737	747	753	759	764	770	776	782	788	794	800	2 1.0
738	806	812	817	823	829	835	841	847	853	859	3 1.5
739	864	870	876	882	888	894	900	906	911	917	4 2.0
											5 2.5
740	923	929	935	941	947	953	958	964	970	976	6 3.0
741	982	988	994	999	*005	*011	*017	*023	*029	*035	7 3.5
742	87 040	046	052	058	064	070	075	081	087	093	8 4.0
743	099	105	111	116	122	128	134	140	146	151	9 4.5
744	157	163	169	175	181	186	192	198	204	210	
745	216	221	227	233	239	245	251	256	262	268	
746	274	280	286	291	297	303	309	315	320	326	
747	332	338	344	349	355	361	367	373	379	384	
748	390	396	402	408	413	419	425	431	437	442	
749	448	454	460	466	471	477	483	489	495	500	
750	506	512	518	523	529	535	541	547	552	558	
N.	0	1	2	3	4	5	6	7	8	9	Proportional parts

TABLE 21 (continued)

Five-place logarithms (continued)

N.	0	1	2	3	4	5	6	7	8	9	Proportional parts
750	87 506	512	518	523	529	535	541	547	552	558	
751	564	570	576	581	587	593	599	604	610	616	
752	622	628	633	639	645	651	656	662	668	674	
753	679	685	691	697	703	708	714	720	726	731	
754	737	743	749	754	760	766	772	777	783	789	
755	795	800	806	812	818	823	829	835	841	846	
756	852	858	864	869	875	881	887	892	898	904	
757	910	915	921	927	933	938	944	950	955	961	
758	967	973	978	984	990	996	*001	*007	*013	*018	
759	88 024	030	036	041	047	053	058	064	070	076	
760	081	087	093	098	104	110	116	121	127	133	**6**
761	138	144	150	156	161	167	173	178	184	190	1 0.6
762	195	201	207	213	218	224	230	235	241	247	2 1.2
763	252	258	264	270	275	281	287	292	298	304	3 1.8
764	309	315	321	326	332	338	343	349	355	360	4 2.4
											5 3.0
765	366	372	377	383	389	395	400	406	412	417	6 3.6
766	423	429	434	440	446	451	457	463	468	474	7 4.2
767	480	485	491	497	502	508	513	519	525	530	8 4.8
768	536	542	547	553	559	564	570	576	581	587	9 5.4
769	593	598	604	610	615	621	627	632	638	643	
770	649	655	660	666	672	677	683	689	694	700	
771	705	711	717	722	728	734	739	745	750	756	
772	762	767	773	779	784	790	795	801	807	812	
773	818	824	829	835	840	846	852	857	863	868	
774	874	880	885	891	897	902	908	913	919	925	
775	930	936	941	947	953	958	964	969	975	981	
776	986	992	997	*003	*009	*014	*020	*025	*031	*037	
777	89 042	048	053	059	064	070	076	081	087	092	
778	098	104	109	115	120	126	131	137	143	148	
779	154	159	165	170	176	182	187	193	198	204	
780	209	215	221	226	232	237	243	248	254	260	**5**
781	265	271	276	282	287	293	298	304	310	315	1 0.5
782	321	326	332	337	343	348	354	360	365	371	2 1.0
783	376	382	387	393	398	404	409	415	421	426	3 1.5
784	432	437	443	448	454	459	465	470	476	481	4 2.0
											5 2.5
785	487	492	498	504	509	515	520	526	531	537	6 3.0
786	542	548	553	559	564	570	575	581	586	592	7 3.5
787	597	603	609	614	620	625	631	636	642	647	8 4.0
788	653	658	664	669	675	680	686	691	697	702	9 4.5
789	708	713	719	724	730	735	741	746	752	757	
790	763	768	774	779	785	790	796	801	807	812	
791	818	823	829	834	840	845	851	856	862	867	
792	873	878	883	889	894	900	905	911	916	922	
793	927	933	938	944	949	955	960	966	971	977	
794	982	988	993	998	*004	*009	*015	*020	*026	*031	
795	90 037	042	048	053	059	064	069	075	080	086	
796	091	097	102	108	113	119	124	129	135	140	
797	146	151	157	162	168	173	179	184	189	195	
798	200	206	211	217	222	227	233	238	244	249	
799	255	260	266	271	276	282	287	293	298	304	
800	309	314	320	325	331	336	342	347	352	358	
N.	0	1	2	3	4	5	6	7	8	9	Proportional parts

TABLE   21   (continued)

Five-place logarithms (continued)

N.	0	1	2	3	4	5	6	7	8	9	Proportional parts
800	90 309	314	320	325	331	336	342	347	352	358	
801	363	369	374	380	385	390	396	401	407	412	
802	417	423	428	434	439	445	450	455	461	466	
803	472	477	482	488	493	499	504	509	515	520	
804	526	531	536	542	547	553	558	563	569	574	
805	580	585	590	596	601	607	612	617	623	628	
806	634	639	644	650	655	660	666	671	677	682	
807	687	693	698	703	709	714	720	725	730	736	
808	741	747	752	757	763	768	773	779	784	789	
809	795	800	806	811	816	822	827	832	838	843	
810	849	854	859	865	870	875	881	886	891	897	**6**
811	902	907	913	918	924	929	934	940	945	950	1 0.6
812	956	961	966	972	977	982	988	993	998	*004	2 1.2
813	91 009	014	020	025	030	036	041	046	052	057	3 1.8
814	062	068	073	078	084	089	094	100	105	110	4 2.4
											5 3.0
815	116	121	126	132	137	142	148	153	158	164	6 3.6
816	169	174	180	185	190	196	201	206	212	217	7 4.2
817	222	228	233	238	243	249	254	259	265	270	8 4.8
818	275	281	286	291	297	302	307	312	318	323	9 5.4
819	328	334	339	344	350	355	360	365	371	376	
820	381	387	392	397	403	408	413	418	424	429	
821	434	440	445	450	455	461	466	471	477	482	
822	487	492	498	503	508	514	519	524	529	535	
823	540	545	551	556	561	566	572	577	582	587	
824	593	598	603	609	614	619	624	630	635	640	
825	645	651	656	661	666	672	677	682	687	693	
826	698	703	709	714	719	724	730	735	740	745	
827	751	756	761	766	772	777	782	787	793	798	
828	803	808	814	819	824	829	834	840	845	850	
829	855	861	866	871	876	882	887	892	897	903	
830	908	913	918	924	929	934	939	944	950	955	**5**
831	960	965	971	976	981	986	991	997	*002	*007	1 0.5
832	92 012	018	023	028	033	038	044	049	054	059	2 1.0
833	065	070	075	080	085	091	096	101	106	111	3 1.5
834	117	122	127	132	137	143	148	153	158	163	4 2.0
											5 2.5
835	169	174	179	184	189	195	200	205	210	215	6 3.0
836	221	226	231	236	241	247	252	257	262	267	7 3.5
837	273	278	283	288	293	298	304	309	314	319	8 4.0
838	324	330	335	340	345	350	355	361	366	371	9 4.5
839	376	381	387	392	397	402	407	412	418	423	
840	428	433	438	443	449	454	459	464	469	474	
841	480	485	490	495	500	505	511	516	521	526	
842	531	536	542	547	552	557	562	567	572	578	
843	583	588	593	598	603	609	614	619	624	629	
844	634	639	645	650	655	660	665	670	675	681	
845	686	691	696	701	706	711	716	722	727	732	
846	737	742	747	752	758	763	768	773	778	783	
847	788	793	799	804	809	814	819	824	829	834	
848	840	845	850	855	860	865	870	875	881	886	
849	891	896	901	906	911	916	921	927	932	937	
850	942	947	952	957	962	967	973	978	983	988	
N.	0	1	2	3	4	5	6	7	8	9	Proportional parts

TABLE 21 (continued)

Five-place logarithms (continued)

N.	0	1	2	3	4	5	6	7	8	9	Proportional parts
850	92 942	947	952	957	962	967	973	978	983	988	
851	993	998	*003	*008	*013	*018	*024	*029	*034	*039	
852	93 044	049	054	059	064	069	075	080	085	090	
853	095	100	105	110	115	120	125	131	136	141	
854	146	151	156	161	166	171	176	181	186	192	
855	197	202	207	212	217	222	227	232	237	242	
856	247	252	258	263	268	273	278	283	288	293	**6**
857	298	303	308	313	318	323	328	334	339	344	1 0.6
858	349	354	359	364	369	374	379	384	389	394	2 1.2
859	399	404	409	414	420	425	430	435	440	445	3 1.8
											4 2.4
860	450	455	460	465	470	475	480	485	490	495	5 3.0
861	500	505	510	515	520	526	531	536	541	546	6 3.6
862	551	556	561	566	571	576	581	586	591	596	7 4.2
863	601	606	611	616	621	626	631	636	641	646	8 4.8
864	651	656	661	666	671	676	682	687	692	697	9 5.4
865	702	707	712	717	722	727	732	737	742	747	
866	752	757	762	767	772	777	782	787	792	797	
867	802	807	812	817	822	827	832	837	842	847	
868	852	857	862	867	872	877	882	887	892	897	
869	902	907	912	917	922	927	932	937	942	947	
870	952	957	962	967	972	977	982	987	992	997	**5**
871	94 002	007	012	017	022	027	032	037	042	047	1 0.5
872	052	057	062	067	072	077	082	086	091	096	2 1.0
873	101	106	111	116	121	126	131	136	141	146	3 1.5
874	151	156	161	166	171	176	181	186	191	196	4 2.0
											5 2.5
875	201	206	211	216	221	226	231	236	240	245	6 3.0
876	250	255	260	265	270	275	280	285	290	295	7 3.5
877	300	305	310	315	320	325	330	335	340	345	8 4.0
878	349	354	359	364	369	374	379	384	389	394	9 4.5
879	399	404	409	414	419	424	429	433	438	443	
880	448	453	458	463	468	473	478	483	488	493	
881	498	503	507	512	517	522	527	532	537	542	
882	547	552	557	562	567	571	576	581	586	591	
883	596	601	606	611	616	621	626	630	635	640	
884	645	650	655	660	665	670	675	680	685	689	
885	694	699	704	709	714	719	724	729	734	738	**4**
886	743	748	753	758	763	768	773	778	783	787	1 0.4
887	792	797	802	807	812	817	822	827	832	836	2 0.8
888	841	846	851	856	861	866	871	876	880	885	3 1.2
889	890	895	900	905	910	915	919	924	929	934	4 1.6
											5 2.0
890	939	944	949	954	959	963	968	973	978	983	6 2.4
891	988	993	998	*002	*007	*012	*017	*022	*027	*032	7 2.8
892	95 036	041	046	051	056	061	066	071	075	080	8 3.2
893	085	090	095	100	105	109	114	119	124	129	9 3.6
894	134	139	143	148	153	158	163	168	173	177	
895	182	187	192	197	202	207	211	216	221	226	
896	231	236	240	245	250	255	260	265	270	274	
897	279	284	289	294	299	303	308	313	318	323	
898	328	332	337	342	347	352	357	361	366	371	
899	376	381	386	390	395	400	405	410	415	419	
900	424	429	434	439	444	448	453	458	463	468	
N.	0	1	2	3	4	5	6	7	8	9	Proportional parts

TABLE 21 (continued)

Five-place logarithms (continued)

N.	0	1	2	3	4	5	6	7	8	9	Proportional parts
900	95 424	429	434	439	444	448	453	458	463	468	
901	472	477	482	487	492	497	501	506	511	516	
902	521	525	530	535	540	545	550	554	559	564	
903	569	574	578	583	588	593	598	602	607	612	
904	617	622	626	631	636	641	646	650	655	660	
905	665	670	674	679	684	689	694	698	703	708	
906	713	718	722	727	732	737	742	746	751	756	
907	761	766	770	775	780	785	789	794	799	804	
908	809	813	818	823	828	832	837	842	847	852	
909	856	861	866	871	875	880	885	890	895	899	
910	904	909	914	918	923	928	933	938	942	947	**5**
911	952	957	961	966	971	976	980	985	990	995	1 0.5
912	999	*004	*009	*014	*019	*023	*028	*033	*038	*042	2 1.0
913	96 047	052	057	061	066	071	076	080	085	090	3 1.5
914	095	099	104	109	114	118	123	128	133	137	4 2.0
											5 2.5
915	142	147	152	156	161	166	171	175	180	185	6 3.0
916	190	194	199	204	209	213	218	223	227	232	7 3.5
917	237	242	246	251	256	261	265	270	275	280	8 4.0
918	284	289	294	298	303	308	313	317	322	327	9 4.5
919	332	336	341	346	350	355	360	365	369	374	
920	379	384	388	393	398	402	407	412	417	421	
921	426	431	435	440	445	450	454	459	464	468	
922	473	478	483	487	492	497	501	506	511	515	
923	520	525	530	534	539	544	548	553	558	562	
924	567	572	577	581	586	591	595	600	605	609	
925	614	619	624	628	633	638	642	647	652	656	
926	661	666	670	675	680	685	689	694	699	703	
927	708	713	717	722	727	731	736	741	745	750	
928	755	759	764	769	774	778	783	788	792	797	
929	802	806	811	816	820	825	830	834	839	844	
930	848	853	858	862	867	872	876	881	886	890	**4**
931	895	900	904	909	914	918	923	928	932	937	1 0.4
932	942	946	951	956	960	965	970	974	979	*984	2 0.8
933	988	993	997	*002	*007	*011	*016	*021	*025	*030	3 1.2
934	97 035	039	044	049	053	058	063	067	072	077	4 1.6
											5 2.0
935	081	086	090	095	100	104	109	114	118	123	6 2.4
936	128	132	137	142	146	151	155	160	165	169	7 2.8
937	174	179	183	188	192	197	202	206	211	216	8 3.2
938	220	225	230	234	239	243	248	253	257	262	9 3.6
939	267	271	276	280	285	290	294	299	304	308	
940	313	317	322	327	331	336	340	345	350	354	
941	359	364	368	373	377	382	387	391	396	400	
942	405	410	414	419	424	428	433	437	442	447	
943	451	456	460	465	470	474	479	483	488	493	
944	497	502	506	511	516	520	525	529	534	539	
945	543	548	552	557	562	566	571	575	580	585	
946	589	594	598	603	607	612	617	621	626	630	
947	635	640	644	649	653	658	663	667	672	676	
948	681	685	690	695	699	704	708	713	717	722	
949	727	731	736	740	745	749	754	759	763	768	
950	772	777	782	786	791	795	800	804	809	813	
N.	0	1	2	3	4	5	6	7	8	9	Proportional parts

TABLE 21 (continued)

Five-place logarithms (continued)

N.	0	1	2	3	4	5	6	7	8	9	Proportional parts
950	97 772	777	782	786	791	795	800	804	809	813	
951	818	823	827	832	836	841	845	850	855	859	
952	864	868	873	877	882	886	891	896	900	905	
953	909	914	918	923	928	932	937	941	946	950	
954	955	959	964	968	973	978	982	987	991	996	
955	98 000	005	009	014	019	023	028	032	037	041	
956	046	050	055	059	064	068	073	078	082	087	
957	091	096	100	105	109	114	118	123	127	132	
958	137	141	146	150	155	159	164	168	173	177	
959	182	186	191	195	200	204	209	214	218	223	
960	227	232	236	241	245	250	254	259	263	268	**5**
961	272	277	281	286	290	295	299	304	308	313	1 0.5
962	318	322	327	331	336	340	345	349	354	358	2 1.0
963	363	367	372	376	381	385	390	394	399	403	3 1.5
964	408	412	417	421	426	430	435	439	444	448	4 2.0
											5 2.5
965	453	457	462	466	471	475	480	484	489	493	6 3.0
966	498	502	507	511	516	520	525	529	534	538	7 3.5
967	543	547	552	556	561	565	570	574	579	583	8 4.0
968	588	592	597	601	605	610	614	619	623	628	9 4.5
969	632	637	641	646	650	655	659	664	668	673	
970	677	682	686	691	695	700	704	709	713	717	
971	722	726	731	735	740	744	749	753	758	762	
972	767	771	776	780	784	789	793	798	802	807	
973	811	816	820	825	829	834	838	843	847	851	
974	856	860	865	869	874	878	883	887	892	896	
975	000	905	909	914	918	923	927	932	936	941	
976	945	949	954	958	963	967	972	976	981	985	
977	989	994	998	*003	*007	*012	*016	*021	*025	*029	
978	99 034	038	043	047	052	056	061	065	069	074	
979	078	083	087	092	096	100	105	109	114	118	
980	123	127	131	136	140	145	149	154	158	162	**4**
981	167	171	176	180	185	189	193	198	202	207	1 0.4
982	211	216	220	224	229	233	238	242	247	251	2 0.8
983	255	260	264	269	273	277	282	286	291	295	3 1.2
984	300	304	308	313	317	322	326	330	335	339	4 1.6
											5 2.0
985	344	348	352	357	361	366	370	374	379	383	6 2.4
986	388	392	396	401	405	410	414	419	423	427	7 2.8
987	432	436	441	445	449	454	458	463	467	471	8 3.2
988	476	480	484	489	493	498	502	506	511	515	9 3.6
989	520	524	528	533	537	542	546	550	555	559	
990	564	568	572	577	581	585	590	594	599	603	
991	607	612	616	621	625	629	634	638	642	647	
992	651	656	660	664	669	673	677	682	686	691	
993	695	699	704	708	712	717	721	726	730	734	
994	739	743	747	752	756	760	765	769	774	778	
995	782	787	791	795	800	804	808	813	817	822	
996	826	830	835	839	843	848	852	856	861	865	
997	870	874	878	883	887	891	896	900	904	909	
998	913	917	922	926	930	935	939	944	948	952	
999	957	961	965	970	974	978	983	987	991	996	
1000	00 000	004	009	013	017	022	026	030	035	039	

N.	0	1	2	3	4	5	6	7	8	9	Proportional parts

Appendix 3

Loan repayments

The truth in lending act passed by Congress has required lenders, in most instances, to disclose the annual percentage rate that the borrower is charged. The annual percentage rate is equivalent to the annual compound interest rate that the borrower will pay by repaying the loan in the manner agreed upon.

Loan repayment methods take various forms including: real estate first mortgage loans; add-on loans; discount notes; open notes, interest paid at maturity; and add-on installment repayment loans. All these forms are discussed within this appendix.

Form 1. Real estate first mortgage loan.[1]
Borrow a sum A and repay it in n annual installments of R each. This is typical of the real estate first mortgage loans described in Example 1, Chapter 5. The mortgage loan A is $20,000. Annual interest i is 6% compound with repayment by 20 annual installments n. To find the annual repayment required R the formula is:

$$R = A \left[\frac{i}{1 - (1 + i)^{-n}} \right].$$

---

[1] See Graph 8, Mortgage loan repayments, and Graph 50, Installment loan repayment.

The value of $\dfrac{i}{1 - (1 + i)^{-n}}$ is given in Appendix 1.

This factor is frequently referred to in real estate circles as the *annual constant*. The solution then is:

$$R = 20,000 \left[\frac{.06}{1 - (1.06)^{-20}}\right]$$
$$= 20,000\,[.087184] = \$1,743.68.$$

Where the amount to be calculated is the sum which can be borrowed, A, with such borrowing to be repaid by regular fixed repayments of a specified amount, R, over a period of n regular payments including a rate of annual compound interest of i, then the formula is:

$$A = R\left[\frac{1 - (1 + i)^{-n}}{i}\right].$$

Applying this formula to Example 2 of Chapter 5 where the problem is to determine the amount, A, which one can borrow today, providing \$3,000 annual repayments (R) are to be made for 22 years, n, at annual compound interest of 8%, i, on the unpaid balance.

$$A = 3,000 \left[\frac{1 - (1 + i)^{-n}}{i}\right]$$
$$= 3,000 \left[\frac{1 - (1.08)^{-22}}{.08}\right]$$
$$= 3,000\,(10.200743)$$
$$= 30,602.23$$

The amount the borrower can obtain today is \$30,-602.23.[2]

Form 2.   Add-on loan (also referred to as a discount loan).

In this type of loan, the lender starts with the sum

---

[2] See Appendix 6 for a discussion of mortgage "points."

that the borrower will receive (P) in cash, e.g., $10,000. To this is added interest (I) on the $10,000 at the discount, or add-on rate, e.g., 10% (i) for 90 days, t, ...

$$I = P(it)$$
$$= 10,000 \times 0.1 \times \frac{90}{365}$$
$$= \$246.58$$

Then interest on the interest is calculated and added.

$$246.58 \times 0.1 \times \frac{90}{365} = \$6.08$$

The borrower then signs a note for $10,252.58, determined as follows:

Cash received by borrower..........	$10,000.00
Interest on $10,000.................	246.58
Interest on $246.58................	6.08
Total, Face Amount of note.......	$10,252.66

Thus, the borrower receives $10,000 and pays back $10,252.66 after 90 days. The true annual compound interest rate on such a loan is:[3]

$$S = P(1 + i)^n,$$

and

$$(1 + i)^n = \frac{S}{P}$$
$$(1 + i)^{90/365} = 1.0253$$
$$\frac{90}{365} \log(1 + i) = \log 1.0253$$

---

[3] In actual banking practice, this type loan would probably be repaid over a longer period of time and by monthly installments. It is similar to the "discount installment loan" described later in this chapter. Banking practice varies as to whether 360 days or 365 days are utilized as constituting a year.

$$\log(1 + i) = \frac{365 \log 1.0253}{90}$$
$$\log(1 + i) = 4.0555 \, (0.01083) = 0.04392$$
$$(1 + i) = 1.1064$$
$$i = .1064, \text{ i.e., } 10.64\%.$$

So, the true annual interest rate is really 10.64% for a 90 day 10% add-on loan (sometimes called a 10% discount loan).

Form 3. Discount Note.

A borrower signs a note for $10,000 on a 10% discount loan repayable 2 years later. The lender computes 2 years interest at 10% per year, total 20%; multiplies this times the note face amount of $10,000 to obtain $2,000 in interest. The $2,000 interest is deducted from the $10,000 note face, S, and the borrower receives the difference of $8,000 in cash, P. What is the true annual compound interest rate i?

$$S = P(1 + i)^n \text{ and } (1 + i)^n = \frac{S}{P}$$

$$n \log(1 + i) = \log\left[\frac{10,000}{8,000}\right] = \log 1.25$$

$$\log(1 + i) = \frac{\log 1.25}{2}$$

$$\log(1 + i) = 0.04845$$

$$(1 + i) = 1.118$$

$$i = 11.8\%$$

The true annual interest rate is 11.8% for this 2 year 10% discount loan.[4]

---

[4] In banking practice, this type loan would probably be for a short duration; i.e., 90 days. Alternatively, this type loan might be calculated as follows: The borrower desires $8,000 cash for 90 days. The bank charges a rate of 10% discount (i.e., 2.5% for 90 days). 100% − 2.5% = 97.5%. $8,000 + .975 = $8,250.13. The note which the borrower must sign and the amount which he must repay at the expiration of 90 days is 8,205.13.

Form 4. Open note, interest paid at maturity.
A borrower obtains $10,000 in cash and agrees to re-
pay $10,000 plus interest of $1,000 at 10% 1 year
later. In this case, the stated interest rate of 10% is
the true annual percentage.

$$S = P(1 + i)^n$$
$$11,000 = 10,000(1 + i)^1$$
$$1.1 = (1 + i)^1$$
$$i = .1 \text{ or } 10\%$$

Form 5 Add-on installment repayment loan.
The borrower needs $10,000 cash which he obtains by
agreeing to repay principal and interest computed by
the lender as follows:

Amount of cash loaned................... $10,000 ($A$)
Interest............................... 6% add-on
Number of years over which note is
   repaid in equal annual amounts........ 5 years*
Number of repayments.................. 5
Interest (6%) × years (5)............. 30%
Total interest = 10,000 × 30%........ $3,000
Note signed by borrower.............. $13,000 (10,000 + 3,000)
Annual repayment, 13,000 divided
   by 5, i.e.,......................... $2,600 ($R$)

The true cost of the 6% add-on installment repayment loan can be computed approximately, but quickly,
as follows:

$$A = R \left[\frac{1 - (1 + i)^{-n}}{i} \right]$$

$$\left[\frac{1 - (1 + i)^{-5}}{i} \right] = 3.8461$$

*This type loan would normally be repaid in monthly rather than an-
nual installments. A monthly repayment loan is described later in this
chapter.

Checking Appendix 1 tables under the column "What $1 payable periodically is worth today" on the line for 5 periods, we find that the factor we seek, 3.8461, lies between 9% and 10%. The value of $\left[\dfrac{1 - (1 + i)^{-5}}{i}\right]$ for 9%, is 3.889151 and for 10% is 3.790786.

Then, the interest rate is approximately 9.44%, which is obtained by interpolation. This may be checked by applying the formula:

$$A = R\left[\frac{1 - (1 + i)^{-n}}{i}\right]$$

$$= 2{,}600\left[\frac{1 - (1.0944)^{-5}}{.0944}\right]$$

$$A = 10{,}000.63.$$

Note that the true rate of 9.44% is much higher than is implied simply by the phrase 6% add-on.

The relationship between the annual percentage rate and the quoted add-on installment repayment rate is not fixed. It varies according to the level of rate and number of repayments and time involved. One can obtain an idea of this varying relationship from the following table.

Number of repayments	Add-on rate	True annual compound rate*
1	10.00%	10%
2	7.62	10
3	6.87	10
4	6.55	10
5	6.37	10

*Monthly rate multiplied by 12 months.

Number of repayments	Add-on rate	Approximate true annual compound rate
36............	3%	5⅝%
36............	4	7½
36............	5	9
36............	6	11⅛
36............	7	12¾
36............	8	14¼

Any add-on rate, discount rate, and so on must be converted to a true annual compound rate of interest in order that a borrower or lender or investor may understand the true cost or profitability of a loan or investment. Add-on rates are used by banks and financing and other firms in conjunction with installment repayment terms.

EXAMPLE:

Assume that a borrower wishes to buy a boat for $1,000 and to borrow the entire sum. The annual percentage rate that he will pay will depend on various factors including the current money market and his financial condition, age, and so on. Assume that the applicable annual percentage rate is 15%. He can afford to pay monthly installments of $62.50 to retire the debt. How many monthly payments will he be required to make?

Refer to Graph 50, "Installment loan repayments." The point at which the line extended vertically from 6.25% meets the line extended horizontally from 15% annual percentage rate determines the solution. See the dashed lines on Graph 50. 18 monthly payments would be required.

194

GRAPH 50

Installment loan repayments—12 to 60 monthly repayments

Annual percentage rate

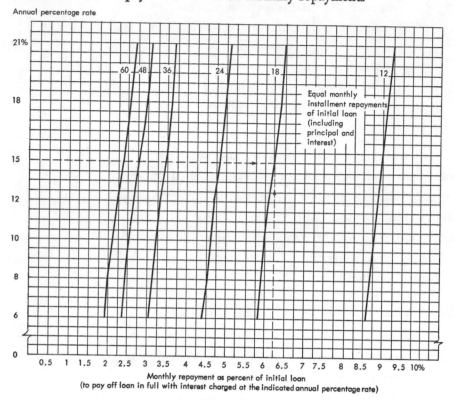

Monthly repayment as percent of initial loan
(to pay off loan in full with interest charged at the indicated annual percentage rate)

EXAMPLE:

A lender is willing to provide a loan of $1,000 and requires 36 equal monthly repayments and charges a 10% annual percentage rate. How much will the monthly payments be to repay the loan? Enter the graph at 10% annual rate, move horizontally to the curve for 36 monthly repayments, then move vertically down. About 3.25% of the original loan; i.e., $35 per month will be required.

This problem may also be solved by formula, as follows:

R = the required monthly payment
A = original loan amount (e.g., \$1,000)
n = number of monthly repayments (e.g., 36)
i = MONTHLY percentage rate (10% divided by 12 = 5/6% per month)

The formula is

$$R = A\left[\frac{i}{1-(1+i)^{-n}}\right]$$

The factor $\dfrac{i}{1-(1+i)^{-n}}$ *for 5/6% per month is* not shown in Tables 1 to 14. However *10% per year* is shown. An approximate answer using Table 12 can be obtained based on 10% *per year* and three *ANNUAL* installment repayments, as follows:

$$R = 1,000\,(.4021) = \$402.10 \text{ per year}$$

The approximate monthly payment is: \$402.10 divided by 12 = \$33.51.

A more accurate solution is:

$$R = A\left[\frac{i}{1-(1+i)^{-n}}\right]^*$$

$$= 1,000\left[\frac{.008333}{1-(1.00833)^{-36}}\right]$$

$$= 1,000\left[\frac{.008333}{1-\dfrac{1}{1.00833^{36}}}\right]$$

$$= 1,000\left[\frac{.008333}{1-\dfrac{1}{1.3366}}\right]^\dagger$$

$$= 1,000\left[\frac{.008333}{.251834}\right]$$

$$= \$33.09 \text{ per month for 36 months}$$

---
* 5/6% per month = .008333
† log 1.008333^{36} = 36 log 1.00833 = 36 × 0.00350 = 0.12600 Antilog 0.126 = 1.3366.

**Add-on
installment
loan**

A borrower obtains $1,000 at 6% add-on repayable in 36 equal installments (n). Computation of the amount of note and monthly repayment amount is shown below.

    a. Cash to borrower—$1,000 ($A$)
    b. 6% × 3 years = 18% add-on
    c. Add-on interest = $180 (18% × $1,000)
    d. Note is for $1,180 ($1,000 + $180)
    e. Monthly repayments are $32.78 ($R$) ($1,180.00 ÷ 36 months).

The annual percentage rate is: Using Graph 50—11.1%.

Using formulas:

$$A = R \left[\frac{1 - (1 + i)^{-n}}{i} \right]$$

$$1,000 = 32.78 \left[\frac{1 - (1 + i)^{-36}}{i} \right]$$

$$\frac{1 - (1 + i)^{-36}}{i} = 30.5064$$

Using Table 2 (36 months), the factor

$$\left[\frac{1 - (1 + 1\%)^{-36}}{0.01} \right]$$

for 1% per month is 30.1075.
And Table 1 for ½% shows—32.8710 as the factor. Our number lies between the two, and thus is between ½% and 1% per month.

Interpolation provides the solution:

½% — 32.8710	30.5064	32.8710
x — 30.5064	−30.1075	−30.1075
1% — 30.1075	0.3989	2.7635

$$\frac{.3989}{2.7635} = \frac{x}{.5} \text{ and } x = .0721$$

$$x = 1.0000 \text{ less } 0.0721 = 0.9279\% \text{ per month}$$

$$0.9279\% \times 12 = 11.1348\% \text{ per year}$$

This is the annual percentage rate for the above loan.

Continuing the example above ($1,000 cash received, 36 monthly payments of $32.78, annual percentage rate about 11.1%). If the borrower wishes to repay his loan in full after having made, let us say, 12 of the 36 payments, what will be the circumstances? That is, how much will he be required to pay and how much true interest cost will be involved?

Banks use a "sum-of-the-digits" system to determine how much they will retain of the interest initially calculated. The interest initially calculated was $180. The "sum-of-the-digits" of the 36 monthly installments is:

Prepaying an installment loan

$$36 + 35 + 34 + 33 + \ldots + 1.$$

This sum is 666.

The "sum-of-the-digits" formula is:

$$\left[\frac{n+1}{2} \right] \times N$$

Where N = the number of payments.

$$\left[\frac{36+1}{2} \right] \times \left[36 \right] = \underline{666}$$

Twelve installment payments have been made. To determine the portion of the $180 interest that is unearned by the bank (and is to be credited to the borrower) as the result of the prepayment of the loan, deduct 12 (payments made, or months elapsed) from the 36-month term; i.e., 24.

Let U = months for which interest unearned = 24.

Then, determine the sum-of-the-digits for U; i.e., $24 + 23 \ldots + 1$.

$$\left[\frac{U+1}{2}\right](U) = \left[\frac{24+1}{2}\right] \times (24) - 300.$$

Unearned interest $= \dfrac{300}{666} \times 180 = \$81.08.$

Original note...............................	\$1,180.00
Less: Payments (12 × \$32.78) made........	−393.36
Balance.....................................	\$ 786.64
Less: Unearned interest....................	− 81.08
Net to payoff loan.........................	\$ 705.56

The true annual percentage rate, if the loan is thus prepaid is:

$$A = R\left[\frac{1 - (1 + i)^{-n}}{i}\right] + x(1 + i)^{-n}$$

Where

A = the cash received (\$1,000)

R = regular monthly payments (\$32.78)

n = 12 (months)

i = what we seek to find; i.e., the annual percentage rate

x = the payment amount to extinguish the debt (705.56).

$$1{,}000 = 32.78\left[\frac{1 - (1 + i)^{-12}}{i}\right] + 705.56\,(1 + i)^{-12}$$

$$30.5064 = \left[\frac{1 - (1 + i)^{-12}}{i}\right] + 21.5241\,(1 + i)^{-12}$$

$12i$ (annual APR) = about 11.4%

Thus, the annual percentage rate (APR) effec-

GRAPH 51

Add-on conversion to annual percentage rates and vice versa
(monthly installment loans—months: 3, 6, 9, 12, 18, 24, 36, 60, 72, and 144)

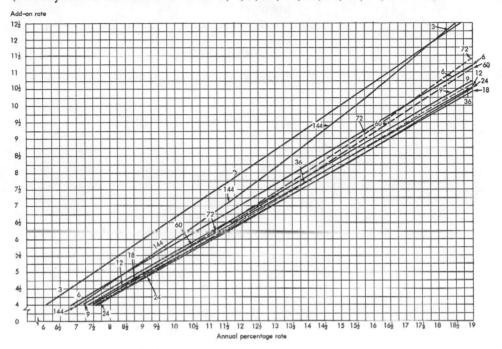

tively charged the borrower resulting from prepayment is just slightly higher than that of the annual percentage rate which would have been applicable had the loan been carried through to maturity.

A borrower needs $1,000 which a bank agrees to lend at 6% discount, repayable in 36 equal monthly installments. The bank requires the borrower to sign a note for $121.51. The amount of note is computed as follows:

Discount installment loan

  a. Cash to be borrowed—$1,000 (*A*).
  b. The discount = 6% × 3 years = 18%.
  c. 100% less the discount, 18% = 82%.

$$d. \quad \frac{\$1{,}000.00 \;(a)}{0.82 \quad (c)} = \$1{,}219.51, \text{ the amount of}$$

the note.

e. Monthly repayments are $33.87 ($121.51 ÷ 36 months) (R).

The annual percentage rate is determinable as follows:

From Graph 52—13.4%

By formula:

$$A = R \left[\frac{1 - (1 + i)^{-n}}{i} \right]$$

$$\$1{,}000 = \$33.87 \left[\frac{1 - (1 + i)^{-36}}{i} \right]$$

$$\frac{1 - (1 + i)^{-36}}{i} = \$29.5246$$

Checking the tables one finds for this factor, for 36 periods, that:

$$1\% = 30.1075, \text{ and}$$
$$\tfrac{1}{2}\% = 27.6607$$
$$\text{Our factor} = 29.5246.$$

Thus, the monthly annual percentage rate is between 1% and ½%. Interpolation produces:

30.1075	1%
29.5246	y
27.6607	1½%

$$\frac{1.8639}{2.4468} = \frac{x}{.5} \qquad x = 0.3808$$

The monthly rate, y, is: 1½% — 0.3808 = 1.1192%.

A monthly rate of 1.1192% per month × 12 months is an annual percentage rate of 13.430.

GRAPH 52

Discount rates converted to annual percentage rates and vice versa
(monthly installments repayments—months: 12, 24, 36, 48, 60, 72, and 144)

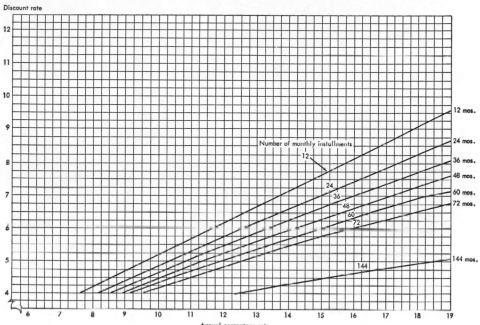

Appendix 4

Interest and dividend income

Investors or savers who desire to keep money invested at attractive and competitive rates should keep abreast of ever-changing "money market" conditions.

The reprints which follow are from *The Wall Street Journal.*

* * *

Money Rates

NEW YORK—Bankers' acceptance rates quoted by one dealer: one to 270 days, 11½% bid, 10¾% offered.

Federal funds in an open market: day's high 12%, low 11⅝%; closing bid 11 13-16%, offered 12%.

Call money lent brokers on stock exchange collateral by New York City banks, 11½% to 12%; by banks outside New York City, 11½% to 12%.

Call money lent on governments to dealers by New York City banks were negotiated; to brokers by New York City banks, 11½% to 12%; to brokers by banks outside New York City, 11½% to 12%.

Commercial paper placed directly by a major finance company: 30 to 89 days, 9⅞%; 90 to 270 days, 8¾%.

Commercial paper sold through dealers: 30 to 270 days, 11⅛% to 12⅞%.

Certificates of deposit ($100,000 or more): top rates paid by major banks in the newly issued market, one month, 11%; two months, 11⅛%; three months, 11¼%; six months, 10⅞%; one year, 10%.

Eurodollar rates in London include: one month, 11 15-16% to 11 13-16%; two months and three months, 11⅞% to 11¾%; four months, 11¾% to 11⅝%; six months, 11¾% to 11⅝%.

Rates shown are only a guideline to general trends, and don't necessarily represent actual transactions.

The money market

Investors must be aware of the way the money market functions, as changes in interest rate levels cause changes in the market prices of debt securities.

The money market specializes in short-term U.S. government securities and prime short-term commercial or financial paper. The money market is characterized by the short-term nature of its activity as opposed to the capital markets, which are for long-term funds.

Money market instruments

Money market instruments are close substitutes for cash and for each other, and are a principal medium of temporary investment by banks, businesses, and financial institutions. In addition to short-term U.S. government securities, other money market media include: negotiable time certificates of deposit, federal funds, banker's acceptances, commercial paper, and call loans.

Certificates of Deposit (CDs) are negotiable or nonnegotiable certificates given by a commercial bank in exchange for a time deposit. Regulation Q of the Federal Reserve Board prescribes the maximum rate of interest that may be paid by member banks on certain time and savings deposits made in the United States.

Federal funds are another name for the deposit balances of member banks at the Federal Reserve bank. Since some banks may have more on deposit than is required, and other banks may be deficient, trading in federal funds takes place. Transactions take place through federal funds houses. The daily volume of transactions is in billions of dollars. Federal funds are also used extensively for other purposes, including large transactions in government issues. With federal funds, settlement of transactions between a buyer and seller may be done on a same-day basis.

A banker's acceptance begins as a draft drawn by, let us say, an exporter against his customer, ordering him to pay a specified sum either at sight or after a specified period of time for goods that have been purchased. When the customer takes possession of the goods, he simultaneously endorses the draft with the word "accepted" and his signature. With this endorsement, the draft becomes an acceptance. The exporter may find it difficult to sell or discount the acceptance if the customer is not well known. Therefore, arrangements are often made for drafts to be drawn against the customer's bank. When such a draft is accepted by the customer's bank, it is known as a banker's acceptance. These acceptances are then traded through banker's acceptances houses.

Commercial paper consists of short-term promissory notes of business firms, which are sold by commercial paper houses to their customers.

Call loans are bank loans to brokers or dealers against listed or government securities as collateral. The proceeds of these loans are used by brokers to finance customers' margin (loan) accounts and by dealers to carry securities they are distributing.

Eurodollars are U.S. dollars on deposit outside the United States and the rate of interest paid on such deposits is not limited by Regulation Q.

Eurodollars

Stock market closing prices include other interesting data as well. In the transactions listed on page 206, the ".80" after the word Dreyfus indicates that the annual dividend per share of this common stock is at the rate of $0.80 per year. The current yield from dividends is:

Stock market prices

$$\frac{\text{Annual dividend (i.e., \$0.80)}}{\text{Current price (\$6\frac{3}{4} \text{ or \$6.75})}} = 11.85\%.$$

New York Stock Exchange Transactions

—1974— High	Low	Stocks Div.	P-E Ratio	Sales 100s	High	Low	Close	Net Chg.
48	37½	Dravo 1.60	11	3	43¾	43½	43¾	+ ½
70¼	40¼	Dresser 1.40	12	238	46⅝	45⅜	46⅜	+ 1⅛
70½	44	Dres pf 2.20	...	18	49⅛	48	49⅛	+ ⅞
63½	39¼	Drssr pfB 2	...	29	43½	43	43½	+ 1
19⅛	15⅜	DrexBd 1.44	...	5	17	16¾	16⅞	— ⅛
9¾	6	Dreyfus .80	7	18	6¾	6¾	6¾	......
20¾	13½	Duk Pw 1.40	6	371	13½	12¾	12⅞	— ⅝
106¼	89½	Duke pf8.70	...	z170	93	92	92	— ½
101½	85	Duke pf8.20	...	z440	86	85	85	......
94	78	Duke pf7.80	...	z100	81½	81	81	+ ¼
84½	67¾	Duke pf6.75	...	1	74	74	74	......
36	24	DunBrad .96	21	120	32	31⅜	31⅞	+ ½
4⅝	2½	Duplan Cp	...	19	2⅞	2⅞	2⅞	......
179	152¾	duPont 5.75e	14	130	172¾	170¾	172½	+ 2
66¾	59¼	duPnt pf4.50	...	2	61	60½	60½	— ¼
21¾	16⅛	DuqLt 1.72	7	79	17⅜	17	17⅛	— ¼
27	22	Dq 4.1pf2.07	...	z100	21½	21½	21½	— ½
27	24	Dq 4.1pf2.05	...	z20	22⅜	22⅜	22⅜	— 1
27	21	DuqLt 4pf 2	...	z380	22	21¼	22	+ ½
14⅜	8¼	Dymoln .28	5	8	10⅛	9½	10⅛	+ ⅝
		— E—E—E —						
22½	18¼	EaglPic 1.04	5	8	18½	18⅜	18⅜	— ⅛
11	9⅛	EascoCp 40	4	26	10½	10¼	10¼	— ⅛
8½	5⅜	EastAir Lin	...	72	6⅞	6⅝	6⅞	+ ¼
27½	20½	East Gs .15r	9	14	21¾	21¼	21¼	— ½
17	9¼	EastUtl 1.50	10	3	10⅜	10¼	10⅜	+ ¼
117½	96⅜	EasKod 1.56	28	510	116½	114⅝	115⅝	+ ⅜
31	25½	Eaton 1.80	5	40	28⅝	28⅝	28⅝	......
34	23⅝	Echlin .38	20	34	28¾	27⅞	28¾	+ ¾
26⅞	18¾	EckrdJk .24	20	233	23¾	22⅞	23½	+ ⅜
16⅛	12⅛	EckdNC .24	10	3	12⅞	12¾	12⅞	+ ¼
25	21	EdisBro 1.32	6	55	23	22½	22½	— ½
19⅞	9⅞	EG&G .10	14	46	12¾	12½	12½	+ ⅛
3½	2	Elect Assoc	...	5	2¼	2¼	2¼	......
25⅜	12¼	EDS .25e	12	17	16¾	16	16¾	+ ½
4⅛	2½	El Mem Mg	4	9	2⅝	2½	2⅝	......
12	7⅜	Elgin Natl	...	3	11	10¾	11	— ⅛
4⅞	2⅛	Elixir Ind	41	3	2⅞	2⅞	2⅞	......
16⅝	11⅞	ElPaso 1b	5	38	12¼	12⅛	12⅛	......
28	22⅛	EltraCp 1.50	5	8	24⅝	24	24¼	+ ¼
45⅜	37¼	EmerEl .70	24	165	40½	39⅜	39⅞	+ ⅜
59½	46¼	EmeryA .96	38	83	56¼	55¾	56	......
10	6¾	EmeryIn .34	8	17	9⅝	9½	9⅝	......
22	16⅞	Emhrt 1.30a	5	17	18	17½	17½	— ¾
3	2½	EMI Lt .19e	5	3	2⅝	2½	2½	......
16¾	11	EmpDE 1.28	9	5	13¼	13¼	13¼	+ ¼
		EmD 5pf.50	...	z350	5⅛	5⅛	5⅛	— ⅜

Prices of Recent Issues

Current quotations are indicated below for recent issues of corporate senior securities that aren't listed on a principal exchange.

Issue		Moody's Rating	Bid	Asked	Chg.	Yield %
		UTILITIES				
CaroP&L	9¾s '04	A	99¾	100	−1	9.75
C & P Md	8⅞s '09	Aaa	99⅜	99⅝	− ⅜	8.91
DetrEd	9⅞s '04	A	95½	96	−1½	10.26
DukePwr	9¾s '04	A	99¾	100	−1	9.75
Fla Pwr	8⅞s '82	Aa	100½	100¾	− ½	8.71
NY Tel	9s '14	Aaa	100	100¼	− ½	8.97
OhioPwr	10⅛s '82	Baa	101⅜	101⅝	− ⅜	9.67
Pac G&E	9⅛s '06	Aa	99¾	100	− ¾	9.12
		INDUSTRIALS				
Carnatn	8½s '99	Aaa	100	100½	.....	8.43
Gen Elec	8½s '04	Aaa	100⅛	100⅜	− ⅛	8.46
GE Credit	8⅞s '82	Aa	101	101¼	− ½	8.60
GMAC-n	8⅞s '99	Aaa	99½	99¾	.....	8.90
PepsiCo	8⅝s '81	A	100	100¼	− ⅛	8.53
PhilipMor	8⅞s '02	A	98½	98¾	− ¼	8.99
PhilipMor	8⅞s '04	A	100¼	100½	− ¾	8.69
Intl Harv	9s '04	A	98½	98¾	− ⅛	9.09

n-New listing.

Bond issues

Usually, new bond issues pay an interest rate that will be competitive with the existing bonds trading in the secondary market. Refer to "Fla Pwr." This is a bond issue of Florida Power, a utility. "8 7/8s '82" means that for each $1,000 bond the annual interest is $88.75 and that the bonds mature (the bondholder is to be repaid $1,000 per bond) in 1982. The asked price 100 3/4 means that one can probably buy the bond for $1,007.50 per bond. The current yield is $88.75 divided by $1,007.50 (neglecting brokerage costs), i.e., 8.81%. The Moody's rating is furnished by an investment advisory and rating or analysis firm and attempts to rate the risk of owning this bond issue. Risk relates to the probability that interest will be paid on schedule and eventually the bond face amount will be paid at maturity. Aaa is the best quality, Aa next best, and so on. Yield % (i.e., 8.71%) is the bond yield to maturity.

Tax-Exempt Bonds

Here are current prices of several active tax-exempt revenue bonds issued by toll roads and other public authorities.

Agency	Coupon	Mat	Bid	Asked	Chg.
Bat Park City Auth NY	6[illegible]s	'14	83½	85½	.....
Chi Calumet Skyway-f	3⅜s	'95	45	48	.....
Chelan Dist	5s	'13	80	82	—1
Chesapeake B Br&Tun-f	5¾s	'00	38	41	—1½
Chgo-O'Hare Int Airpt	4¾s	'99	85	89	+1
Dallas-Ft Worth Airpt	6¼s	'02	88	92	.....
Delaware Riv Port Auth	6½s	'11	95	97	— ½
Delaware Riv Port Auth	6s	'10	65	67	—1
Douglas Cnty PU Dist	4s	'18	65	68	.....
Florida Turnpike	4¾s	'01	78½	80½	— ½
Gr'ter New Orl Expr	4.9s	'06	75	78	.....
Illinois Toll	3¾s	'95	78	80	.....
Indiana Toll	3½s	'94	70	72	.....
Kentucky Turnpike	6⅛s	'08	88½	92½	.....
Maine Turnpike	4s	'89	75	78	.....
Maryland Br&Tun	5.2s	'08	86	89	.....
Massachusetts Turnpike	3.3s	'94	72	74	.....
NJ Turnpike Auth	5.7s	'13	88½	90½	.....
NJ Turnpike Auth	7s	'09	108½	110½	.....
NJ Sports & Expos	7½s	'09	87	90	—2½
NY State Power Auth	5⅜s	'10	84	86	.....
NY State Thruway	3.1	'94	59	61	.....
NY Urban Development	7s	'14	93½	95½	— ½
Ohio Turnpike	3¼s	'92	88½	90½	.....
Penn Turnpike	3.1s	'93	84	87	— ½
Port of NY Auth	5½s	'08	80½	83½	.....
Port of NY Auth	6s	'08	89	92	.....
Richmond-Met Auth	5.6s	'13	84	88	.....
West Virginia Turnpike-f	3¾s	'89	68	72	.....

f-Trades flat without payment of current interest.

Tax-exempt bonds

Tax-exempt bonds are bonds whose interest is not taxable (for the federal income tax) to its owner. The Kentucky Turnpike 6 1/8s of 2008 are selling for $925 each. The bond pays $61.25 annual interest. The current yield ($61.25 divided by $925) is 6.62%. Yield to maturity may be determined as explained in Chapter 6.

Refer to ATT 8 3/4 2000. This is a bond issue of American Telephone and Telegraph. Annual interest per $1,000 bond is $87.50. The bonds can be purchased for about $1,006.25 (i.e., 100 5/8). The cur-

New York Exchange Bonds

CORPORATION BONDS

Volume, $12,180,000

Bonds	Cur Yld	Vol	High	Low	Close	Net Chg
Abex 8¾s77	9.0	10	96½	96½	96½	.....
AirRe 3⅞87	cv	15	57½	57⅜	57½	− ½
AlaP 9s2000	9.2	1	97½	97½	97½	− ½
AlaP 8⅞s03	9.4	9	94½	94⅛	94⅛	− ⅝
AlaP 8½s01	9.3	2	90⅞	90⅞	90⅞	.....
AlaP 7⅞s02	9.1	3	85¾	85¾	85¾	+ ¾
Alison 8¾79	10.	6	80	80	80	+1
AldCh 5.2s91	7.1	23	72⅞	72⅞	72⅞	+ ⅜
AlldPd 7s84	9.2	2	76	76	76	+1
AlldSt 4½92	cv	5	63½	63½	63½	.....
AldSu 5¾87	cv	5	51	50	51	.....
Alcoa 6s92	7.5	20	80	79¼	80	+ ¾
Alcoa 5¼s91	cv	19	91	90	91	+ ½
Alcoa 4¼s82	5.5	5	77⅛	77⅛	77⅛	.....
AAirFil 6s90	cv	12	70¼	70	70	−1
AAirln 11s88	10.	5	101	101	101	.....
AAirl 10⅞88	10.	2	101	101	101	.....
AAirl 4¼s92	cv	59	45½	45	45½	+1
ABrnd 8⅞75	8.8	5	100	100	100	− ¼
ABrnd 5⅞92	7.7	5	76	76	76	+1
AExC 6½77	6.9	5	94	94	94	+1⅞
AHoist 5½93	cv	1	66	66	66	.....
AMF 4¼s81	cv	8	76	75⅝	75⅝	.....
AMetCl 8s86	9.0	47	89	88⅝	88⅝	.....
AmMot 6s88	cv	11	69½	69½	69½	+ ¼
ATT 8.80s05	8.7	1253	100½	100¼	100¼	− ½
ATT 8¾2000	8.7	483	100⅝	100¼	100⅝	− ¼
ATT 8.7s02	8.7	184	100⅜	99⅞	100	.....
ATT 7.75s77	7.8	70	99⅜	98¾	99⅜	+ ⅜
ATT 7⅛s03	8.4	44	84½	84½	84½	.....
ATT 7s01	8.3	69	84	83¼	84	.....
ATT 6½s79	7.0	119	92⅜	92	92	− ½
ATT 4⅜s85	6.1	20	71½	70¾	71½	.....
ATT 4⅜s85r		4	70½	70½	70½	.....
ATT 3⅞s90	6.4	54	60¼	59½	60	− ⅞
ATT 3¼s84	4.9	6	66½	66	66	.....
ATT 2¾s75	2.9	24	94⅞	94½	94½	.....
ATT 2¾s80	3.6	81	75	74¼	75	+ ¾
ATT 2¾s82	4.0	13	68⅝	68⅝	68⅝	+ ⅜
ATT 2⅝s86	4.4	13	60	59	59	−1½
Amfac 5¼94	cv	25	62⅝	62⅝	62⅝	

Government, Agency and Miscellaneous Securities

Thursday, June 13,

Over-the-Counter Quotations: Source on request.

Decimals in bid-and-asked and bid changes represent 32nds (101.1 means 101 1-32). a-Plus 1-64. b-Yield to call date. d-Minus 1-64.

U.S. TREASURY BONDS

Rate	Mat. date		Bid	Asked	Bid Chg.	Yld.
3⅞s,	1974	Nov	98.0	98.8	— .1	8.26
4s,	1980	Feb	81.30	82.14	— .6	7.90
3½s,	1980	Nov	78.2	79.2	— .6	7.70
7s,	1981	Aug	96.2	97.2	.....	7.54
6⅜s,	1982	Feb	91.26	92.26	— .2	7.63
3¼s,	1978-83	Jun	72.30	73.30	.....	7.25
6⅜s,	1984	Aug	91.26	92.26	— .2	7.39
3¼s,	1985	May	72.16	73.16	— .2	6.71
4¼s,	1975-85	May	75.30	76.30	— .2	7.34
6⅛s,	1986	Nov	90.0	91.0	— .2	7.24
3½s,	1990	Feb	72.16	73.16	.....	6.16
4¼s,	1987-92	Aug	72.30	73.30	— .2	6.76
4s,	1988-93	Feb	72.22	73.22	— .2	6.44
6¾s,	1993	Feb	87.12	88.12	.....	7.96
7½s,	1988-93	Aug	95.2	95.18	.....	7.96
4⅛s,	1989-94	May	72.20	73.20	— .2	6.51
8½s,	1994-99	May	103.24	104.8	— .8	8.10
3s,	1995	Feb	72.16	73.16	— .2	5.09
7s,	1993-98	May	89.20	90.20	— .10	7.88
3½s,	1998	Nov	72.16	73.16	.....	5.48

U.S. Treas. Notes

Rate	Mat	Bid	Asked	Yld
5⅝	8-74	99.10	99.14	8.96
6	9 74	99.1	99.5	8.90
5¾	11-74	98.17	98.21	9.10
5⅞	12-74	98.9	98.13	8.98
5¾	2-75	97.28	98.4	8.71
5⅞	2-75	97.31	98.7	8.69
5⅞	5-75	97.4	97.22	8.57
6	5-75	97.19	97.27	8.51
[illegible]	8-75	96.28	97.4	8.32
8⅜	9-75	100.2	100.10	8.12
7	11-75	98.7	98.15	8.17
7	12-75	98.0	98.8	8.24
5⅞	2-76	95.30	96.6	8.38
6¼	2-76	96.2	96.30	8.25
8	3-76	99.14	99.18	8.27
5¾	5-76	95.14	95.22	8.23
6½	5-76	96.31	97.7	8.10
8¾	6-76	100.25	100.29	8.25
6½	8-76	96.14	96.22	8.20
7½	8-76	98.1	98.25	8.12
6¼	11-76	95.19	95.27	8.18
8	2-77	99.22	100.30	8.03
6⅞	5-77	96.14	96.18	8.22
7¾	8-77	98.26	99.2	8.09
6¼	2-78	94.30	95.6	7.78
8¾	8-78	102.2	102.6	8.12
6	11-78	92.7	92.15	8.06
6¼	8-79	92.22	92.30	7.95
6⅝	11-79	93.22	93.30	8.00
7	11-79	95.10	95.14	8.06
6⅞	5-80	94.12	94.20	8.01
7	2-81	94.26	94.30	7.79

U.S. Treas. Bills

Mat	Bid	Ask	Mat	Bid	sk
	Discount			Discount	
6-20	9.05	7.67	10- 3	8.34	8.06
6-21	8.48	7.46	10-10	8.36	8.10
6-27	8.36	7.60	10-17	8.36	8.08
7- 2	8.25	7.71	10-22	8.30	7.96
7- 5	8.27	7.71	10-24	8.37	8.15
7-11	8.13	7.73	10-31	8.37	8.15
7-18	8.27	7.69	11- 7	8.36	8.14
7-26	8.27	7.71	11-14	8.33	8.09
7-30	8.25	7.79	11-19	8.27	8.01
8- 1	8.31	7.95	11-21	8.34	8.08
8- 8	8.31	7.95	11-29	8.30	8.02
8-15	8.28	7.94	12- 5	8.38	8.18
8-22	8.28	7.94	12-12	8.44	8.34
8-27	8.33	7.99	12-17	8.17	7.85
8-29	8.34	7.96	1-14	8.23	7.95
9- 5	8.38	8.16	2-11	8.26	7.96
9-12	8.36	8.26	3-11	8.27	8.01
9-19	8.37	8.15	4- 8	8.28	8.02
9-24	8.31	8.01	5- 6	8.25	8.01
9-26	8.34	8.06	6- 3	8.28	8.20

World Bank Bonds

Rate	Mat	Bid	Asked	Yld
5⅞	9-74	98.28	99.12	8.39
6¾	3-75	98.24	99.0	8.14
3⅜	5-75	95.	95.24	8.32
8⅝	9-75	99.16	100.8	8.39
6½	1-76	96.16	97.16	8.22
3	3-76	91.16	92.16	7.78
6.90	3-76	97.0	97.24	8.30
4½	1-77	90.8	91.0	8.52
6⅜	1-77	94:16	95.8	8.44
4¼	5-78	85.24	86.16	8.41
4¼	1-79	83.16	84.8	8.47
4¾	11-80	81.8	82.8	8.40
3¼	10-81	72.0	73.0	8.25
4½	2-82	77.8	78.8	8.42
5	2-85	75.24	76.24	8.33
4½	2-90	65.16	66.16	8.39
5⅜	7-91	72.8	73.8	8.34
5⅜	4-92	71.24	72.24	8.34
5⅞	9-93	75.0	76.0	8.42
6½	3-94	80.16	81.16	8.44
6⅜	10-94	79.8	80.8	8.42
8⅝	8-95	99.16	100.16	8.57
8⅛	8-96	94.0	94.24	8.55

Inter-Amer. Devel. Bk.

Rate	Mat	Bid	Asked	Yld
¼	12-82	74.24	75.24	8.28
½	4-84	73.24	74.24	8.32
½	11-84	72.24	73.24	8.33
.20	1-92	70.0	71.0	8.38
½	11-92	81.0	82.0	8.44
⅝	11-93	81.24	82.24	8.45
⅝	10-95	99.16	100.12	8.57

Bank for Co-ops

Rate	Mat	Bid	Asked	Yld
.95	7-74	99.27	99.31	8.45
.15	8-74	99.24	99.28	8.92
.15	9-74	99.14	99.18	9.08
.20	10-74	99.19	99.23	9.04
.65	11-74	99.23	99.27	8.97
.90	12-74	99.28	99.30	9.01
.70	4-77	97.16	98.0	8.51

Postal Service

Rate	Mat	Bid	Asked	Yld
6⅞	2-97	82.24	83.8	8.62

FIC Bank Debs.

Rate	Mat	Bid	Asked	Yld
5.95	7-74	99.24	99.28	8.93
9¾	7-74	99.29	100.1	8.36
7.95	8-74	99.22	99.26	9.05
8.60	9-74	99.22	99.26	9.08
7.95	10-74	99.15	99.19	9.06
8	11-74	99.13	99.17	9.00
7.15	12-74	98.31	99.3	9.02
6.05	1-75	98.4	98.16	8.94
8.15	1-75	99.13	99.17	8.90
8.80	2-75	99.25	99.29	8.86
9	3-75	99.27	99.29	9.11
5.70	7-75	96.24	97.8	8.52
6.65	1-76	97.0	97.16	8.49
7.10	1-77	96.16	97.0	8.43
7.10	1-78	95.12	95.28	8.47

FNMA Issues

Rate	Mat	Bid	Asked	Yld
7.85	9-74	99.16	99.24	8.77
5.65	9-74	98.30	99.6	9.11
6.10	12-74	98.12	98.24	8.80
6.45	12-74	98.16	98.22	8.88
7.55	3-75	98.16	99.8	8.60
6.35	3-75	97.20	98.12	8.67
5¼	6-75	96.8	97.0	8.50
7½	9-75	98.8	98.28	8.46
6.80	9-75	97.16	98.0	8.53
5.70	12-75	95.20	96.4	8.54
8¼	12-75	99.8	99.24	8.43
5.65	3-76	94.20	95.12	8.57
7⅛	3-76	97.8	97.24	8.54
5.85	6-76	94.16	95.4	8.58
6.70	6-76	96.0	96.24	8.52
5.85	9-76	94.4	94.20	8.54
6⅛	9-76	94.20	95.4	8.56
7.45	12-76	96.20	97.20	8.53
6¼	12-76	94.16	95.0	8.53
8.45	12-76	99.8	99.16	8.68
4½	2-77	89.20	90.20	8.53
6.30	3-77	94.0	94.20	8.54
7.05	3-77	96.0	96.16	8.51
6⅜	6-77	93.24	94.16	8.50
6½	6-77	94.4	94.24	8.53
7.20	6-77	96.4	96.20	8.50
6⅞	9-77	94.24	95.12	8.53
7.85	9-77	97.16	98.0	8.56
7¼	12-77	95.20	96.4	8.56
7.55	12-77	96.16	97.0	8.56
8.45	3-78	99.2	99.10	8.66
7.15	6-78	94.28	95.12	8.54
7.15	9-78	94.16	95.0	8.58
6¾	12-78	92.20	93.20	8.49
7¼	3-79	94.20	95.4	8.52
7.85	6-79	96.28	97.12	8.51
6.40	9-79	90.8	91.8	8.50
6.55	12-79	90.16	91.16	8.52
6⅞	3-80	91.16	92.16	8.55
8½	6-80	99.4	99.12	8.64
7½	9-80	94.24	95.8	8.49
6.60	12-80	89.20	90.20	8.51
7.05	3-81	91.20	92.20	8.51
7¼	6-81	92.20	93.20	8.48
7¼	9-81	92.16	93.16	8.47
7.30	12-81	93.4	93.28	8.42
6.65	6-82	89.16	90.16	8.30
6.80	9-82	90.4	91.4	8.31
7.35	12-82	93.20	94.4	8.33
6¾	6-83	88.28	89.28	8.38
7.30	6-83	92.12	93.12	8.36
6¾	9-83	88.28	89.28	8.34
6¼	6-84	85.8	86.8	8.30
6.90	12-84	89.12	90.12	8.29
7	3-92	87.8	88.8	8.27
7.05	6-92	87.24	88.24	8.26
7.10	12-97	86.8	87.8	8.35

Fed. Home LoanBk.

Rate	Mat	Bid	Asked	Yld
9⅝	8-74	99.28	100.4	8.74
7.65	8-74	99.12	99.24	8.79
5⅜	8-74	99.0	99.8	9.21
7.05	11-74	98.28	99.8	8.76
8	11-74	99.8	99.24	8.55
6.10	2-75	97.28	98.8	8.75
8.20	2-75	99.8	99.20	8.74
5⅞	2-75	97.20	98.4	8.73
8.05	5-75	98.24	99.16	8.60
6.80	5-75	97.28	98.12	8.62
7.15	5-75	98.4	98.20	8.68
7.15	8-75	97.24	98.8	8.72
7⅞	8-75	98.24	99.8	8.53
7.95	8-75	98.24	99.12	8.50
6½	11-75	96.20	97.12	8.47
7.05	11-75	97.20	98.4	8.45
9.10	11-75	100.12	100.20	8.62
8¾	2-76	100.0	100.16	8.41
7⅜	2-76	97.28	98.12	8.42
8.70	2-76	99.27	99.31	8.71
7.20	5-76	97.8	97.24	8.48
7.45	5-76	97.24	98.8	8.44
7.80	8-76	98.4	98.20	8.49
7.20	2-77	96.12	96.28	8.52
6.95	5-77	95.16	96.0	8.51
8.70	5-77	99.27	99.31	8.71
7.15	8-77	95.20	96.8	8.51
8.80	8-77	100.2	100.10	8.68
6.75	11-77	94.8	94.24	8.54
7.45	11-77	96.12	96.28	8.51
7.60	5-78	96.16	97.0	8.51
8.65	2-79	99.29	100.1	8.64
8¾	5-79	100.6	100.14	8.64
7.05	2-80	93.0	93.16	8.51
7¾	2-80	96.16	97.16	8.31
7.80	10-80	96.16	97.16	8.31
6.60	11-81	89.20	90.20	8.31
7.30	5-83	92.20	93.20	8.32
8¾	5-84	101.0	101.16	8.52
7⅜	11-93	89.16	90.16	8.37

Federal Land Bank

Rate	Mat	Bid	Asked	Yld
5.85	7-74	99.16	99.24	8.25
5.30	10-74	98.16	98.28	8.59
7.15	1-75	98.24	99.8	8.45
8⅜	1-75	99.20	100.4	8.13
[illegible]	4-75	96.4	96.28	8.37
7.65	4-75	98.24	99.8	8.57
5.70	7-75	96.20	97.4	8.50
[illegible]	7-75	99.16	99.28	8.41
7.20	10-75	97.28	98.12	8.49
7.40	10-75	98.4	98.28	8.49
6¼	1-76	96.4	96.24	8.47
5	2-76	93.20	94.20	8.48
6¼	4-76	95.28	96.12	8.40
8¼	4-76	99.12	99.24	8.39
5⅜	7-76	93.12	94.12	8.36
7.05	7-76	96.28	97.18	8.44
7.15	10-76	96.28	97.18	8.40
8¼	4-77	99.8	99.24	8.34
7½	7-77	97.4	97.20	8.34
6.35	10-77	93.20	94.4	8.40
4⅛	2-78-73	85.20	86.20	8.43
5⅛	4-78	88.12	89.12	8.42
6.40	7-78	92.8	93.8	8.38
7.35	10-78	95.20	96.4	8.43
5	1-79	86.4	89.4	8.43
7.10	1-79	94.16	95.0	8.43
6.85	4-79	92.28	93.28	8.40
7.15	7-79	94.8	94.24	8.43
6.80	10-79	92.0	93.0	8.45
6.70•	1-80	91.16	92.16	8.40
7½	7-80	95.4	95.28	8.49
6.70	4-81	90.8	92.8	8.47
6.90	4-82	90.20	91.20	8.38
7.30	10-82	93.0	94.0	8.31
7.30	10-83	92.4	93.4	8.37

rent yield is $87.50 divided by $1,006.25 (i.e., 8.70%). The yield to maturity (not shown) can be determined by the methods shown in Chapter 6.

Government issues

There are a variety of bonds or other evidences of debt issued by the U.S. Treasury and other governmental agencies and authorities. On page 209, under U.S. Treasury Notes, the first line shows a note maturing August 1974. The annual interest is $56.25 (5 5/8%). The current yield is $56.25 divided by the

---

Interest is Exempt, in the opinion of Bond Counsel, from all present Federal Income Taxes.

Moody's Rating: Con (Aa)
Standard & Poor's: A

NEW ISSUE

$17,000,000

Jefferson County Community Improvement District, Kentucky

Special Tax Revenue Bonds, Series 1974

Payable at the Bank of Louisville—Royal Bank and Trust Company; Louisville, Kentucky.

This announcement is not an offer to sell nor a solicitation of an offer to buy these securities. Offering is made only by means of the Circular, copies of which may be obtained from the undersigned.

Amounts, Coupon Rates, Maturities and Yields or Prices

(dated April 1, 1974)
(due January 1, as shown below)

$ 465,000	6¾%	1975	5.25%
490,000	6¾	1976	5.25
520,000	6¾	1977	5.30
550,000	6¾	1978	5.30
580,000	6¾	1979	5.40
615,000	6¾	1980	5.45
655,000	6¾	1981	5.50
695,000	6¾	1982	5.55
735,000	6¾	1983	5.60
780,000	6¾	1984	5.70
825,000	6½	*1985	5.80
875,000	6¼	*1986	5.90
930,000	6.20	*1987	6.00
985,000	6.20	*1988	6.00
1,045,000	6.20	*1989	6.10
1,105,000	6.20	*1990	100
1,175,000	6.30	*1991	100
1,245,000	6.40	*1992	100
1,320,000	6½	*1993	100
1,410,000	4¾	*1994	6.85

*Callable in accordance with the Optional Provisions as set forth in the Official Statement.

asked price of $994.275 (99.14 is 99 14/32 which multiplied by 10 is the price); i.e., 5.66%. The yield shown is the yield to maturity of 8.96%.

Treasury bills do not pay interest. Instead they sell at a price below their maturity value (a discount). They are quoted and trade on the basis of yield to maturity.

The advertisement for the Jefferson County bond issue was placed by the bonds' underwriters. The table within the ad shows the variance in yields to maturity at which the issue is being offered to investors depending on the year of maturity.

Variance in yields

For example, the bonds maturing in 1985 are offered to provide a tax-exempt yield to maturity of 5.80% and those maturing in 1994—6.85%.

The reader is cautioned that the foregoing is but a brief explanation of a complex subject—investment analysis.

Investors must consider a variety of fundamental and technical factors including the general level and direction of interest rates, inflation, callable, convertible and other bond characteristics as well as the soundness of the issuer, the industry of the issuer, and the state of the economy.

An introduction to the securities industry for prospective or actual investors may be found in *Go Where The Money Is,* published by Dow Jones–Irwin.

Appendix 5

Return on investment—
Discounted cash flow

A businessman has proposed to him two alternate courses of action by his staff.

Proposal 1:

This proposal requires a capital investment of $100,000 and the estimated revenues for the first five years are forecast below:

Year	Estimated revenues
1	$ 0
2	10,000
3	10,000
4	50,000
5	60,000
Total	$130,000

The revenues forecasted are net, after expenses, taxes, and so on, and the businessman has investigated the underlying assumptions which he believes to be accurate.

Proposal 2:

The capital investment required is also $100,000 and revenues forecast are given below:

Year	Estimated revenues
1.	$ 40,000
2.	20,000
3.	20,000
4.	20,000
5.	20,000
Total.	$120,000

The businessman's financial limitations are such that he must choose between the two proposals. He decides that he will select that which offers him the best return on investment during the ensuing five years. Which proposal does he choose?

In both cases it is necessary to determine what the future revenues are worth today based on discounting such revenues back from the date they occur to the present at an appropriate interest rate. The interest rate selected should be at least that which the company could obtain by investing its funds elsewhere. Let's assume that 10% per year is selected.

Determination of the present value of future revenue

Proposal 1:

The formula is:

$$P = a(1 + i)^{-n} + b(1 + i)^{-n_1} + \text{etc.}$$

where,

P = present value of the future revenues

i = 10%

$n, n_1, n_2, \ldots$ = the number of years hence that the revenues of a, b, and so on will be received.

Note: See Chapters 2 and 3 for details of the computation method and the use of graphs to expedite the calculations.

Thus,

$$P = 10,000\,(1.1)^{-2} + 10,000\,(1.1)^{-3} + 50,000\,(1.1)^{-4}$$
$$+ 60,000\,(1.1)^{-5}$$
$$P = 8,264 + 7,513 + 34,151 + 37,653$$
$$P = \$87.681.$$

Proposal 2:

$$P = 40,000\,(1.1)^{-1} + 20,000\,(1.1)^{-2} + 20,000\,(1.1)^{-3}$$
$$+ 20,000\,(1.1)^{-4} + 20,000\,(1.1)^{-5}$$
$$P = 36,364 + 16,529 + 15,063 + 13,602 + 12,418$$
$$P = \$93,976.$$

As Proposal 2 affords the businessman the prospect of about $6,300 more in present value of future income, it (other things being equal) should be chosen even though Proposal 1 would produce $10,000 more total cash over the entire five-year period.

The above analysis is commonly known as the "discounted cash flow" method of investment analysis. It illustrates a key element in decision making with respect to investments—that it is important to note both the amount of money one expects to earn as well as when one will receive it.

Appendix 6

Mortgage "points"

State usury laws (or FHA or VA regulations) sometimes set a maximum interest rate that is below prevailing national mortgage rates. In such a case granting of loans would practically cease (without a special solution) because a significant portion of mortgage loans are sold by the originator to other financial institutions in the national market. And, in selling such loans they would have to be discounted to bring the yield to the secondary market purchaser to competitive national levels.

To compensate for an artificially low rate of interest on real estate mortgages, where the borrower is paying the maximum allowable interest rate, which is below national prevailing rates, the following chain of events may take place.

Either the buyer (borrower) pays an additional fee (expressed as a percentage of the loan) to the lender under the guise of being a "service fee" or some other type of fee (as opposed to interest) or the following type of solution prevails.

The *seller* of the property pays "points" (1% = 1 point) expressed as a percentage of the loan to the lender. The seller compensates by increasing the price at which he sells the property to the buyer.

EXAMPLE:

The loan is for $10,000. It is to be repaid in 20 annual level repayments which include principal and interest. The interest rate is 8%. Annual repayments are $1,018.52. The annual percentage rate is also 8%.

EXAMPLE:

Same circumstances as above and the buyer pays a 2% service fee to the lender, total $200 (.02 × $10,000). The annual percentage rate is determined as follows.

Net cash to the borrower............ $9,800
Annual repayments................. $1,018.52

$$A = R\left[\frac{1 - (1 + i)^{-n}}{i}\right]$$

$$9,800 = 1,018.52\left[\frac{1 - (1 + i)^{-20}}{i}\right]$$

$$\frac{1 - (1 + i)^{-20}}{i} = 9.621804.$$

By interpolation, then

8%........................ 9.818147
x........................ 9.631804
9%........................ 9.128545

$$\frac{.493259}{.689602} = \frac{x}{1.0}$$

$$x = 0.71528$$

The annual percentage rate is 9.00000 less 0.71528 = 8.28472%. Thus the effect of the buyer paying 2 points at the inception of the loan is to increase the annual percentage rate from 8.0% to 8.28472%.

Appendix 7

Finding yield to maturity
by mathematical solution

Yield to maturity may be determined mathematically by either trial and error methods, or by solving a complex formula.

EXAMPLE:

A bond is purchased for $1,130. It matures five years hence and the coupon rate is 8%. What is the yield to maturity?
The formula is

$$A = R\left[\frac{1 - (1 + i)^{-n}}{i}\right] + S[1 + i]^{-n}$$

and

$A =$ purchase price of $1,130
$R =$ annual interest of $80
$S =$ maturity value of $1,000
$n =$ number of years to maturity; i.e., 5
$i =$ yield to maturity.

The equation may be restated to the following:

$$\frac{A}{R} = \left[\frac{1 - (1 + i)^{-n}}{i}\right] + \frac{S}{R}[1 + i]^{-n}$$

$$14.125 = \left[\frac{1 - (1 + i)^{-5}}{i}\right] + 12.5[\underline{1 + i]^{-5}}$$

Trial and error solution

From Table 5 we seek various values of i for the underlined factors in the formula where the values for such factors are from the appropriate column for 5 periods. We seek to find the rate of i where the factors involved, when inserted in the formula, produce a total of 14.125 or very close to it.

if i is	then $\left[\frac{1 - (1 + i)^{-5}}{i}\right]$ is	and $12.5(1 + i)^{-5}$ is	And the total is
a. .03	4.579707	10.7826	15.363307
b. .04	4.451822	10.274087	14.725909
c. .05	4.239476	9.794075	14.123551

The total in (a) was too large so a higher rate of interest was tried.

The total in (b) was also too large and a still higher rate was attempted.

The total in (c) of 14.123551 is almost exactly equal to the desired total of 14.125. Thus the yield to maturity is almost exactly 5%.

Mathematical solution

The basic formula for determining yield to maturity is used. However, in addition, both a binomial expansion and the use of the quadratic formula are required as explained in the footnotes at the end of this appendix.

$$A = R\left[\frac{1 - (1 + i)^{-n}}{i}\right] + S(1 + i)^{-n}$$

$$1{,}130 = 80\left[\frac{1 - (1 + i)^{-5}}{i}\right] + 1{,}000(1 + i)^{-5}$$

$$14.125 = \left[\frac{1 - (1 + i)^{-5}}{i}\right] + 12.5(1 + i)^{-5}$$

$$14.125i = 1 - (1 + i)^{-5} + 12.5i\,(1 + i)^{-5}$$

14.125i $(1 + i)^5 =$
$(1 + i)^5 - 1 + 12.5i$ (See footnote 1.)
14.125i $(1 + 5i + 10i^2 + 10i^3 + 5i^4 + i^5) =$
$(1 + 5i + 10i^2 + 10i^3 + 5i^4 + i^5) - 1 + 12.5i$
14.125$i + 70.735i^2 + 141.25i^3 + 141.25i^4 + 70.125i^5$
$+ 14.125i^6 =$
$1 + 5i + 10i^2 + 10i^3 + 5i^4 + i^5 - 1 + 12.5i$

See footnote 2 regarding elimination of powers of
i greater than i^3.

$0 = -3.375i + 60.625i^2 + 131.25i^3$

$0 = 131.25i^2 + 60.625i - 3.375$ (see footnote 3 on
solution by use of
quadratic formula.)

$$i = \frac{-60.625 \pm \sqrt{(60.625)^2 - 4(131.25)(-3.375)}}{2(131.25)}$$

$$i = \frac{-60.625 \pm \sqrt{5447.265625}}{262.5} = \frac{-60.625 \pm 73.805}{262.5}$$

$$= \underline{.0502}$$

And, .0502 is 5.02% which is the yield to maturity.

---

[1] To determine $(1 + i)^5$ use the binomial expansion formula.
For example, using the formula one obtains the following:

$$(a + b)^5 = a^5 + 5a^4b + 10a^3b^2 + 10a^2b^3 + 5ab^4 + b^5$$
$$(a + b)^4 = a^4 + 4a^3b + 6a^2b^2 + 4ab^3 + b^4$$
$$(a + b)^3 = a^3 + 3a^2b + 3ab^2 + b^3$$
$$(a + b)^2 = a^2 + 2ab + b^2$$

and, where the problem is of the nature that $(a + b)$ is in the format,
$(1 + i)$, then

$$(1 + i)^5 = 1 + 5i + 10i^2 + 10i^3 + 5i^4 + i^5$$
$$(1 + i)^4 = 1 + 4i = 6i^2 + 4i^3 + i^4$$
$$(1 + i)^3 = 1 + 3i + 3i^2 + i^3$$
$$(1 + i)^2 = 1 + 2i + i^2$$

The binomial formula for the expansion of positive integral
powers of a binomial (where $r =$ the number of terms) is:

$$(a + b)^n = a^n + na^{n-1}b + \frac{n(n - 1)}{2!} a^{n-2}b^2$$
$$+ \frac{n(n - 1)(n - 2)}{3!} a^{n-3}b^{n-3} + \cdots$$
$$\cdots + \frac{n(n - 1)(n - 2) \cdots (n - r + 2)}{(r - 1)!} a^{n-r+1}b^{r-1} + \cdots$$

In expanding a power of a binomial, it is usually easier to build up each successive term from the preceding one rather than substitute in the formula. Note that if the coefficient of any term be multiplied by the exponent of a in that term, and if this product be divided by the number of terms already written down, the result is the coefficient of the next term. The exponent of a decreases by one in each successive term (until the exponent becomes 0 in the last term) and the exponent of b increases by one (starting with $b^0 = 1$ in the first term).

For example, to expand $(a + b)^6$ we need remember only that the first term will be a^6. Then

$$(a + b)^6 = a^6 + \frac{6 \times 1}{1} a^5 b^1 + \frac{6 \times 5}{2} a^4 b^2 + \frac{15 \times 4}{3} a^3 b^3 + \frac{20 \times 3}{4} a^2 b^4$$
$$+ \qquad + \qquad +$$
$$+ \frac{15 \times 2}{5} a^1 b^5 + \frac{6 \times 1}{6} a^0 b^6$$
$$= a^6 + 6a^5 b + 15a^4 b^2 + 20a^3 b^3 + 15a^2 b^4 + 6ab^5 + b^6$$

Usually the multiplication and division can be done mentally and the resulting coefficient written down immediately. It can be shown that the coefficients will build up to a maximum at the middle term (or two middle terms if the number of terms is even) and then decrease symmetrically as in the above example. The number of terms in the expansion is always $n + 1$.

[2] Values larger than i^2 or i^3 may be disregarded to simplify the solution. Such values are practically insignificant. For example, if $i = .04$, then $i = .000002$.

[3] Once the equation is in the form $ax^2 + bx + c = 0$, then the quadratic formula is used to solve for x.

$$x = \frac{-b \pm \sqrt{b^2 - 4ac}}{2a}$$

Appendix 8

Yield to call

Most bonds are callable by the issuer at a premium prior to the maturity date of the bonds. The reason that bonds include a "callable" provision is to allow the issuer to redeem the bonds (and perhaps issue new ones) in the event that interest rates drop materially after the original issuance of the bonds. Such a re-financing would reduce the issuer's interest costs.

Therefore, investors who purchase bonds at a premium (over $1,000) MUST BEWARE of callable provisions.

For example, consider the following situation.

Bond purchase price...........................	$1,103
Years to maturity............................	30
Coupon rate.................................	10%
Yield to maturity (refer to Graph 48)...........	9%

The yield to maturity is 9% if the bond is held for 30 years and redeemed at maturity for $1,000. (Technically, it is also presumed that the interest received will be invested upon receipt to also earn 9%. Actual reinvestment of interest at rates higher than 9% will cause the realized yield to exceed the 9% yield to maturity and vice versa.) However, if the bond is callable, then —in the event that the bond is called prior to maturity

223

—the yield will not be 9%. Let us assume that the aforementioned bond is callable as follows:

Call date............................ 5 years hence
Call price............................ $1,034

To determine the yield to call, several methods are available.

Formula

The formula is

$$A = R \left[\frac{1 - (1 + i)^{-n}}{i} \right] + S(1 + i)^{-n}$$

Where,

A = purchase price of $1,103
R = annual interest of $100
n = years to call, 5
S = call price, $1,034
i = yield to call.

Then,

$$1,100 = 100 \left[\frac{1 - (1 + i)^{-5}}{i} \right] + 1,034(1 + i)^{-5}$$

This equation may be solved by the same mathematical techniques described in Appendix 7. The yield to call is ONLY 8%. Thus if the bond is called, the investor's yield would be reduced by 100 basis points; i.e., from 9% to 8%.

To summarize,

The 30-year yield to maturity is.................... 9%
The 5-year yield to call is........................ 8%

Graphs or tables

Bond yield to maturity graphs (or other published bond tables) may be used to determine YIELD TO

CALL if, and only if, adjustments are made by converting the call price to a $1,000 base as described below. First, determine the ratio of $1,000 to the call price.

$$\text{Ratio} = \frac{1,000}{1,034} = 96.7117\%$$

Then, multiply the purchase price by this ratio.

$$1,103 \times 0.967117 = 1,066.73$$

Then multiply the coupon rate by this ratio.

$$0.10 \times 0.967117 = 0.0967117$$

No adjustment is made to the number of years to call, which in this case remains at five years.

> Revised purchase price.............. $1,066.73
> Revised coupon.................... 0.0967117
> Years to call..................... 5

The above revisions convert the terms of the bond to a $1,000 base rather than $1,034 and the adjustment is such that the interest per dollar invested ($0.090661) and the maturity value per dollar invested ($0.969317) remain the same.
Prior to revision, the situation was:

$$\frac{100 \text{ interest}}{1,103 \text{ purchase price}} = .0907 \text{ interest per dollar of purchase price}$$

$$\frac{1,034 \text{ maturity (call) value}}{1,103 \text{ purchase price}} = 0.93744 \text{ maturity value per dollar of purchase}$$

After the revision, the relationship is unchanged.

$$\frac{96.7117 \text{ interest}}{1066.73 \text{ purchase price}} = 0.0907$$

$$\frac{1,000 \text{ revised maturity}}{1,066.73 \text{ revised purchase price}} = 0.93744$$

Using the revised coupon rate and revised purchase price, the yield to call (8%) may be determined from the graphs (see Graph 23) or from conventional bond yield tables. The revisions are necessary because both the graphs and yield tables are based on a $1,000 maturity value.

Appendix 9

Probability

The same mathematical technique as explained in Appendix 7, footnote 3, may be applied in determining the probability of card splits—as for example, in the game of bridge. If declarer and dummy have 8 trumps, what is the probability that the remaining 5 cards will be split 5–0?

Apply the number of outstanding cards; i.e., 5, as the exponent in the expression $(a + b)$. Then expand $(a + b)^5$ to

$$a^5 + 5a^4b + 10a^3b^2 + 10a^2b^3 + 5ab^4 + b^5.$$

The coefficients of each term are added (remember that 1 is the coefficient of both the a^5 and b^5 terms).

$$1 + 5 + 10 + 10 + 5 + 1 = 32.$$

The split probabilities are then as follows:

Type of split	Probable occurrences out of 32 possibilities	Coefficient of terms applicable	Percent probability
5–0.........	2	a and b	6.25
4–1.........	10	a^4 and ab^4	31.25
3–2.........	20	a^3b^2 and a^2b^3	62.5
			100.00

Thus as shown above the probability of a 5–0 split is 6.25%. The same method of computation is applicable for any number of outstanding cards. The table below provides the probabilities of various splits.

Number of *outstanding cards*	
2...........	2–0, 50%; 1–1, 50%
3...........	3–0, 25%; 2–1, 75%
4...........	4–0, 12.5%; 3–1, 50%; 2–2, 37.5%
5...........	5–0, 6.25%; 4–1, 31.25%; 3–2, 62.5%
6...........	6–0, 3.125%; 5–1, 18.75%; 4–2, 46.875%; 3–3, 31.25%
7...........	7–0, 1.5625%; 6–1, 10.9375%; 5–2, 32.8125%; 4–3, 54.6875%
8...........	8–0, 0.7812%; 7–1, 6.25%; 6–2, 21.875%; 5–3, 43.75%; 4–4, 27.3437%

Appendix 10

Personal financial planning

Personal financial planning essentially involves a determination of:

1. What one has now in the way of investments.
2. What one will need in the future to meet his financial goals.
3. What one needs to save and invest in order to reasonably achieve his goals.

For example, let's assume that Mr. Planner is 35 and has already invested $10,000 in savings, mutual funds, and insurance cash values. He desires to retire at *age 65*. His present annual cost of living is $20,000 per year.

1. Based on today's cost of living, and one's knowledge of his likely circumstances 30 years from now (children grown, and so on), how much annual income would he like to have per year to retire on? Answer ($10,000).

2. But, this sum, $10,000, is based on today's cost of living. If we assume (5%) per year inflation, then the amount required per year (30 years from now) will be ($43,000). (Refer to Graph 2 for the calculation.)

Analysis

229

3. Of the required *$43,000* per year, how much will be provided by annual income from social security and company pension plans? Answer (*$6,000 per year*).

4. Then, the net annual income needed is *$43,000* less *$6,000;* i.e., *$37,000.*

5. How long after age 65 does Mr. Planner wish to have this level of income? Answer (*15 years*).

6. Then, the capital sum of money one needs to accumulate *30* years hence is the amount which, when invested, will produce *$37,000* per year for *15* years. At the end of *15* years, this capital sum will be exhausted. Let's assume that the capital sum can be invested to earn *8%* per year. Then the capital sum required is *$296,000.* (Refer to Graph 6; $37,000 = 12.5% of the capital sum required. And, 37,000 divided by .125 is $296,000.)

7. However, the existing investments of *$10,000* —if they can be kept continuously invested—and assuming that they will earn *8%,* will be worth *$100,000, 30* years from now. (Refer to Graph 3).

8. Thus, the additional capital sum needed is *$196,000* (*$296,000* less *$100,000*).

9. To produce an additional *$196,000, 30* years from now, the amount Mr. Planner needs to save and invest per year—assuming *8%* compound earnings per year—is *$1,730.* (Refer to Graph 55).

The type of analysis used above is appropriate for most people and is quite flexible and adaptable to the varying circumstances that may exist.

The graphs which follow (53 to 58) may be used to determine solutions to the following types of problems.

1. If an investment earns 5%, how much must one save each year to accumulate $100,000 within 20 years? Refer to Graph 53. Enter the graph on the horizontal base at $100,000; proceed vertically to the 20-year curve, then horizontally to the left margin. The necessary annual amount to save is about $3,025.

2. If one saves $3,025 per year for 20 years at 5% compound interest, how much capital will be accumulated? Refer to Graph 53. This is the problem above in reverse. $100,000 would be accumulated.

232

GRAPH 53

Annual investments to accumulate capital (to $260,000) at 5%

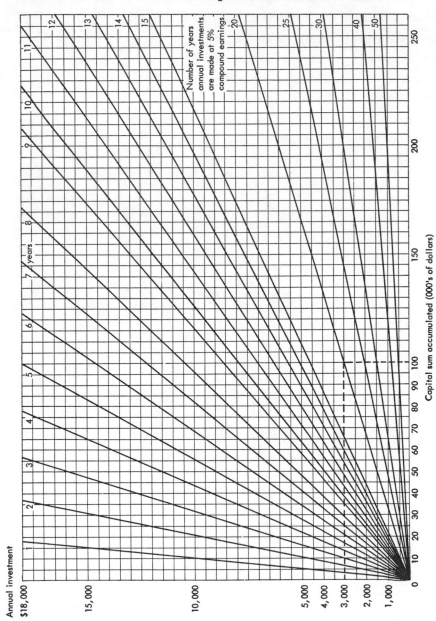

GRAPH 54

Annual investments to accumulate capital (to $2,600,000) at 5%

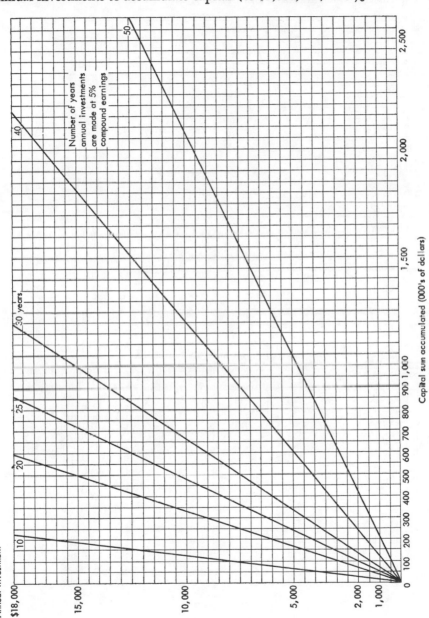

234

GRAPH 55

Annual investments to accumulate capital (to $260,000) at 8%

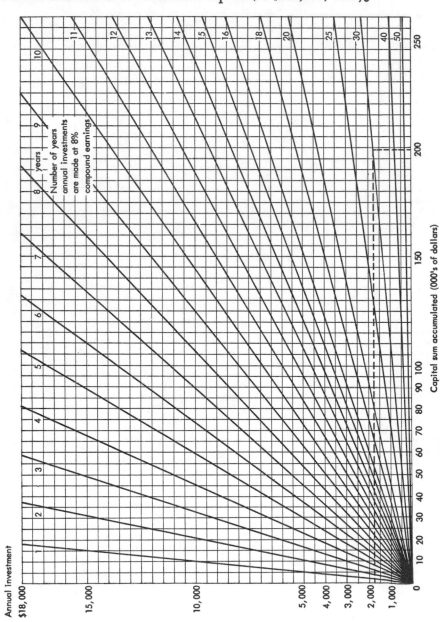

GRAPH 56

Annual investments to accumulate capital (to $2,600,000) at 8%

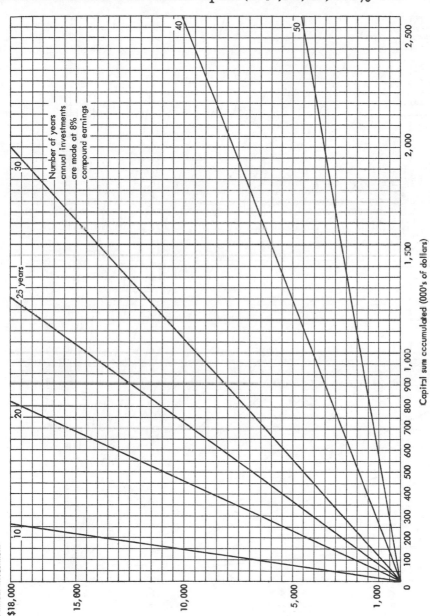

236

GRAPH 57

Annual investments to accumulate capital (to $260,000) at 10%

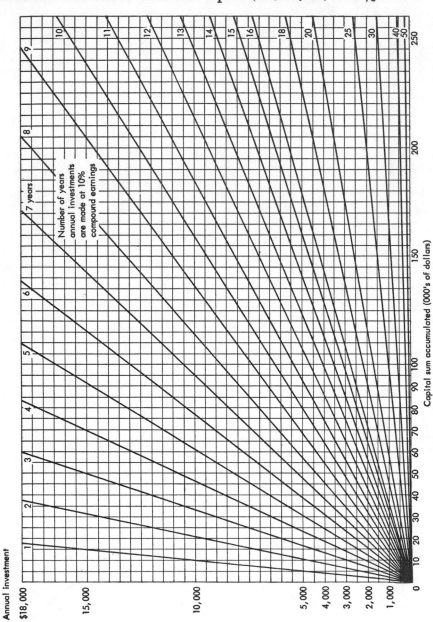

GRAPH 58

Annual investments to accumulate capital (to $2,600,000) at 10%

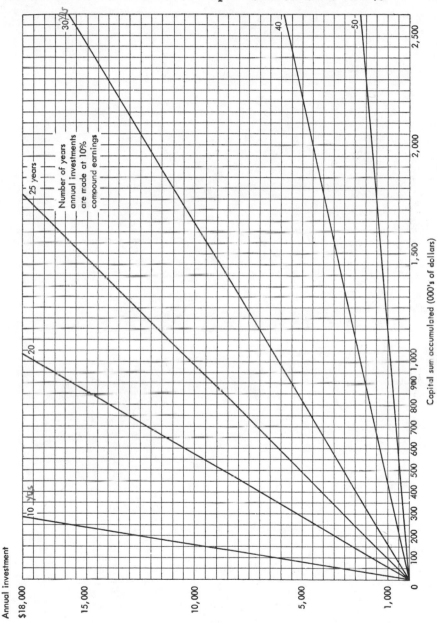

Index

239

240